COLD WAR IN A COLD LAND

COLD WAR
IN A
COLD LAND

*Fighting Communism on
the Northern Plains*

DAVID W. MILLS

University of Oklahoma Press : Norman

Material examining the politics in South Dakota during the Cold War appeared in earlier form as "Politics, Piety, and Patriotism: Cold War Politics in South Dakota," in *The Political Culture of South Dakota*, edited by Jon K. Lauck, John E. Miller, and Donald C. Simmons, Jr. Pierre: South Dakota State Historical Society Press, 2014.

Material on the Cold War in North Dakota appeared in earlier form as "The Cold War in the Peace Garden State," *On Second Thought* (Spring 2013): 22–29.

Material in chapter 4 on the Ground Observer Corps was published in an earlier form as "An Unlikely Team: Social Aspects of the Ground Observer Corps," in *Cold War and McCarthy Era: People and Perspectives*, edited by Caroline Emmons, 63–77. Perspectives in American Social History. Santa Barbara, Calif.: ABC-Clio, 2010.

Library of Congress Cataloging-in-Publication Data

Mills, David W., 1965–
  Cold War in a cold land : fighting communism on the northern plains / David W. Mills.
    pages cm
  Includes bibliographical references and index.
  ISBN 978-0-8061-4694-2 (hardcover) ISBN 978-0-8061-6912-5 (paper) 1. Great Plains—History, Military—20th century. 2. Cold War—Social aspects—Great Plains.
  3. Intercontinental ballistic missile bases—United States—History—20th century.
  4. North Dakota—History, Military—20th century. 5. South Dakota—History, Military—20th century. 6. Montana—History, Military—20th century. 7. Cold War—Social aspects—United States. 8. Anti-communist movements—United States—History—20th century. 9. Civil defense—Great Plains—History—20th century. 10. Air power—Great Plains—History—20th century. I. Title. II. Title: Fighting communism on the northern plains.
  F595.2.M53 2014
  355.00978—dc23

                    2014030894

The paper in this book meets the guidelines for permanence and durability of the Committee on Production Guidelines for Book Longevity of the Council on Library Resources, Inc. ∞

Copyright © 2015 by the University of Oklahoma Press, Norman, Publishing Division of the University. Paperback published 2021. Manufactured in the U.S.A.

Contents

Illustrations

Figures

Maps

Acknowledgments

There are so many people to thank for their assistance in writing this book that I cannot begin to name them all. A few deserve mention, particularly Tom Isern, who was my dissertation advisor and my friend throughout this process. Thanks, Tom. Thanks to Kayla Westra for her help in initially editing the manuscript and to Kathy Lewis, Stephanie Attia, and Chuck Rankin at the University of Oklahoma Press for their assistance in bringing the book together.

My greatest thanks are reserved for my family. My boys—Sam, Joey, and Jacob—put up with long absences when I was off on research trips or locked in my office, revising and rewriting. Thanks, guys. Words cannot express my gratitude to my wife, Ann, for her support. One evening I told her that I intended to quit my corporate job so that I could go to graduate school and pursue my dream of writing and teaching history. Her response: "Go for it." Thanks, dear.

COLD WAR IN A COLD LAND

Introduction

Master Sergeant James Lessman was a United States Army recruiter serving in South Dakota in January 1948, when he invited President Harry S. Truman to vacation in the Black Hills. Hoping to combine military business with the president's trip, Lessman envisioned Truman administering the oath of enlistment to new members of the armed services at the foot of Mount Rushmore. Having the president involved in recruiting, the sergeant thought, would greatly assist in attracting new members of the military. "It would be a ceremony heard around the world," claimed Lessman. He added: "It would serve as a notice to all those who wish to deny us our freedoms that there are a lot of Americans who think differently."[1]

The four members of the congressional delegation from South Dakota —senators Chan Gurney and Harlan J. Bushfield and representatives Francis Case and Karl Mundt, all of whom were Republicans—endorsed the plan to bring the Democratic president to the Black Hills. The four members of Congress jointly penned a letter, asking Truman to consider the sergeant's request favorably, adding: "The Mount Rushmore Memorial, which is fittingly called the Shrine of Democracy, would form a perfect backdrop for such a ceremony."[2] Within a week the Republican governor from South Dakota, George T. Mickelson, joined the congressional members and Master Sergeant Lessman in extending the invitation to President Truman. In referring to the proposed ceremony, Mickelson responded: "I am sure that such an event held before this beautiful monument . . . would greatly aid the current recruiting program."[3]

The president never came to South Dakota that year, but the invitation suggests that the political representatives enthusiastically supported the federal government's effort to recruit service members and that the people would appreciate the gesture and respond positively to it. In fact, this is exactly the case. South Dakota and the other northern plains states, North Dakota and Montana, enthusiastically supported the federal government's effort to combat Soviet communism. Moreover, the effort to bring the president to such a majestic site as Mount Rushmore suggests that South Dakota's congressional delegation was following a program developed at the federal level and enacting it at the local level. They knew that federal officials often used monuments or other historic sites as a stage to deliver a patriotic or anticommunist message.

Civilian and military leaders on the national stage continuously developed plans to undermine Communist influence in America then pushed these programs down to the state and local level, where they became reality. Such programs included tactics to expand patriotic and religious sensitivities among the populace and to curtail Communist activity or sympathy toward that ideology. Federal authorities sanctioned a civil defense initiative to protect civilians from the effects of nuclear war, allocating plans and costs to the state and local level. Military authorities developed plans to defend the United States from Soviet attack, necessitating the reactivation of closed air bases or the construction of new ones. They built offensive nuclear missile sites and a defensive nuclear missile complex on the northern plains. This book examines the effect of the national government's Cold War initiatives and ways in which they took shape in one particular region: the northern Great Plains, including the states of North Dakota, South Dakota, and Montana.

A particular theme that does not permeate this examination of the Cold War is the sense of fear that so many historians have described. This is not to suggest that people in this area did not experience sleepless nights over the fear of Communist insurgency or nuclear war. To imply that no one was afraid is as problematic as suggesting that everyone was. In this study the term "fear" is used to describe a collective emotion, not an individual one. For example, the analysis shows that people in this region generally did not participate in civil defense measures, demonstrate against military construction projects, or demand anticommunist legislation from their state and local governments as people in some other places did. Citizens probably discussed the international situation among themselves, but these conversations did not translate into action in this area at this time. Explicitly or implicitly, each chapter addresses fear.

The people who live in the region appear dissimilar in many respects from the Dakotas to Montana. They do not fit into homogeneous categories, but commonalities are more apparent than demographics might suggest. Catherine McNicol Stock describes the conservative nature of citizens in North Dakota and South Dakota during the Depression era and refers to them as hard working, willing to help their neighbors, and overwhelmingly Republican in voting patterns. She also notes that they were "ardently patriotic and demonstrated it through lively and rich political activities."[4] Historian Jon Lauck describes the settlers of the Dakota Territory as veterans of the Civil War who brought with them "a devotion to the Union, a common commitment to the Republican Party, a deeply entrenched patriotism, an attachment to Midwestern agrarianism, support for late-nineteenth-century Midwestern reform efforts, and long experience with the American political tradition." According to Lauck, 80 percent of the settlers in the Dakota Territory were members of the Republican Party and the overwhelming majority of the population was Protestant. He also argues that a sense of civic duty and devotion to their neighbors motivated the first settlers.[5]

The settlement patterns in Montana were much different. The Irish were the largest immigrant group, bringing their perpetual allegiance to Ireland and unwavering Catholicism with them to America and the northern Great Plains. They dominated the mining region and many other cities in Montana and had a church membership of 25,000 in Butte by 1901. St. Patrick's alone had 10,000 members, while no Protestant church in the city had more than 800.[6] The numerous Irish miners in the state bowed deeply to the power of the miners' unions and the Democratic Party. This is not to say that the miners embraced party ideology; they did not. The Irish in Montana voted with the Democrats because the party ran candidates who were politically acceptable and actively courted the Irish vote. If a Democratic candidate forgot the necessity of the Irish vote, the Irish could vote en masse for a Republican. The most acceptable political candidate to the Irish would be an Irish Catholic.[7]

The people of the northern plains were somewhat differentiated then. The Dakotas were far more agrarian, Protestant, and Republican.

Montana had significant mining concerns in additional to agrarian interests, was more Catholic, and tended to vote Democratic. Whatever their differences on the surface, however, these groups shared many collective traits. They were highly influenced by their mining and agricultural industries, church affiliation, ethnic identity, community attachment, and cooperative relationships. Harvard public policy professor Robert Putnam asserts that people from the northern plains have the largest rates of "social capital" in the nation, which he defines as a sense of belonging and social obligation that an individual feels toward a group.[8]

These people could be called regionally minded or inward looking, a trait honed by the particular style of colonialism and dependency that shaped the region. Colonialism means simply extracting more resources from an area than a controlling interest contributes. The most famous villains in these cases are banking and corporate entities from the East who invest in western infrastructure and reap financial rewards at the expense of inhabitants. Historian William G. Robbins wrote one of the best articles reviewing this contention. He recalls Bernard DeVoto's 1934 claim that the sole objective of those financing western development was to turn the region's resources into marketable commodities. During the 1930s and 1940s other prominent authors built upon DeVoto's claim, including Walter Prescott Webb, A. G. Mezerik, Wendell Berge, Joseph Kinsey Howard, and Ladd Haystead.[9] When thoroughly installed, colonialism inevitably leads to dependency on the part of the exploited region. Esteemed historian Elwyn B. Robinson identifies dependency as one of the six themes dominating the North Dakota story. Sociologist Carl Kraenzel accepts the idea of dependency but explores what he calls the "minority behavior" of the plains and the contradictory, contrary, and cranky behavior of the people in the region.[10]

Colonial peoples are in fact contradictory. They do things that seem to be odd and inconsistent unless we consider that as colonial peoples they are fundamentally pursuing their own interests. They do not go along with everything that outside powers propose. Plains people have a resistance mentality within the colonial system; but they also support the maintenance of the system, through which they prosper to a degree. It may seem a contradiction that they are sometimes in opposition to the outside power and sometimes rally to support it, but these responses come from the same colonial circumstances. The consistency within the apparent inconsistencies is the predominance of regional interests in a colonial area.

This seeming inconsistency explains why the people on the northern Great Plains readily welcomed some Cold War measures, adopted others with lukewarm enthusiasm, and rejected others outright. While much of the nation expended time, energy, and financial resources to detect or oust Communist sympathizers, this phenomenon largely bypassed the region, with a few noted exceptions. When the people of the area were called on to demonstrate their patriotic commitment, however, their intensity and numbers astounded federal officials. The citizens in the region ignored civil defense initiatives. But they eagerly supported one particular program known as the Ground Observer Corps (GOC), a volunteer organization directed to report unknown aircraft to a United States Air Force representative to prevent a surprise attack by the Communists. By far the most popular Cold War strategy in the region, however, was the construction of military bases and weapon systems. The people enthusiastically supported this, because of the guaranteed influx of federal dollars into the area.

Watching people from the northern plains energetically supporting the government's Cold War effort may have surprised those who knew of the region's reputation for shunning international entanglements. Some have called people from this region "isolationist," meaning that they often opposed U.S. international efforts. They preferred to keep American soldiers and tax dollars at home. While many residents were certainly isolationist, politicians were often responsible for perpetuating this label. Many citizens in North Dakota opposed entry into World War I before the formal declaration in 1917. But most residents of the state supported the war effort once the United States was committed to the conflict, even though Asle Gronna was one of only six senators to vote against entry into the war. In fact, some citizens were a bit overzealous in their support of the war effort, such as those North Dakotans who stole one hundred steers and one thousand sheep from Hutterite communities—known for their pacifist viewpoints—and used the money from the livestock sale to buy war bonds. The War Department sent over thirty-one thousand North Dakotans, including two National Guard units, into the conflict. At the conclusion of the war the North Dakota legislature gave each returning veteran a $25 bonus for each month served overseas.[11]

South Dakotans also opposed entry into the war at an early stage but overwhelmingly supported the war effort after Congress declared war, sending over thirty-two thousand soldiers to the conflict, including the state's National Guard unit. The South Dakota governor established a State Council of Defense a month after the declaration of war and charged the organization to assist the prosecution of the war in every way. The council organized war bond drives, solicited Red Cross donations, assisted local draft boards, and fostered loyalty in general. South Dakota was also home to many Mennonites, who opposed the war for religious reasons. Although it is unclear how many Mennonites the state drafted, almost all refused to serve. The government gave them war-related work instead of military service, though some refused to perform any work linked to the war effort. Most of these citizens earned prison sentences in Fort Leavenworth. Mennonites, who generally spoke only German, also found themselves the target of mobs that burned their houses. State laws targeted other members of the German-speaking population within the state, forbidding instruction in any foreign language in public schools and use of the German language on the telephone system.[12]

While North and South Dakota sent the number of soldiers that the War Department requested to fight in World War I, Montana sent a disproportionate number, including a fourteen-year-old boy named Mike Mansfield. Mansfield lied about his age to join the navy and later became a political force in Washington as a Montana senator. Twelve and a half thousand Montanans volunteered for service in the war. Apparently due to confused population estimates, the Selective Service drafted twenty-eight thousand more. Forty thousand Montanans served in the armed forces during the conflict, some 10 percent of the population.[13] Popular support for the war ran so high that a mob broke into the high school in Lewistown and burned all of the German textbooks in 1918. Ironically, with so many young men and women from the state in uniform, U.S. representative Jeannette Rankin from Montana was one of fifty members of Congress to vote against entry into the war, further inspiring isolationist characterizations of the area. She ran for reelection in 1918 and was soundly defeated because of her pacifist views.[14]

The northern plains states did their part in World War I, but sentiment changed between the wars. Citizens and politicians opposed intervention as Europe moved toward another world war. In fact many

Americans opposed involvement in Europe. This sentiment was as much an example of regional pragmatism as it was of isolationism. The consensus emerged throughout the region that intervention in World War I had led to nothing but unpaid debts and dead soldiers and that another war would probably mean more of the same. Besides, plains states seemed to gain little material or financial benefit by joining any effort to prepare America for war. So the isolationist label remained.[15]

As World War II approached, many politicians on the northern Great Plains tried to stay out of the conflict. Senator Gerald P. Nye from North Dakota led an investigation into the munitions industry in 1934, connecting industry's desire for profits with participation in World War I. Nye was also a prominent member of the America First Committee, an organization determined to keep America out of the World War II. Before the June primary in 1940 not a single North Dakota candidate supported Franklin Delano Roosevelt's plan to keep out of war by aiding the allies. Students at North Dakota Agricultural College organized a movement to keep America out of the war, while North Dakota senator William Langer vigorously opposed any action that could lure the United States into the war and argued that America had to defend the Western Hemisphere first.[16] Many South Dakotans also opposed entry into the war. Republican Karl Mundt went to the House of Representatives in 1939, claiming that he was not an isolationist but an "insulationist." He rejected President Roosevelt's proposals to aid Great Britain's struggle against Nazi Germany. Mundt's position was common in South Dakota, where citizens generally opposed the United States' entrance into the war. A bloc of states from the Midwest and plains formed the base against such measures as Lend-Lease and the destroyers-for-bases deal, including Nebraska, Minnesota, Wisconsin, North Dakota, South Dakota, Montana, Iowa, Kansas, and Michigan. Mundt noted that the opposition was geographic, not political. Most of the congressional representatives voting for the Lend-Lease package came from regions with industrial or seafaring traditions that would likely prosper from such a change.[17]

When the Japanese bombed Pearl Harbor, many of the citizens and politicians who had argued against war changed their stance. But it was difficult for North Dakota's Senator Nye to change quickly. When he heard about the bombing, he remarked: "Just what the British had planned for us. . . . We have been maneuvered into this by the President." The next day Nye, along with every other member of Congress from North Dakota, voted for the declaration of war.[18]

South Dakota's Senator Mundt worked hard to distance himself from his isolationist stance in his state, with some success. He and other active members of the America First Committee, who had advocated staying out of the war, became its most ardent supporters. Shortly after Roosevelt declared war on Japan, Mundt emptied his office of every newspaper clipping, speech, or memorandum that recorded his opposition to the conflict. He wrote to the secretary of war, Henry Stimson, a week after the bombing and offered his services to the U.S. military. He was forty-one years old but eligible for service under the new rules that Congress had adopted days before. Stimson replied that Mundt could best serve his country in his current capacity in the House of Representatives.[19]

Another South Dakota politician had similar ideas about staying out of the war before Pearl Harbor. Francis Case was a representative and then a senator from South Dakota who emphasized international cooperation early in his political career, which began in the 1920s. He was disillusioned with the idea by 1935, when he advocated a more no-nonsense approach. Case, like many midwestern members of Congress, opposed Roosevelt's Cash and Carry proposal because it permitted trade with belligerents, increasing the likelihood of an incident leading to United States involvement in the war. Case introduced a House Joint Resolution in 1937, known as "The Unknown Soldier Amendment," which proposed a constitutional amendment that required the government to submit a referendum to the people in order to send soldiers into battle. Case later abandoned his proposal in favor of a similar amendment that had a better chance of success, although the Roosevelt administration defeated the later measure.[20] Despite the setback, Case continued to oppose any actions that might lead the United States into war. He voted against the repeal of the embargo on arms to belligerents in 1939 after the outbreak of war on the continent. He and other Great Plains politicians were in the minority by this point: Congress continued to repeal the several neutrality acts, thus allowing Roosevelt to support the efforts of France and England. South Dakotans solidly supported Case's position of trying to keep the United States out of war. Case's mail ran approximately thirty to one against repeal of the neutrality acts: 3,230 against repeal and 117 in favor.[21]

Case's position began to shift as the nation drew closer to war at the end of 1941. He no longer opposed legislation that would prepare the country for war and voted to arm merchant ships that delivered Lend-Lease material to Europe. There is no evidence to suggest what Case thought when he heard news of the Pearl Harbor attack, but the next day he voted for the declaration of war and telephoned the commandant of the Marine Corps to offer his services. Lieutenant General Thomas Holcomb told Case that he was serving in the most important capacity he could as a congressional representative and good-naturedly suggested that it had been a long time since Case had served in uniform back in 1918.[22]

Before the Japanese attack on Pearl Harbor, President Roosevelt tried to free himself from the shackles of the neutrality acts, though he had few supporters from the northern plains. One of the few senators from that region to support the president was Democrat James Murray of Montana. Murray told his constituents that the United States faced domination from the east and the west and that a free market economy could not withstand the assault of totalitarian regimes. "Under our American system," Murray argued, "where industry and labor are free and where we enjoy the highest plane of living in the world, we would be utterly unable to compete with Hitler."[23] Support of the Lend-Lease agreement, Murray argued, would keep America out of the war by supporting England, letting the British do their own fighting.[24]

While Senator Murray supported the president, the other Democratic Montana senator, Burton K. Wheeler, opposed Roosevelt every step of the way. He said that lifting the neutrality acts was a prelude to sending troops to Europe to fight in the war and vowed "never to send an American boy across the water to fight on foreign soil, though I am hanged in effigy." Wheeler fought the Lend-Lease proposal, arguing that it would "plow under every fourth American boy," a statement that Roosevelt called "the most untruthful, the most dastardly, unpatriotic thing that has been said." The secretary of war accused Wheeler of "near treason."[25]

When the Japanese attacked Pearl Harbor, Wheeler told the press: "Let's lick hell out of them."[26] The attack united the nation: the politicians from the northern Great Plains and the citizens who lived there were nearly unanimous in their support of President Roosevelt and his strategy to win the war. The primary source of dissent on the northern plains came from Jeannette Rankin, the representative from Montana who had voted against U.S. entry into World War I. Rankin's message of staying out of the war was popular before Pearl Harbor. She was serving a second term in the House of Representatives in 1941 when she cast the only vote against entry in World War II. Voters denounced her at home and referred to her as "Japanette." Her pacifism had continued between the wars. She had written a number of articles, lectured before crowds, and organized groups sympathetic to her message that the world should solve its problems peaceably. Her message was largely unheard or forgotten after Pearl Harbor. Montanans threw themselves into the war effort, as did people in every other state in the nation.[27]

Citizens of the northern plains displayed regional pragmatism between the wars, preferring that foreign nations do their own fighting. But this sentiment changed after Pearl Harbor, when citizens responded to their country's call after the attack. North Dakotans bought $397 million in war bonds and in 1944 put 11 percent of their income into series E savings bonds, the largest percentage of any state, even though some 20 percent of the state's citizens were of German ethnic origin. By July 31, 1945, the state's fifty-five draft boards had registered nearly 145,000 men. In spite of numerous agricultural deferments, 60,079 North Dakotans served in the armed forces, of whom 1,939 paid the ultimate price.[28] South Dakotans played an important role in World War II as well, sending approximately 64,560 citizens into military service, with 2,044 laying down their lives. Citizens there exceeded all expectations in their purchase of war bonds worth $328 million and gave over $2 million in donations to the Red Cross. Local colleges accelerated courses in sciences and math to prepare soldiers for technical duties in the military, while schoolchildren collected milkweed pods (a buoyant material) during the summer for use in life jackets.[29]

Montana also sent a large number of its sons and daughters into the military, 1,553 of whom never returned. The Shultz family of Glasgow had seven sons serving their country. Hubert Zemke was a former University of Montana football player, then a P-47 ace, then a prisoner of war. The Montana Jaycees elected him Man of the Year while he was serving in a German prisoner of war camp. Montanans stoically accepted that the

Montana Education Association canceled state high school champion-
ship tournaments for the duration of the war. They waited for victory
over America's enemies and for life to return to normal.[30]

Citizens on the northern plains volunteered for the war and submit-
ted when drafted. Approximately one-third of the trainees going into the
military from the northern plains were volunteers, not draftees. The citizens in the region participated in scrap drives for all metals, rubber, and
grease to contribute to the war effort. They volunteered to serve on the
many state draft boards and withstood the strict rationing program that
drastically reduced their consumption of gasoline, sugar, meat, shoes,
tires, and automobiles, all intended to provide the raw materials for the
thriving military machine.[31] Citizens from the northern plains served in
the armed forces and responded to every government request. Agricultural commodities coming from the region's farms were one of the most
important contributions to the war effort, all of which earned handsome
profits for farmers who enjoyed federal agricultural subsidies.

President Franklin Roosevelt initiated the era of farm subsidies when
he extended aid to farmers through the Agricultural Adjustment Act,
ostensibly to take land out of production to preserve the soil. The result
was an artificial price support for farmers during the Great Depression.[32]
One-third of the North Dakota's farmers had their farms and homes
foreclosed, and more than 15 percent of the population left the state in
search of jobs during the Depression. Half the population received some
sort of government relief, while South Dakota and Montana suffered
similarly.[33] Federal money mitigated circumstances, marking a shift
away from dependence upon eastern powers and toward federal largesse.

Industrial and military efforts resulted in victory. The Allies—the
United States, Great Britain, and the Soviet Union—defeated Germany
and Japan in World War II, but this cooperation did not translate into
close relations. The United States and Great Britain distrusted the Soviet
Union throughout the war, a feeling that the Soviets reciprocated. U.S.
political and military leaders continuously worried that the Soviet Union
would ask the Germans for a separate peace, leaving the United States
and England to finish the war without their eastern ally. The Soviets
constantly harangued their allies to start a second front in the West.
The Americans and British needed to relieve the pressure on the Soviets,
Stalin begged, as the Russians did not enjoy the luxury of minimizing

casualties as the Americans and British were doing. The Soviets suspected that the United States and Britain hoped to inflict the maximum damage upon the Soviet Union by forestalling a cross-channel attack.[34] The United States, Great Britain, and the Soviet Union were allies in the common cause of defeating Nazi Germany, but the alliance was a matter of convenience, not one of trust. Throughout the war and in the early stages of the peace, the United States and the Soviet Union continued to view each other with suspicion. Each nation saw itself carrying out a series of defensive measures in the postwar world against the other nation's offensive maneuvers. Each viewed the other with alarm, convinced that the other's actions indicated the darkest intent.[35]

Americans pointed to Soviet premier Joseph Stalin's broken promises at Yalta as evidence of a sinister Soviet Union with designs on all of Western Europe. At the conference Stalin agreed to allow the Baltic States, Poland, and other Eastern European countries—under Soviet control as territory conquered during the war—to hold free elections in exchange for territorial demands. Stalin required a buffer zone between his nation and Germany, which had twice launched invasions against the Soviet Union in the early twentieth century. American and British leaders agreed to territorial concessions at Poland's expense, moving the Soviet Union's borders hundreds of miles to the west and compensating Poland with German territory. Stalin reneged on his promise to allow these nations to hold free elections, imposing Communist governments instead. The United States was not in a position to push Stalin too far, however: the dictator controlled all of the lands in question and could proceed as he wished, regardless of American opposition.

President Truman came under enormous criticism from political rivals who claimed that he had not done enough to curtail the advancement of communism, although he amassed a lengthy resume that indicated otherwise. Truman developed the containment policies that led to confrontations with the Soviets over Iran, Turkey, Greece, and South Korea and negotiated treaties with 50 nations that enabled the United States to position soldiers in 117 countries around the world, corralling the Soviet Union and Communist China. Truman rearmed Germany, created the North Atlantic Treaty Organization (NATO), and set up the Marshall Plan. He signed the National Security Act in 1947 that established the National Security Council, the Central Intelligence Agency (CIA), the

United States Air Force as a separate branch, the Department of Defense, and the Joint Chiefs of Staff. Truman did not carry out these actions to appease critics but because he and many other members of the federal government believed that the Soviet Union constituted a vital threat.[36]

Still, opponents charged that the national government teemed with subversives, compelling Truman to institute a loyalty program in 1947 that required all federal employees to sign a loyalty oath and submit to a background investigation. Despite these actions, the revelation of spy rings operating in the United States indicated that the Soviet Union had penetrated secret projects within the American government, had used this information to develop and then detonate an atomic bomb in 1949, and was intent upon worldwide domination. Truman's critics pointed to deceits in Poland; Communist actions in Iran, Greece, Turkey, Berlin, and Czechoslovakia; the takeover of China; and the invasion of South Korea as concrete evidence of Soviet offenses and argued that the Communists were on the march around the world.

Perhaps the greatest shock to Americans came not from an invasion but from one of their own citizens who had turned his back on the finest education available and the highest positions of power in order to transfer secret information to Soviet agents. Alger Hiss was a graduate of the Harvard Law School, a Supreme Court clerk for Justice Oliver Wendell Holmes, Jr., a highly regarded government attorney during the New Deal, a member of the American delegation at the Yalta conference, the secretary-general of the inaugural meeting of the United Nations, and the president of the Carnegie Endowment for International Peace. He was also accused of being a Soviet spy who passed secret information to Whittaker Chambers, an active Communist in the 1930s but a reformed one in the late 1940s when he implicated Hiss. Hiss seemed to be guilty of treason; but the statute of limitations had ended, so he was not eligible for prosecution under that charge. Twice Hiss faced prosecution for perjury when the first trial ended in a hung jury on July 7, 1949. The next jury convicted Hiss at his second trial on January 21, 1950. He spent the next forty-four months in prison. If Alger Hiss with all of his advantages could be a spy, it seemed, anybody could be a spy.[37]

A few months after the Hiss conviction, Julius and Ethel Rosenberg faced prosecution as atomic spies. Their lives had been rather obscure to that point, but signs pointed to their political leanings. Julius earned a degree as an engineer and served in World War II but was discharged for being a Communist, a charge that he vehemently denied. U.S. Communist Party authorities canceled his subscription to the *Daily Worker*, the newspaper of the Communist Party of America, perhaps to protect one of their important informants. The Federal Bureau of Investigation (FBI) untangled a web of Communist agents operating in America, catching the Rosenbergs in the process. A jury convicted them of conspiracy to commit espionage in March 1951. They died in the electric chair in June 1953.[38] The news that average Americans had acted as spies for the Soviet Union again stunned the nation.

Because the Soviet Union emerged as a clear and obvious danger, countless Americans supported the government's Cold War initiatives. Residents of the northern plains followed many of these programs simply because they were patriotic, but other considerations also emerged. Farmers knew that government officials could use the region's crops to provide food for the millions of starving people in Europe and expected farm subsidies to continue after the war, perpetuating substantial profits. Farm subsidies were about to realize a considerable shift in support, however, as they came under attack in the 1950s.[39] While politicians thanked providence that the American farmer was so productive during the war, that quality proved a curse soon after the conflict ended, as stockpiles of excess crops continued to grow. Government subsidies lasted until 1954, when President Eisenhower and his secretary of agriculture, Ezra Taft Benson, told farmers that the artificial price supports simply cost too much money. They wanted to allow market forces to determine commodity prices and permit surpluses to disappear. The states on the northern plains flexed their muscles and rallied against the measure. Eisenhower's plan ultimately did not cut subsidies nearly as much as he wished, but he found new outlets for farm products through school lunches and by sending surpluses overseas to American allies. Farm prices continued to decline from their World War II high point, and residents on the northern Great Plains looked for other financial opportunities.[40]

If agriculture did not promise long-term economic salvation, then the growing international situation did. Western states benefited in at least four ways through Cold War spending: military installations, defense contracts and manufacturing, major science laboratories, and university research.[41] All but the possibility of military bases eluded the northern plains during the Cold War. Manufacturing facilities that were growing in other parts of the West bypassed the plains, which had no industrial base upon which to build. Additionally, corporations and universities on the northern plains could not compete with major science laboratories and research universities that other western cities already had at the start of the Cold War.

In addition to defense spending, the federal government also contributed to the region's economy through building projects such as the federal highway system and a number of dam projects. The 1956 Interstate Highway Construction Act provided up to 90 percent of the cost of building thousands of miles of interstate highways cutting through the region. The highway project brought millions of federal dollars and thousands of jobs to the northern plains in the 1950s. The Pick-Sloan Plan, also known as the Flood Control Act of 1944, authorized the construction of four major dams on the Missouri River in South Dakota and one major dam in North Dakota. In its entirety the plan called for the construction of some 107 dams at a cost of $1.5 billion. The recreational opportunities that the flat-water lakes created were also important financially, but the project had its costs as well. American Indian tribes lost over 250,000 acres of fertile, timber-rich land.[42] Nonetheless, the people in the region had learned how to attract federal dollars and no longer resisted federal intrusion. They worked the system to secure benefits.

This book can be broken down into three parts, each consisting of three chapters. The first three chapters examine endeavors designed to root out those actively engaged in subversion and discourage people from experimenting with Communism, to encourage participation in religious observance, and to inspire pro-American feelings and patriotism. Chapter 1 shows the ways in which the states copied anticommunist programs developed at the national level and carried them out at the state and local level.

Chapter 2 assesses national attempts to encourage religious veneration during the Cold War, as federal and church officials used spiritual adoration as a bulwark against atheistic Communist ideology. The Catholic Church mobilized its worldwide congregations to oppose communism, especially when the Soviets persecuted church officials in Eastern Europe.

Chapter 3 examines the federal government's attempt to push patriotism or "Americanism" down to the state and local level, encouraging people to get involved in the fight against communism.

The second part of the book deals with civil defense measures in the region. As chapter 4 points out, civil defense was a federal endeavor, but the central government refused to fund the project. Thus the federal government recommended that American citizens privately fund their own fallout shelter and defensive plans, ensuring that little was done. Chapter 5 is a look at one of the most successful and little-known civil defense programs of the Cold War era. The Ground Observer Corps was a volunteer organization directed by the air force that looked to the skies for Soviet aircraft in an era before effective radar coverage. Chapter 6 is a description of the Cuban Missile Crisis in 1962 and the ways in which the event played out in the region. State and local governments were not organized for the emergency, despite years of government warnings to prepare.

The third part of this book is concerned with military expenditures on the northern plains. Congress funneled more than $100 billion into western military installations between 1945 and 1973, and the politicos and citizens of the northern plains states were determined to get a share.[43] Chapter 7 compares the Berlin Airlift in Europe with "Operation Haylift," which took place in the Great Plains during the winter of 1948–49. Cargo planes from various units dropped hay bales to livestock and other supplies to stranded people during a series of blizzards that paralyzed the region. The event demonstrated the need for airpower and the parallels between two simultaneous events.

Chapters 8 and 9 examine the offensive and defensive nature of atomic missiles. The United States developed the capability to deliver a nuclear weapon by placing it atop a missile in the 1950s. After a number of improvements, the air force developed the Minuteman missiles in the early 1960s and stationed them throughout the northern plains.

Finally, chapter 9 examines the construction of the Safeguard Anti–Ballistic Missile (ABM) Complex in northern North Dakota, built to defend America from a Chinese nuclear strike. It was one of a dozen sites planned for the United States, but the Safeguard Complex was controversial. Government officials reduced the number of Safeguard sites to just two and finally to just one. When federal officials realized that the single existing facility offered no real defense against a Soviet nuclear attack, the government shut down the complex after spending $6 billion in construction costs and expenses for operating about one week.[44]

The northern Great Plains benefited from the Cold War economically but contributed to the federal government's overall Cold War strategy through patriotism and religious observance, if not through civil defense and anticommunist measures. This book consists of separate but overlapping chapters that describe the daily experiences of citizens in a particular place during the Cold War. It is primarily concerned with the early Cold War era of the late 1940s and 1950s. The book considers broad topics yet examines individual encounters in detail, explaining what the Cold War meant to the people who lived in this region. Secondary sources provide an outline of what was happening at the national and international level, while archival and newspaper sources from the region provide the local and individual narrative. Few historians have attempted to investigate the Cold War at the state or regional level, instead looking at national events on a grand stage. Historians who have considered important topics affecting the states use evidence from throughout the nation, often citing the most extreme or interesting example. This work is not the definitive answer to what the Cold War meant to the states: many more questions remain. For example, this study does not address the topics of race, class, or gender in any meaningful way. It is a starting point, meant to invite conversation and to entice others to break new ground.

Chapter 1

Anticommunism

Joseph McCarthy was an obscure senator from Wisconsin when he gave the annual Lincoln Day address to the Republican Women's Club of Ohio County in Wheeling, West Virginia, on February 9, 1950. McCarthy's stature was so low in the Republican Party at that point that he called the party headquarters and volunteered to give speeches around the country to bolster his public image. Even then, the party assigned him to areas such as Wheeling, Salt Lake City, Reno, Las Vegas, and Huron, South Dakota.[1] McCarthy began his anticommunist crusade as the Soviet ideology appeared to be gaining momentum globally. China had fallen to communism, the Soviet Union had the atomic bomb, and Communist North Korea had invaded its southern neighbor.[2] People were looking for answers.

When McCarthy left West Virginia he continued his crusade, eventually arriving in Huron, South Dakota. His arrival was exciting to citizens there, and some three hundred spectators crammed into the basement of the First Presbyterian Church to hear McCarthy's grim description of communism on the march around the world. He gave the audience more of his fearful rhetoric. "The chips are down right now in the struggle against communism," he warned, "and the past six years have seen U.S. power gradually deteriorate."[3] The venue in a church basement indicates that South Dakota political officials had little expectation that a capacity crowd would show up to hear McCarthy speak. He was, after all, an obscure senator with little name recognition. Three hundred citizens showed up, however, which is an indication that his message was interesting, if not appealing, to some citizens. Though it was the middle of

February on the northern plains, the number of bodies crammed into the basement must have made the heat nearly unbearable after a short period. Despite the conditions, McCarthy's message mesmerized the citizens in South Dakota. According to journalist Haynes Johnson, McCarthy "had barely left the state when a state senator introduced a concurrent resolution in the legislature demanding that Congress and the president check on 'the loyalties of the men employed in the State Department from Dean Acheson on down.'" The resolution passed the Senate and the House only four days after it was introduced, with no debate.[4]

Joe McCarthy was nothing if not controversial. Across America he gathered a wide following of true believers and an equal number of critics throughout the five years known for "McCarthyism." Regardless of their sentiment toward McCarthy, the evidence suggests that most citizens on the northern plains saw his fight as one waged outside of the region, against an invisible enemy based in Washington and other major urban centers. His crusade did not lead to the identification of a Communist movement in North Dakota, South Dakota, or Montana. Some politicians such as South Dakota senators Karl Mundt and Francis Case attempted to emulate McCarthy for political gain, but the Communist issue did little for their careers. Other politicians such as William Langer of North Dakota consistently opposed McCarthy and his Communist issue. But he was repeatedly reelected until his death in 1959.

Many on the northern plains appreciated McCarthy's efforts to stop the spread of communism as he gained popularity in 1950. W. E. Bond of Grand Forks, North Dakota, asked Senator Langer what he was doing to assist McCarthy in exposing Communists. "It is time to quit fooling with communism in our country," Bond declared.[5] A constituent asked Montana senator James Murray why she had not heard Murray's response to McCarthy's charges. "Perhaps Senator McCarthy used the wrong words, if 'Communist' is not the right word, perhaps 'traitor' would be more appropriate," she wrote.[6] A. E. Godfrey wrote to South Dakota senator Karl Mundt: "The stench arising from the State Department is nauseating to every citizen." He, too, expressed his support for McCarthy's actions.[7] Others remained unconvinced as McCarthy spread his message of fear in early 1950. Although few constituents wrote to their senators to object to McCarthy's antics early on, among those who did were two citizens from South Dakota. Pauline de Sherbinin of Yankton wrote: "I object to the manner in which Senator Joseph McCarthy is carrying on his search for Communists. If he were primarily interested in searching out Communists . . . he would go about his work quietly with the aid of the FBI."[8] Dan Grigg of Mitchell was more direct: "We're getting fed up with McCarthy's accusations. Is he a crackpot? We feel he is doing more harm than good for the nation's foreign policy."[9]

McCarthy's rally against communism was controversial, which demonstrates that people were concerned about the subversion to which he often alluded. Seditious forces rarely operated out in the open, and officials worried that clandestine organizations or individuals were scheming in secret, obliging government and civic leaders to root out the conspirators before they could act. Those who suggest today that government leaders overreacted to the Communist threat forget that Joseph Stalin, who came to power in the 1920s, advocated the overthrow of capitalist nations to secure the Soviet state. As people watched the old dictator install governments friendly to the Soviet Union throughout the nations he occupied, suspicions grew into outright fear, renewed each time the media reported the existence of spy networks unearthed throughout Western nations. At the same time, officials could see the Soviet propaganda machine at work and knew what Stalin meant by "freedom." It did not match the American definition, and citizens and governments had reason to fear Soviet strategies.[10]

State and federal officials employed three methods to expose subversives: the passage of Communist-control laws to hinder the operation of radical organizations, the formation of investigation committees to find subversives, and the initiation of loyalty oaths. Communist-control laws attempted to regulate the actions of suspected subversives by restricting the meetings of radical elements, often ordering that subversive organizations and their members register with a branch of the federal or state government. The federal government led the way in passing anticommunist legislation and attempting to root out subversives through investigation committees. Senator Mundt from South Dakota helped to write one of the most comprehensive federal laws designed to destroy the Communist movement. He worked closely with Senator McCarthy, who was probably the best-known Communist-hunter from the early Cold War era and the chair of a federal investigation committee. Loyalty oaths were the least aggressive of the three methods, though supporters argued that

Senator Joseph McCarthy. No date given. Courtesy Senate Historical Office.

anyone who lied about supporting a revolutionary organization committed perjury, a crime punishable through the court system.[11] State and local governments copied the federal example and implemented similar laws and committees.

Americans scorned radicals during the Cold War, but they had enjoyed wide support at the beginning of the twentieth century. They found their base in the urban centers and generally ignored the radical farmers who demanded an egalitarian class system. Despite collectivization of the nation's farms as the endgame of Communist ideology, thousands of farmers across the nation embraced the revolutionary ideas of the Communist Party of America (CPA).[12] Fighting between and within the various Communist and socialist organizations precluded any serious recruitment of farmers in the early stages of the movement, and the Nonpartisan League (NPL) enjoyed the support of radical farmers on the northern plains.[13] This organization did not advocate socializing farmlands but did endorse state ownership of grain elevators, flour mills, packing houses, cold storage plants, statewide hail insurance, and state-owned banks, ideas radical enough to earn it a variety of leftist labels. Once the NPL lost momentum, many farmers turned to the CPA in the early 1920s.[14]

After the Russian Revolution and throughout the 1920s, representatives from the CPA toured the region and advocated a new economic and political system that put money in the pockets of those who produced agricultural commodities, not the banks or industrialists with a long history of exploiting farmers. Many of these radical spokespersons and their American leaders had been to Moscow and received training and direction from the directors of the Communist Party there. By far the most successful party organizing had taken place in Sheridan County, Montana, where party members purchased the weekly newspaper, *Producer News*, in 1918.

Charles Taylor arrived in Plentywood, Montana, shortly after the paper changed hands, to become its chief editor. Even before he came, the town was crowded with Communists. Between 1920 and 1924 they controlled the county government and extended their influence into neighboring counties. Taylor won a seat in the Montana legislature in 1922, with little pretense that he and his paper were not instruments of the Communist Party. The paper used the terms "Bolshevik" and "Red" in almost endearing ways.[15] Taylor remained a fixture in the state legislature until his defeat in 1932, the same year he was appointed to the executive board of the Communist Party in New York City. Just when the movement should have reached new heights on the northern plains, momentum began to wane. The people in northeast Montana had grown weary of inept leadership and absurd edicts emanating from Moscow and New York that failed to address their problems. The federal government in the form of the Works Progress Administration (WPA) and the Civilian Conservation Corps (CCC) came into the region and helped solve the problems, undermining the influence of the Communist Party. Ironically, the Great Depression increased agrarian radicalism nationally due to problems of price and yield just as the CPA lost influence on the northern plains.[16]

Extremists populated the northern plains in the early twentieth century, but the view that radicalism equaled unpatriotic behavior led to violence. As the nation continued the march toward war in 1917, conservatives throughout the region reacted to this movement from the left. The North Dakota National Guard disrupted a meeting led by Max Eastman, a journalist and Industrial Workers of the World (IWW) organizer, while police in Minot, North Dakota, jailed citizens for even showing support for the IWW. Additionally, Minot police fire-hosed protesters, raided the IWW headquarters, and deported members of the office staff the same year. State and local police also deported IWW employees working in Aberdeen, South Dakota, in 1917, and then broke up a state convention of the Socialist Party of America. Police arrested 134 people and convicted 52 of them for violating Montana's criminal syndicalism and sedition laws in the eight months after the law went into effect in 1918. Federal troops patrolled areas of the state containing copper mining camps throughout 1920 and 1921. They broke up attempted strikes and protests, raided IWW and other union halls, and arrested and detained miners. Troops under the command of General Omar Bradley in Montana had a reputation for viciously beating and arresting miners in Butte.[17]

Controlling communism and repressing radicals continued on a national level after World War I, when a series of strikes and labor disputes around the nation made Americans look for causes other than unfair management practices in large corporations. The culprits were left-wing radicals, according to journalists and government officials.[18] A series of labor riots in May and June 1919 frightened many people, who demanded action. Attorney general A. Mitchell Palmer pursued a policy of deportation for suspected radicals, as numerous members of the CPA and other radical organizations were foreign born. Palmer authorized the arrest of thousands of suspected radicals, although the Red Scare died out after only a year. The idea of exposing those with radical agendas never completely evaporated, however.[19]

Fears of subversives infiltrating the government and undermining American values resurfaced during the Great Depression, sparking a number of congressional investigations. Republican representative Hamilton Fish chaired one such committee, which determined that the Communist Party posed a danger to the United States. The Fish Committee established that the CPA was just as revolutionary as it claimed to be and owed its allegiance to the Soviet Union. The committee was determined to outlaw the Communist Party, although this was not done. The McCormick-Dickstein Committee formed in 1934 investigated both fascist and Communist movements, warning against their growing influence. A conservative Texas Democrat named Martin Dies created the Special House Committee on Un-American Activities in 1938, continuing the hunt for subversives. The Dies Committee named more radicals in one year than Senator McCarthy did in a lifetime. Dies understood that the "Communist issues" played well throughout the country and drew wide support during the 1930s and 1940s.[20] Congress passed the Hatch Act in 1939, which in part forbade the employment of any individual who belonged to a party or organization that advocated the overthrow of the American government by force. By 1941 the Navy Department and War Department had authority to dismiss any employee in the "interests of national security." Congress appropriated $100,000 for the FBI to investigate members of the federal government suspected of belonging to subversive organizations. Between July 1, 1940, and March 31, 1947, 1,313 people lost their jobs for reasons of security.[21]

The Dies Committee ceased to exist during World War II because the Soviets were American allies and persecution of Communists would undermine the fragile wartime alliance. Additionally, the American government perpetuated the view that Joseph Stalin was a friend.[22] Even before the end of the war, however, government officials discovered evidence of Soviet espionage, and another organization arose in 1945 from the ashes of the Dies Committee. The House Un-American Activities Committee (HUAC) held a series of hearings that investigated the loyalty of many citizens and organizations in the United States. The committee members believed that American workers were entirely too comfortable with communism, and labor leaders found themselves the target of these investigations. The most spectacular hearings focused on the film industry and Hollywood, as the committee heard from a number of prominent stars. Evidence mounted at the end of 1945 and throughout 1946 that Communist sympathizers had ties to various government entities, as congressional investigations increased in volume and intensity. President Truman, for whatever reason, did not react to these allegations of radicals working to raze the government. Subversion became a pivotal topic during the 1946 midterm elections, when Republicans swept both houses of Congress and controlled twenty-five governorships to the Democrats' twenty-three. The allegation that destabilizing elements were undermining national security was a decisive issue in the election.[23]

Two weeks after the 1946 election Truman had to act, issuing Executive Order 9806 and establishing the President's Temporary Commission on Employee Loyalty. The commission was a temporary one because

Truman did not really believe in a threat brewing within the federal government. But events soon took on a life of their own as agencies in and out of government warned of the red menace. The United States Chamber of Commerce estimated that 400 Communists held high governmental positions. FBI director J. Edgar Hoover warned HUAC that the goal of the Communist Party was to overthrow the government of the United States by force. He also stated that the fifth column operating within the United States was better organized than the Nazi fifth column of World War II. Hoover lectured that Communists should be barred from government. When he spoke in March 1947, no less than six bills in Congress were designed to limit or destroy the CPA in the United States. When his temporary commission warned that Communists in government were a substantial threat, Truman responded. He issued Executive Order 9835, which outlined the procedures to enact a loyalty program aimed at federal employees. Every single one of the 2 million federal employees had to sign a loyalty oath and submit to a cursory background examination and then a full inquiry if investigators suspected subversion.[24]

The loyalty oath was the most prolific method used to uncover subversives. Its use rose to absurd levels at the height of the Cold War as the federal government asked millions of employees to sign the oaths. National officials even encouraged all recipients of public housing, numbering some 16 million people, to sign loyalty affidavits. The futility of the gesture was overwhelming, but the implementation of loyalty oaths nonetheless became popular at the state level. Many objected to these oaths, but once a constituent or political representative suggested a loyalty oath it became difficult to avoid. The obvious implication was that anyone who objected to a loyalty oath must have something to hide. Thus state governments often followed the federal example, requiring their employees to sign loyalty oaths.[25] Most of the states employed some or all of these methods with differing levels of success, but the intent was always to stop or control subversive elements.

Truman ordered loyalty oaths for federal employees in 1947. By 1953 over 80 percent of states had followed the federal example and imposed some sort of loyalty oath, usually aimed at state employees, who signed millions of oaths across the nation in the early stages of the Cold War. The conservative press and organizations such as the American Legion and the Daughters of the American Revolution (DAR) often played a key role in convincing legislators to propose and then pass the bills requiring such oaths.[26] No other state surpassed California in its passage of loyalty legislation. Los Angeles County required its employees to disavow subversive activities and the intentions of 150 blacklisted organizations. California state senator Jack Tenney proposed thirteen anticommunist bills in the legislature.[27]

One of these bills proposed a loyalty oath for the state's University of California system, based on the success of a similar proposition in the state of Washington. Three professors lost their jobs for refusing to sign the loyalty oath implemented there. Tenney pushed the university's board of regents to institute its own loyalty oath. When thirty professors refused to sign the oath, they lost their teaching positions. Soon California required a loyalty oath to be signed by every state employee. Those who refused to sign had their paychecks withheld until they complied. The California court system was overwhelmed with cases associated with employees who refused to sign their oaths, including professors, schoolteachers, social workers, and nurses. Cases made their way to the state supreme court, where the employees lost their battles. California even passed a law that required churches, veterans' groups, and nonprofit organizations to submit loyalty affidavits to retain their tax-free status.[28]

Other states also adopted loyalty oaths. Oklahoma's American Legion pushed the state to adopt a loyalty oath in 1951. As the bill wound its way through the legislative system, politicians tacked a number of provisions onto it, such as the requirement that all signatories must bear arms for the state if required. The governor had initially favored a loyalty oath more as a patriotic gesture than anything else, but he and some members of the state legislature had reservations about the bill in its final form. Public pressure soon forced the governor's hand, and he signed the bill into law. At least one hundred people left government service within a few months of the bill's passage, some by resignation and some by force when state officials fired employees for refusing to sign the oath or allowed employment contracts to expire. A coalition of professors from the University of Oklahoma and the Agricultural and Mechanical College took the matter to the state supreme court, arguing that the law violated religious freedoms of those forced to sign and thus guarantee that they would bear arms if required. The Oklahoma Supreme Court upheld the law, arguing that the state had the right to define the conditions under which employees would retain their employment, but the United States Supreme Court struck down Oklahoma's loyalty act in 1952. The conservative press and veterans' groups lobbied for a new law that met the court's intent, and the legislature enacted a more acceptable version in 1955.[29]

Loyalty oaths on the northern Great Plains were tame in comparison to the rest of the country. The Montana and North Dakota legislatures never enacted a statewide loyalty oath, though South Dakota veterans believed that their state needed one. Representatives of the American Legion and the Veterans of Foreign Wars studied several loyalty oaths from other states, drew up one of their own, and sent it to representatives in the South Dakota state legislature. The bill required the signers to swear support for the Constitution of the United States and for the constitution of the state of South Dakota and affirm that they did not belong to a group that advocated the overthrow of any government in the United States by force or violence. The veterans pressured the South Dakota legislature to enact a loyalty program in 1955, rather late compared to most other states but much to the annoyance of many of the state employees who had to sign it. Supporters for the bill argued that any citizen who wanted to work for the government should not object to such an oath. It passed the South Dakota Senate 33 to 0 and the House 72 to 2. This was an easy bill for legislators to support, for arguments against it might raise concerns with constituents at home. Governor Joe Foss signed the bill into law in February 1955. The new law required all state employees to sign the oath, including all teachers and college professors.[30]

A number of teachers in Lead, South Dakota, felt humiliated by the gesture. "There are four thousand adults in my community, and a hundred of us have been singled out by the legislature to stand up by ourselves and defend our allegiance to our country by taking a loyalty oath," said R. V. Hunkins, the superintendent of the school system.[31] The loyalty oath caused no major confrontations at the University of South Dakota, but one faculty member recalled that "we all held our noses and signed it and then forgot about it."[32] Other groups with no need to sign the loyalty oath also opposed it; the Aberdeen Ministerial Association passed a resolution opposing loyalty oaths for public employees in the state.[33] Most people denounced the loyalty oath simply because it called into question the loyalty of every citizen asked to sign one.[34] Critics argued that even Communists could sign a loyalty oath, while proponents urged the program to facilitate perjury charges against those who signed the oaths and belonged to subversive groups.

North Dakota did not mandate a statewide loyalty oath, though some individual cities attempted to enact their own loyalty programs. Fargo city commissioner Gladys Zube proposed a loyalty oath for the 300 city employees in November 1954, but two citizens stood up at that meeting to voice their opposition to the measure. One of those opposed was Dr. C. Maxwell Brown, pastor of the First Methodist Church, who told the assembled crowd that he represented the Fargo-Moorhead Ministerial Organization and that he and the organization opposed the loyalty oath under consideration. With Brown that evening was Rabbi Steven S. Schwarzchild, a member of a ministerial group and an opponent of the loyalty oath, though he did not speak at the event. The other speaker was E. J. McCanel, a former Fargo city commissioner, who also spoke against the need for a loyalty oath. Each speaker called the loyalty oath demeaning to city employees and reminded the assembly that loyalty oaths really accomplished nothing. The city council concluded the meeting by directing the city attorney to draw up a loyalty oath at the end of the meeting but not to require a signature.

The city council met again in January 1955, when Zube proposed a specific loyalty oath for all Fargo city employees, including a measure that called for the termination of any employee who did not sign the oath within thirty days. There was no second for the motion, so she moved on to her next proposal, which included a mandated loyalty oath with no clause for dismissal. This time her proposal was seconded. In the discussion that followed Zube gave an impassioned speech in which she described subversive elements that stole America's nuclear secrets and caused the deaths of American soldiers in Korea and chastised the ministerial organization for opposing the loyalty oath. She also questioned the patriotism of Brown and McCanel for opposing the measure. She told the audience that Brown did not represent the wishes of everyone in his organization but perpetuated the illusion that he did. She cited the separation of church and state, telling the assembled audience that the church should not bring unfair influence upon the proceedings, and found it unjust that the clergy should meddle in city government affairs.[35]

Dr. Brown again rose to address the city council and made six points as to why the council should oppose the measure. The first reason was that requiring an oath infringed on the principle of religious liberty, as oaths were solemn vows or a pact between the individual and God. Second, the oath was discriminatory in singling out a specific group to sign it. Third, the oath involved an implication of guilt without a legal procedure. Fourth, there were enough laws already to deal with traitors. Fifth, loyalty oaths implied guilt by association. Finally, Brown argued that bad means never achieved good ends. When he finished his oration, the city council voted on the proposal. The final measure failed to pass by a vote of 3 to 2, to the applause of the assembled spectators. Mayor Herschel Lashkowitz, at the final defeat of the motion, suggested that the "defeat or rejection of the loyalty oath . . . must be regarded as a vote of confidence in the integrity and loyalty of our Fargo city employees."[36]

The Montana legislature never enacted a statewide loyalty oath, though the State Personnel Commission established a four-person committee that considered a loyalty oath and background questionnaire for all state employees in late 1953. The proposed loyalty oath asked state workers to swear that they would not take part in any movement to alter or change the form of Montana's government currently in existence. The questionnaire asked a series of detailed questions regarding participation in organizations that were Communist in nature or had as their stated goal the overthrow of the government. A number of state employees might have been exempt from taking the oath or completing the questionnaire, however. Those exemptions generally included state legislators and their staff members, members of the National Guard, and members of the state court system. Many states stipulated that employees in similar positions should swear to support the state and federal constitutions.

With so many exemptions, it was unclear as to what state employees remained to take the oath and complete the questionnaire. The reason for so many exemptions was that the Montana Constitution stipulated that state employees only had to take one oath. Persons in the above-mentioned positions had already sworn their allegiance to the Constitution of the United States and the constitution of the state of Montana in that oath. Additionally, state school laws required university professors, instructors, and teachers within the university system to sign loyalty pledges to the United States and Montana as well as to promote respect for the flag, reverence for law and order, and undivided allegiance to the government. The commission had prepared 6,000 copies of the oath and questionnaire to send to 4,500 state employees through the mail but waited for the state attorney general to rule that such a move was constitutionally acceptable.[37]

The effort was apparently a colossal waste of time and resources. The Montana attorney general, Arnold H. Olsen, declared that state employees were only required to take one oath and could not be compelled to take another, as the new proposal required. The oath mandated under the Montana Constitution already commanded employees to support, protect, and defend the Constitution of the United States. The new oath affirmed this requirement but also required employees to swear that they would not take part in any movement that would alter or change the form of government and would not belong to any group or organization that advocated such a change. While Olsen personally supported such an oath and lauded the attempts to stamp out communism, the new oath was confusing. It did not define what constituted a prohibited organization. The groups in question could actually include the Democratic and Republican Parties, because each intended to oust the other from power. Olsen also ruled that the questionnaire requested of state employees was a violation of state law because it conflicted with the initial oath required of all state employees. Thus the committee abandoned the idea of a new loyalty oath.[38]

Many state legislatures found loyalty oaths easy to enact to appease conservative constituents, but investigation committees were also popular throughout the nation. According to a 1953 American Civil Liberties Union (ACLU) survey, only seven states did not set up an investigations committee based on the HUAC model: Wyoming, Idaho, Nevada, Nebraska, North Dakota, South Dakota, and Maine.[39] Though North Dakota and South Dakota legislatures never set up an investigation committee aimed at Communist subversives, the Montana legislature did, but it was a rather short-lived experiment. The Republican-dominated Senate set up a study group to consider anticommunist legislation in 1949 but dropped the measure until 1953. The lower chamber then enacted House Bill No. 231, entitled "An Act Relating to the Creation of the

Interim Committee to Investigate Subversive and Un-American Activities in the State of Montana," to mirror Senator McCarthy's investigative committee. The bill passed overwhelmingly, because it was politically inadvisable to oppose such a measure. The committee in Montana, however, was rather tame in comparison to McCarthy's organization.[40]

The Montana committee was supposed to investigate Communists in the state and expose them. It had the necessary powers to issue subpoenas and hold hearings as well as an appropriation of five thousand dollars. The committee consisted of four members of the Montana House and Senate. All of them were reluctant to serve on it except E. V. "Sonny" Omholt, a Republican representative from Teton County.[41] The committee only met once, in Butte, to confer with an FBI agent who told members that the committee was of minimal value because "there were no Communists in Montana, and if there were, the FBI would know their location." The members returned to their hotel, where they voted three to one to disband. The committee took no further action, and the five thousand dollars went back into the state budget.[42]

The FBI agents had the interests of Montana citizens in mind when they advised the committee to stop investigating, but they were incorrect in suggesting that there were no Communists in the state. In 1950 the FBI reported that eighty Communists resided there. That same year, Communists in Butte distributed propaganda when a well-known anticommunist gave a stirring speech inside the local high school. Members of the Communist Party in Montana signed hundreds of pamphlets and placed them on the windshields of vehicles parked outside.[43]

Even so, one reason why citizens on the northern Great Plains did not enact the legislation that other states did was because relatively few Communists lived there. Notwithstanding the socialist and other left-wing movements that had colored the region's history in the early twentieth century, the tension of the emerging Cold War reduced the number of Communists across America. The number of CPA members fell from eighty thousand members nationally in 1944 to fewer than sixty thousand members in 1946. More than thirty thousand members of the Communist Party lived in New York when the anticommunist crusade began in 1948; almost seven thousand Communists lived in Illinois; and almost nine thousand lived in California.[44] The CPA recruited most successfully in urban-industrial areas with large numbers of trade unionists, educators, welfare workers, students, and racial and ethnic minorities—elements uncommon on the northern Great Plains.[45] Furthermore, anti-communist campaigns across the nation had eliminated the majority of members by 1955, when CPA membership in the United States had declined to only 22,000.[46] Dynamics within the region itself led to the diminution of Communists, such as the large number of agrarian land-holders, a deeply religious and spiritual tradition, fewer cities, and numerous fraternal organizations concerned with civic duty. In 1946 the FBI counted 124 Communists in North Dakota, 103 in South Dakota, and just 71 in Montana. By 1955 the number of Communists in North Dakota fell from 124 to 45; South Dakota membership dropped from 103 to 38; Montana membership actually rose from 71 to 80.[47]

One of the reasons for the nationwide decline in CPA membership was the federal use of the Smith Act, ratified in 1940, which allowed for the arrest of those who advocated the overthrow of the American government by violence. Use of Communist-control laws such as the Smith Act began in earnest in 1948, when President Truman sought to convince the American people that international communism remained a threat to domestic security. The Republican Party constantly attacked Truman for being soft on communism. In response Truman's attorney general and federal prosecutors indicted twelve of the highest-ranking members of the CPA under the provisions of the Smith Act. Prosecutors later declined to pursue one defendant due to health reasons, but the federal trial of the other eleven members in New York City captured the attention of the American people in January 1949.[48] It also would resonate in one community of the northern plains.

At the center of the trial was Harold R. Medina, who was appointed a judge in the Southern District of New York by Truman in 1947, after having given up a lucrative law practice. When the trial ended in the conviction of the eleven defendants, the American people hailed Medina as a hero. Medina not only upheld the jury's decision to find the defendants guilty but also remanded six defense lawyers to prison sentences of thirty days to six months for disruptive tactics used during trial. Citizens in Medina, North Dakota, so respected the judge for his actions that the city (pronounced Meh-dine-ah) voted to change its name to the Hispanic pronunciation. Mayor Dan Preszler said: "It would be one way to pay some tribute to a judge, who by his conduct of the Communist trial, showed himself to be a great man and a great American."[49] Although the revised pronunciation failed to catch on in North Dakota, the story illuminates the support of its citizens for anticommunist actions.

While the federal government prosecuted the eleven Communist leaders, Senator Mundt of South Dakota began his most notorious crusade as a House member in 1947. He outlined a plan that included registering Communists with the attorney general of the United States.[50] The Mundt-Nixon bill, which Representative Mundt wrote and HUAC chair Richard Nixon approved, passed the House of Representatives by an overwhelming majority on May 21, 1948. But the Senate did not take up the bill even though many people nationally supported anticommunist legislation.[51] More than a quarter of American citizens supported outlawing the Communist Party, and a majority approved imprisonment in the event of war with the Soviet Union for those who subscribed to Communist ideology. About 13 percent of the population even approved shooting or hanging every known Communist.[52]

The Mundt-Nixon bill had advocates at the grassroots level on the northern plains: George C. Fullinweider of Huron, South Dakota, wrote to Senator Case recommending that the process be "speeded up."[53] Harry L. Burns of Chinook, Montana, wrote to Senator Murray, who did not support the bill, outlining his frustration. "You are a member of the Democratic Party which is the party in power at the present time," Burns wrote, "and it is difficult for me to understand . . . why your party is dodging its responsibility and has for so long failed to enact any anti-subversive laws along the line of the Mundt-Nixon bill."[54] L. A. Forkner of Elm Springs, South Dakota, also wrote to Case, advising the senator that "no country can hope to live unless they retain the right to curb any subversive doctrine." As democracy implied majority rule, "the senate should put the question to the people to decide whether the preaching of communism is profitable in this country. There would be a majority so large that the ballot would need no count."[55]

Jack Williams of Fargo, North Dakota, wrote to Senator William Langer endorsing the bill and questioning Langer's patriotism for opposing it. Langer responded: "I am 100 percent against communism or Communists in every way, shape, form and manner. Under the proposed measure of these reactionaries, members of the Nonpartisan League could be barred without hearing and the appeal would be futile. Also under the proposed reactionary bill any man can be branded as a communist without hearing and his only appeal is not to a federal court where he lives but to federal court only in the District of Columbia, which may be 3,000 miles away from his home and prohibits a poor man from getting a hearing."[56]

Langer's remarks showed that public officials and citizens from the northern plains did not necessarily stampede into excessive anticommunism. L. S. Boe of Whitefish, Montana, asked: "Is the shouting to promote Democracy in other nations for the purpose of covering up the sound of bulldozers digging democracy's grave in our own nation?"[57] Another Murray constituent wrote: "This bill, if passed, will destroy our present democracy and take away the civil liberties of all American people. In reality, this Mundt-Nixon bill is a step towards making this country a police state."[58]

An article in *Time* called the measure "Logical, But Not Practical" by arguing that the bill endangered civil liberties, could be used as a weapon against any unpopular group, and could be interpreted in a variety of ways. Even the attorney general of the United States spoke out against the bill, arguing that existing laws were effective against the Communist threat and that this legislation would unduly tax the Justice Department. The bill died because the Senate did not take action, most likely due to the controversy surrounding it.[59] One of the most prominent senators from the northern plains had originated the Mundt-Nixon bill and another had been one of its most valiant opponents, though constituents returned both to office repeatedly.

Two years later the House again took up the Mundt-Nixon bill. It passed by an even larger majority of 354 to 20 in August 1950. This time the senators took up the bill when Nevada senator Pat McCarran proposed several key amendments. The new bill, called the McCarran Act or Internal Security Act of 1950, contained most of the provisions of the Mundt-Nixon bill but also included the "Emergency Detention Act of 1950," which now authorized the internment of Communists in camps in the event of an "internal security emergency."[60] A small but effective group of senators rose to oppose the bill, including Minnesota senator Hubert Humphrey, who spoke passionately against the bill during a four-hour speech and predicted: "The Congress of the United States will regret the day it ever passes S. 4037. . . . It will prove to be one of the darkest pages in American history."[61] Joining Humphrey was Senator Langer, who opposed the bill even during debate in the Judiciary Committee. Langer warned that, if enacted, the bill "would constitute the greatest threat to American civil liberties since the Alien and Sedition Laws of 1798," arguing further that it was "the product of hysteria, and frantic, unthinking fear. Like that bill, it merits the opposition of all who cherish liberty."[62] Many groups joined in opposition to the bill, including the Communist Party of America, which produced a number of pamphlets arguing that the bill was anti-American and violated the Bill of Rights. Simon W. Gerson, an admitted Communist and legislative chair of the New York Communist Party, argued before HUAC that the majority of Americans opposed the measure as a threat to civil liberties, upon which their ancestors had founded the nation. The Communist Party later published Gerson's testimony in the pamphlet *Either the Constitution or the Mundt Bill, America Can't Have Both.*[63] The Senate passed the measure in an overwhelming vote of 70 to 7, and the bill went to Truman for his signature. The president vetoed the measure on September 22, 1950, but the bill passed both houses of Congress over his veto.

On the heels of the McCarran Act, a number of states enacted laws aimed at Communists. All professional wrestlers had to sign loyalty oaths in Indiana, while Communists could not legally collect unemployment benefits in Ohio. Pennsylvania prohibited Communists from receiving any form of state aid, while Birmingham, Alabama, officials ordered all Communists to leave the city. The city of Jacksonville, Florida, made it a crime to communicate with active or former Communists, and the state legislature in Tennessee ordered the death penalty for anyone attempting to overthrow the state government.[64] The northern plains states were exceedingly mild in comparison. Montana enacted a subversive registration law based on the federal example. House Bill 333, introduced by Republican representative Leonard J. Esp in 1950, was also known as the "Subversive Organization Registration Law." Esp said that the law would define subversive individuals and organizations, requiring them to register with Montana's secretary of state by July 1, 1951, and to divulge membership information of officers with complete names and addresses for each, as well as a list of any affiliations or chapters. Additionally, the groups would have to provide the secretary of state with a detailed description of their aims, purposes, and activities and a list of the property that the groups owned, copies of their charters or bylaws, and oaths of membership, if any. In addition to the definition of subversive groups already set forth under the proposal, the bill also explained that an association could be considered subversive if it was under the control of a foreign power or if it appeared on the list of organizations declared subversive as defined by the attorney general of the United States. The House bill passed the Senate within days of its introduction and became law on July 1, 1951.[65] Subversives who did not register in Montana risked a fine of $10 to $1,000 and from ten days to one year in jail. For officers who had not confessed their roles in such groups the punishment was much more severe, with fines ranging from $500 to $5,000 and from six months to five years in prison. For organizations in which all officers did not register with the secretary of state, the group could have been ordered to pay an additional $1,000 to $10,000. No subversive organizations ever registered with the secretary of state, despite the teeth put into the bill.[66]

No Communist ever registered in Montana, but FBI agents arrested John C. Hellman in Butte in 1956 as a leading Communist Party organizer operating in Montana and Idaho. Officials charged Hellman in the membership section of the Smith Act, which made it illegal to belong to the Communist Party because it advocated the overthrow of the U.S. government by force and violence. Hellman had difficulty in finding counsel to represent him: the only lawyer in Butte willing to do so had not heard a criminal case in over forty years. H. L. Maury told the court that he would not continue representing Hellman in the future but felt that he deserved representation, if only temporarily. United States commissioner David Holland quickly arraigned Hellman and assigned him a $20,000 bail, though Hellman could not pay that amount and remained in jail.[67]

The first real evidence against Hellman emerged during the course of a 1955 trial of another suspected Communist in Denver, where a witness testified that Hellman was present at a 1952 meeting of Communist Party officials in Yellowstone National Park. Another witness identified Hellman as a leading Communist organizer in Montana and reported that Hellman had conducted some sort of training in Bigfork, Montana, in August 1952. Additionally, Hellman had once run for a position on the Montana Railroad–Public Service Commission, garnering over six thousand votes in the general election but losing the race. If Hellman was a subversive, it appeared that he was trying to infiltrate a government organization through the election. It was Hellman's position as a notary public that caused Governor J. Hugo Aronson the most unrest. Hellman had registered over five hundred voters in Silver Bow County through this office, and his association with Communist front organizations concerned many public officials. The U.S. attorney general had indicated that the International Union of Mine, Mill, and Smelter Workers was Communist-infiltrated, and Hellman was one of the principals of that organization. The governor revoked Hellman's notary public commission and invited him to a public hearing over the decision. Hellman did not attend the hearing and did not challenge the decision.[68]

In the days following Hellman's arrest, stories outlining his alleged activities began to surface in Montana papers. FBI officials noted that Hellman had been a vocal advocate of Communist issues for approximately ten years at the time of his arrest, writing articles and giving speeches endorsing the Communist position. FBI chief J. Edgar Hoover even noted that Hellman was a high-ranking member of the Communist Party who had traveled to many communities in both Montana and Idaho to carry out his subversive actions. FBI officials pointed to one speech attributed to Hellman in which he described the American participation in the Korean conflict as "mass murder" on the part of the United States. While most citizens were probably thrilled that another Communist organizer was behind bars, federal judge William D. Murray handled the preliminary aspects of the case and was not pleased that Hoover and other federal officials felt the need to give statements to the press. "I condemn in the strongest terms," Murray stated, "the issuance of statements by police officials or investigating officers with reference to the facts of the case, presenting them to the public, in an effort, apparently, to try the case outside of court." Had this case been assigned to him, Murray went on to say, he would have called FBI director Hoover and his men to stand before him and account for such "un-American and unfair tactics." Murray took one further step to accentuate his displeasure. Hellman's bond was originally set at $20,000, but Murray lowered it to just $5,000, allowing Hellman to leave the Silver Bow County Jail while he awaited trial.[69]

Hellman went to trial in Butte in May 1957. After a lengthy process, a jury found him guilty of violating the Smith Act. Judge Murray, now presiding over the trial, raised Hellman's bond from $5,000 to $10,000 but allowed him three days of freedom to raise the additional funds. Murray eventually sentenced Hellman to serve five years in federal prison for his crime, though the punishment could have been as severe as a ten-year sentence plus a $10,000 fine. After Hellman's arrest, a new federal law went into effect that raised the maximum sentence to twenty years and a $20,000 fine, but Hellman was exempt from that possibility. Hellman gave a short speech just before Murray handed down the sentence. He claimed that he was completely innocent of the charges and had never advocated the violent overthrow of the government but added that socialism could heal many of the problems that Americans faced. Murray, in a sort of rebuttal of Hellman's portrayal of socialism as a positive influence, told the convicted man that he had no tolerance for Marxism, which had no regard for the rights of the people. Only a violent confrontation between democracy and Marxism could replace our existing government.[70]

Other examples of anticommunism also emerged on the northern Great Plains. A professor at the University of Montana, never identified by name, lost his position after accusations of Communist sympathies surfaced.[71] A high school teacher from McHenry, North Dakota, was fired, "in view of his known Communist leanings."[72] School officials suspected that an unnamed faculty member at the University of South Dakota Medical School was actually a Communist, leading the president of the university, I. D. Weeks, to order the man's dismissal. The dean of the Medical School, Dr. Walter Hard, refused to fire a professor on hearsay, especially because the dean had renewed the professor's position for the following year. In the end Hard told the professor in question that he was not in the long-term plans of the department, and the professor left voluntarily.[73]

One of the most notorious accusations of Communist associations on the northern Great Plains involved the Farmers Union, a well-known organization with thousands of members in the region. The incident was the result of the federal legislation ordering the loyalty oaths, when attorney general Thomas Clark released a list of known or suspected subversive organizations in December 1947. After all, it would be difficult for the new loyalty review boards to know whether a person was actually trustworthy unless the government knew the subversive organization to which a person might belong. The original list actually dated back to 1919, when attorney general A. Mitchell Palmer started a list of twelve known Communist organizations, but that list had grown to forty-seven organizations under attorney general Francis Biddle in 1938. The 1947 list contained the names of eighty-nine organizations that Clark had whittled down from three hundred under consideration, though the exact number continued to fluctuate. Inclusion on this list was only possible, the attorney general explained, if the organization met all of the six criteria defined by the Justice Department, which generally included subversive activities with the aim of overthrowing the U.S. government.[74]

Clark had assured liberals that the federal government would conduct loyalty investigations in a fair manner that promised to put an end to suspicions of all government employees. Additionally, the attorney general assured skeptics that membership in one of the dissident organizations should only count as a small piece of evidence and not constitute an entire case. Before the publication of the list, critics charged that the attorney general wielded too much power in determining who was subversive, while others pointed out that no organization had the opportunity to defend itself from accusations of disloyalty before inclusion on the list. The attorney general rebuffed the claims and insisted that the Justice Department had scheduled a hearing with each organization listed. Despite the attorney general's claims, membership in any organization listed as subversive was enough to brand individuals as traitors, regardless of their actual knowledge of Communist activities or infiltration of the group.[75]

The attorney general's list never included the Farmers Union in its list of dissident groups, but another list did. The American Legion (or more correctly the Legion's National Americanism Commission's Subcommittee on Subversive Activities) published a list of hundreds of suspected revolutionary organizations and publications. Among the organizations that the American Legion suspected of subversion was the Farmers Educational and Cooperative Union of America (Farmers Union). The organization had 450,000 members nationally and was by most accounts a leftist organization until the outbreak of the war in Korea. Perhaps this is why New Hampshire senator Styles Bridges attacked the National Farmers Union, claiming that it was a tool of international communism. "The time has come," Bridges argued, "to rid the Farmers Union, composed for the most part of fine and loyal Americans, of the evil and subversive forces within the organization."[76] No one else in the Senate rose to support Bridges and his accusations, but the attack prompted a quick rebuke from senators from the northern Great Plains. The attack on the Farmers Union was not new, as the FBI, the State Department, and HUAC had initiated investigations of the organization with the intent of proving Communist ties.[77]

The Farmers Union did in fact have many Communist members in the 1920s, even until 1950. A kind of alliance had emerged during World War II between the Farmers Union and its leftist members, and no one seemed in a hurry to end the relationship. The initiation of the Korean War, however, proved a turning point in the Farmers Union, which cleaned up its membership and its public image. Bridges referred to the Communist membership from an earlier era. The many pamphlets and articles that the Farmers Union published clearly outlined Communist sympathies that gave Bridges the ammunition that he needed. For example, North Dakota Farmers Union president Glenn Talbott reported that he knew of at least three men who were both Communists and members of the Farmers Union in 1946. Additionally, a 1948 pamphlet published at Farmers Union expense criticized capitalism for its emphasis on creating wealth rather than emphasizing the welfare of people. Finally, the Farmers Union received positive recognition in the *Daily Worker*, the publication of the Communist Party of America throughout the 1940s.[78]

The values of the Farmers Union were on a collision course with American public opinion as the Cold War intensified. The organization had rejected as dangerous and misguided the Truman Doctrine, the Marshall Plan, NATO, universal military training, and the peacetime draft only the year before. By 1950 the Farmers Union was trying to improve its image and announced its support for President Truman, the war in Korea, and other Cold War initiatives. New ideologies require time to take hold, however, and the revised organization was still an object of scorn to ardent anticommunists. To demonstrate its support for American foreign policy and to put a new face on the Farmers Union, the organization fired one of its own workers in 1950 for handing out leaflets opposing the intervention in Korea.[79]

The attack on the Farmers Union precipitated a confrontation between national anticommunism and regional values. The Farmers Union was a powerful establishment on the northern Great Plains, and Senator Langer of North Dakota rose quickly to defend it in light of the new accusations. Days after Senator Bridges attacked the Farmers Union, Langer stood before the Senate and gave a two-hour defense of the organization. Senator Mundt of South Dakota, a conservative and eager anticommunist, joined him, stating that a number of constituents had asked if the Farmers Union of South Dakota was Communistic. Mundt stated that he only got his information on Communist activities from one place, the House Committee on Un-American Activities, which reported no connection between communism and the leaders of the Farmers Union in South Dakota.[80]

North Dakota senator Milton Young also rose to defend the Farmers Union in the Senate. He did so, he told a grateful member of the union, because he had been a member of the group since 1930. He had been president of his local organization and had played a major part in organizing a Farmers Union elevator in his hometown of Berlin, North Dakota. "As a result," he said, "I think I know pretty well what the thinking of the Farmers Union is."[81] Another member of the Farmers Union who appreciated Young's defense of the organization was Harry Miller, the editor of the Wisconsin Division of the *Farmers Union Newsletter*, who sent information to Young and Styles Bridges concerning the position of the Farmers Union on communism. Miller sent the information, he said, "Because it appears the two Senators from our state did not speak in defense of the Wisconsin Farmers Union," referring to Joseph McCarthy and Alexander Wiley. "They certainly are well aware of our position—including the fact, as you will note, that we have a constitutional prohibition against Communists in our Union."[82] Following the Bridges accusations, the National Farmers Union issued a lengthy statement denouncing Communists and denying that the organization had members with Communist sympathies.[83]

One eastern critic who suspected that Communists existed within the Farmers Union was Harvey M. Matusow of New York, who was a former member of the Communist Party and later claimed that he was a spy for the FBI. Matusow was never a paid informant for the government but apparently told FBI officials certain snippets of information on a voluntary basis.[84] He was in Montana to give speeches supporting Republican senator Zales Ecton in his contest with Democratic candidate

Mike Mansfield and to give the impression that Mansfield was sympathetic to Communist ideologies. Matusow touched off a significant controversy in a speech in Great Falls when he mentioned that Communists infested a number of state and national organizations, including the media network CBS (the Columbia Broadcasting System), the State Department, the Boy Scouts, the United Nations, the Voice of America, and the Farmers Union. The Montana Farmers Union, holding a convention in Great Falls at the time, took exception to Matusow's accusation and extended an invitation to him to come before the organization and explain his charges. Unsure of his exact location, the Farmers Union purchased radio time in twelve Montana cities to issue its challenge. "It is a matter of record that the Farmers Union faces squarely to challenges as that of Matusow," the announcement read.[85]

The issue exploded when the Farmers Union insisted that Matusow, or whoever had sponsored him, post a $25,000 bond "to cover any actions which might be brought because of any statements which you might make being slanderous to any persons concerned, including our organization."[86] The Great Falls chapter of the American Legion, the Speakers Bureau, and the Chamber of Commerce had initially sponsored Matusow, thinking that he was simply a former Communist trying to rally support for a Republican candidate. When the controversy with the Montana Farmers Union broke open, all of the local organizations quickly withdrew their support and denied any association with Matusow. Who actually sponsored Matusow remained a mystery until Vic Overcash, former state commander of the American Legion and a right-wing ultra-conservative, clarified the situation. Overcash claimed that the Montana Citizens for Americanism, of which Overcash was the president, had sponsored the speaker and used the other organizations as a cover. When Matusow appeared before the convention with neither sponsor nor bond, the convention refused to allow him to speak.[87]

Overcash responded with a nine-page tract entitled "Documentation of Communist Infiltration Tactics and Strategy," in which he claimed that the Montana Farmers Union attached a $25,000 price tag to free speech. He challenged the Farmers Union to discuss Communist infiltration of the organization, which it declined, calling the idea "preposterous and insincere."[88] Overcash further documented the Communist issue in Montana, citing references to the state and its citizens in pro-Communist literature and listing the different Montana organizations that had opposed the Mundt-Nixon bill, intended to outlaw the Communist Party. Any organization that opposed such a bill, Overcash argued, was obviously Communist, including the Farmers Union.[89] The controversy lingered in the region but eventually died out when the Farmers Union took less controversial stands in the following years.

Matusow was in Montana at the invitation of Joseph McCarthy, who made a name for himself in national politics by claiming that Communists had infiltrated the State Department and were shaping foreign policy. Now he was in Montana and other states to assist the Republican Party with winning as many seats as possible in the fall election. One of the senators McCarthy tried most desperately to defeat, and failed, was Mike Mansfield. The ninety-six members of the Senate were almost equally divided going into the 1952 election, with forty-nine Democrats and forty-seven Republicans. Montana was a battleground state, with each party sending its top political figures into the state to aid in the campaign.[90]

The Democrats brought a number of political figures to campaign with Mansfield, including President Truman and presidential and vice presidential nominees Adlai Stevenson and John Sparkman. The Republicans also brought an impressive list of political figures to campaign for the Ecton, including candidates Dwight Eisenhower, Richard Nixon, and sixteen incumbent senators who campaigned throughout the state. Undoubtedly the most notorious senator campaigning against Mansfield was McCarthy, who addressed an overflowing crowd in Missoula on October 14 and cited positive references to Mansfield in the *Daily Worker*, the newspaper of the Communist Party. McCarthy did not blatantly accuse Mansfield of being Communist but called him "either stupid or a dupe."[91] In the campaign for Ecton—or against Mansfield—Matusow toured nine cities, visiting parochial schools, civic clubs, and American Legion halls. He also gave radio addresses, in which he would pull from his briefcase an article that Mansfield supposedly wrote for the Communist Party's journal *New Masses*. The article allegedly showed Mansfield's support for communism but was actually a report on his trip to China, printed in the *Congressional Record*. Matusow later admitted that he had known nothing of Mansfield; McCarthy's staff had given him the article.[92]

Ecton also continued to assert that Mansfield had Communist sympathies by sending to Montana households a flyer that claimed: "Mansfield Aided Communist Line Which Led to Korean War!"[93] Republicans took out newspaper ads headed "From a Father Whose Son Was Killed in Korea" that attacked Mansfield's ties with communism.[94] Perhaps most disturbing was the thirteen-minute radio address from a Great Falls woman whose husband was a soldier and prisoner of the North Koreans, who blamed Mansfield's blunders for her husband's situation.[95] Stations played the message more than two hundred times in the weeks leading up to the election. The Ecton campaign also telephoned members of the Mansfield campaign, saying "Mike Mansfield is a Communist" and then hanging up.[96]

Mansfield kept above the fray during the campaign, but he addressed Montana listeners through a radio program in the closing hours before the election. He resented, he said, the attack from outside the state on his character, religious faith, integrity, and patriotism. He concluded by asking: "Is it not intolerable that a man seeking high office . . . would suffer the indignity of having to defend, not his political beliefs, but the very honor of his soul?" Montanans apparently agreed with him: they overwhelmingly voted for a Republican president and governor but elected Mansfield by a margin of 6,000 votes of 262,000 votes cast.[97]

The attempt to discredit Mansfield and thus win another seat for the Republican Party failed to play out in Montana. People there did not subscribe to the allegation that Mansfield had Communist sympathies and that the region faced an imminent peril. Thus Mansfield managed to overcome the smear campaign directed against him. The slurs originating from the East over national issues did not gain as much traction in the plains. Mansfield was able to connect with Montanans on a regional level, about issues such as farm bills, and managed to overcome the best efforts of Joe McCarthy to oust him.

By this point in McCarthy's career, people began to wonder about his tactics and his charges. His initial charges had produced excitement and anxiety, though he was never overwhelmingly popular or admired. A Gallup Poll in May 1950 indicated that 84 percent of those surveyed had heard of McCarthy's charges: 39 percent of respondents thought that he was doing more good than harm, while 29 percent thought that he was doing more harm than good.[98] Another poll the following month revealed that 41 percent of the population approved or believed his charges of Communists in the State Department.[99] The initial reaction seems to have been followed by several years of cautious optimism that the Communist threat would subside, as McCarthy and his methods lost popularity. When McCarthy "uncovered" the case of a Communist dentist in the army in late 1953 and investigated the commanding officer in charge, General Ralph W. Zwicker, in early 1954, McCarthy's name recognition soared. He remained in the news as he and Secretary of the Army Robert Stevens moved toward their famous hearings to determine whether, as McCarthy claimed, the United States Army teemed with subversives.

With McCarthy's agency at the center of the hearings, he could not chair the committee that was investigating him, so he stepped down and allowed Karl Mundt, the senior Republican on the committee, to chair the investigation. Mundt tried desperately to have another committee conduct the investigations, knowing that McCarthy was engendering controversy. Many of Mundt's constituents wrote to voice their concern about the Wisconsin senator. Elmer Thurow of Aberdeen, South Dakota, was one of many people who wrote to Mundt to express their disgust with McCarthy. Thurow asked if every senator was a coward, noting that "there are nearly a hundred senators who apparently are going to let this McCarthy ride until President Eisenhower will have to take the situation in hand. The Senate should have gumption enough to straighten out its own sordid affair."[100]

It looked like another committee might actually conduct the hearings at one point. Mundt felt sure that the administration would never let the hearings go forward, but he was mistaken on all counts. Mundt would chair the investigations, on which most of America had strong opinions. McCarthy's approval rating had begun dropping in the polls in the months after reports of the Zwicker case emerged and his tactics became better understood. Many who earlier had no opinions on the matter now zealously opposed McCarthy.[101] While few sources shed any light on the events that put the South Dakota senator in charge of the investigations, Mundt's appointment to the position cannot be overlooked. Perhaps his peers selected him to lead the investigation because his constituents would forgive him, whatever the outcome. As long as Mundt continued to deliver for the farm bloc, his position as senator was relatively secure. Few people envisioned the hearings accomplishing much.

McCarthy lost much of his following throughout the nation and on the northern plains as Americans became familiar with his methods. Attorney Joseph Welch defended the army against McCarthy's attack and exposed McCarthy's brutish tactics in the Army-McCarthy Hearings, one of the first televised congressional investigations. Maude Ridenour of Kalispell, Montana, wrote to Senator Murray, telling him: "People in our area are becoming increasingly concerned over the actions and maneuverings of McCarthy. We feel that his current thrust at the army is another aspect of the blind destruction of democracy by McCarthyism."[102] Emma Reppert of Lead, South Dakota, was outraged at the disgrace that the trial heaped upon the Republican Party. "Shame, Shame, Shame!" she wrote. "Do you have to let McCarthy wreck the nation as well as the Republican Party?"[103] Fred Christopherson, the editor of the *Daily Argus-Leader* in Sioux Falls, saw the problems that McCarthy was creating. "I wonder if McCarthy himself," Christopherson observed, "realizes that he is taking a bad licking in the public mind as a result of the hearings. I fear that those of you who are very close to the detailed testimony do not appreciate the impression being acquired by the casual observer."[104] C. S. Rothwell was disgusted listening to the hearings on the radio and sent a personal note to McCarthy at his Senate office. The Montanan from Park City wrote: "Even the sound and tone of your voice is revolting to me. I presume now you wish to place my name on your list and to, in due time, have your Gestapo shadow me and snoop on me. I say to you, go to it."[105] Even as the criticism increased, McCarthy continued to enjoy support from his most dedicated supporters. Paul Noren of Pierre, South Dakota, wrote a note to encourage him in those troubling times. "I am frank in saying," he wrote to McCarthy, "that this country is definitely in need of men and women with convictions of right and wrong, and I congratulate you on your efforts to root out Communists in government."[106]

While many in the country increasingly blasted McCarthy, Mundt came under increasing attack as well. Government officials and the public attacked Mundt for the way he handled the hearings. He constantly allowed McCarthy to interrupt the hearings, as with McCarthy's constant refrain: "Point of order, Mr. Chairman, point of order!" As the hearings dragged on and McCarthy's popularity diminished, Mundt realized that the hearings were not helping him with his constituents at home. The differences between McCarthy and Stevens were best handled through both men testifying and leaving it at that, Mundt thought, but the hearings dragged on with no clear direction. John E. Griffin of Sioux Falls summed up the mood of other South Dakotans when he wrote to Mundt that "every person who mentions the subject feels the big hearing is damaging you."[107] Others in the state thought that Mundt was doing a good job fighting communism, but during the election year the people of South Dakota wanted to know what he was doing for South Dakota.[108]

Mundt knew the hearings were hurting him politically but did not realize how badly, even though many tried to warn him. Among those who expressed their concern over the hearings was his friend Fred Christopherson, who told Mundt: "There was growing disgust over the proceeding throughout this area."[109] Christopherson wrote an editorial and then a personal letter to Mundt, outlining his views. "Mundt has been trying too hard to please everybody. He has been too tolerant, too eager to lean over backward to give all an opportunity to speak freely. The time has come to swing an iron fist," he concluded.[110] Mundt was up for reelection in November and had to scramble to make up ground politically.

Mundt, hoping to distance himself from McCarthy, opted not to join the Wisconsin senator as he traveled to Sioux Falls near the end of the hearings in June 1954, in contrast to Senate tradition. McCarthy arrived in the city to address an American Legion convention, to that point some of McCarthy's most ardent followers. His supporters, however, were abandoning him in droves: only eighty of sixty thousand Sioux Falls residents turned out to hear the senator. During his presentation McCarthy told listeners that he did not expect a decisive conclusion to the hearings and took the opportunity to praise Mundt, who was running for reelection in the fall. Whether Mundt appreciated the reference remains unclear.[111] The contrast between McCarthy's latest reception in Sioux Falls and his reception in Huron in 1950 is unavoidable. While he was treated with a great deal of interest during his first visit to the state, he was virtually ignored during his final visit. Officials made little preparation for McCarthy's initial visit, and the venue was overwhelmed. Yet his last visit involved a great deal of preparation for the few people that attended the event. This example demonstrates how far McCarthy had fallen in the eyes of people from the region.

After the hearings, senators that McCarthy had insulted or threatened over the years lined up to punish him through the Senate's traditional measure, a vote to "censure" one of its own members. Though the measure sounds tame, it was quite serious in the Senate's tradition of decorum. To examine the motion for censure, Senate party leaders assembled a bipartisan committee of six senators that included three respected Democrats and three conservative Republicans, including Senator Case of South Dakota. Few people knew Case outside of South Dakota or the Senate. But his integrity was beyond question for those that knew him, and he was not up for reelection that fall. Perhaps Case's peers thought that he was safe politically and was thus a sage choice to serve on the committee. Leading the hearings on the censure motion was Republican Arthur V. Watkins, the devout Mormon elder from Utah. Historians credit Lyndon Johnson, the Democratic Senate minority leader, with assembling a committee that no one could accuse of liberal bias. Johnson made sure that a panel of his peers, free of partisan politics, judged McCarthy.[112]

Watkins established the rules for the committee, prohibiting the television coverage that McCarthy obviously relished, and insisted that all participants conduct themselves with discipline and order. The committee and bipartisan Senate leadership wanted to ensure that the censure hearings did not become a debacle along the lines of the Army-McCarthy Hearings. Watkins established his leadership credentials on the first day, when McCarthy grabbed the microphone during testimony and began to shout: "Just a minute, Mr. Chairman, just a minute." Watkins was prepared and stopped McCarthy cold. "The senator is out of order." Watkins slammed the gavel down and exclaimed: "We are not going to be diverted from these diversions and sidelines. We are going straight down the line," banging his gavel down again and adjourning for the day.[113]

On August 31, 1954, the same day the committee met to discuss the censure issue, the members of the Army-McCarthy investigation committee published their report. After months of testimony, the partisan report indicated that the hearings were inconclusive. The hearings held no one accountable or guilty of dishonorable conduct. All of the Republican members of the committee absolved McCarthy of any wrongdoing, while the Democrats found merit in the charges. This lack of judgment upon McCarthy only heightened interest in the censure motion.[114]

South Dakota leaders: Governor Joe Foss (*left*), Senator Francis Case (*center*), and Senator Karl Mundt (*right*). No date given. Courtesy Mundt Archives, Dakota State University, Image 69-778.

Though McCarthy lost much support after the hearings, he was not through. According to the Gallup Poll, 34 percent of Americans questioned thought that he should stay on as the head of the Senate Investigations Committee.[115] Senator Case also thought that McCarthy was on the right track in his government investigations, as he saw the nation facing a serious threat from internal subversion. The only question was the extent of the methods employed, believed Case, who had endorsed a plan to end free speech for Communists in 1948. He approved of McCarthy's crusade to expose Communists, adopting the theme in his own reelection bid in 1950.[116]

The matter of appropriate punishment was the main point in the censure motion. Case began backing away from the idea of censuring McCarthy during the investigations and was solidly against the motion at the conclusion of the hearings. McCarthy still had a small but active core of supporters in South Dakota, and Case did not want the negative publicity to damage the senate or divide the Republican Party. Some suggested that Case's newfound support for McCarthy was the result of political pressure, speculating that South Dakota governor Joe Foss, an outspoken supporter of McCarthy, threatened to run against Case in 1956. Both Case and Foss denied the reports, but Case's actions did raise questions. He had originally supported censure for the Zwicker case and had even helped to draft that section of the report. Case now led a movement to allow McCarthy to escape censure, if he would only apologize. Case explained before the Senate that he did not condone McCarthy's actions but did not want to censure a senator who had tried to inform the nation of the dangers of communism. The committee soundly rejected Case's proposal. No one, not even McCarthy, gave any indication of support.[117]

The suggestion of an apology enraged H. R. Davidson of Riverdale, North Dakota, as McCarthy continued to lose support. "It ought not need saying, but apparently, it does," he wrote. "The Senate appointed a committee to review the censurable actions of Senator McCarthy. The report of the committee was unanimous. Now the papers write of 'compromise' resolutions which McCarthy—the accused—will accept." Davidson concluded his letter with the following observation: "If the Senate does not follow through the action it has begun firmly and unequivocally, it does indeed deserve McCarthy's contempt and the voters also."[118]

Had McCarthy accepted the compromise and apologized, the censure movement would probably have disappeared. Most senators had no desire to reprimand one of their own, and even the president would have welcomed a way out of the embarrassing predicament. When McCarthy refused to apologize, it set in motion a partisan contest. The Democrats had to oppose McCarthy, while most Republicans felt they had to defend him for the good of the party.[119] Case and Mundt were in a particularly awkward position, having defended McCarthy's earlier actions. But to censure him would be tantamount to giving the Democrats a victory.

The citizens on the northern plains had their ideas on the censure issue and wrote to their senators, urging them to act one way or another. Jesse M. Olson of Yankton, South Dakota, wrote to Karl Mundt on behalf of himself and his wife, urging him not to censure McCarthy, not because he supported McCarthy but because the Republican Party needed to work together in the coming years.[120] Douglas Hancock wrote that "we ought to put an end to Joe McCarthy's caveman tactics."[121] Others wrote their senators in Montana, such as Mary Lear of Choteau, who asked Senator Murray to "back Senator McCarthy. We are fighting communism and this fight amongst ourselves is a disgrace."[122] Maude Gushart shared this opinion, telling Murray: "It is difficult to understand why all good Americans are not one hundred percent behind Senator McCarthy and why his work is being hampered by stupid charges."[123]

The committee had trouble identifying specific charges against McCarthy and in the end replaced all previous charges with only one charge: conduct "contrary to Senate tradition," for calling the censure investigating committee the "unwitting handmaiden of the Communist Party."[124] The final vote was a partisan matter for the Democrats, with all voting to censure McCarthy. The Republicans split over the issue, with twenty-two voting for censure, including Senator Case, who had been an outspoken critic of the censure movement. Some suggest that the large number of South Dakotans who wrote to him and expressed their outrage at McCarthy may have changed his mind. Twenty-two Republicans also opposed censure, including Mundt and William Langer and Milton Young of North Dakota. The senate also dropped the word "censure" in its final actions and instead substituted the word "condemned." The only members who did not vote were McCarthy, his fellow senator from Wisconsin, Alexander Wiley, and the Democratic senator John F. Kennedy.[125]

The public on the plains was as divided over the censure vote as over any other aspect of the entire affair. C. Maxwell Brown of Fargo, North Dakota, wrote to Senator Young: "I was greatly disappointed to read that you had found it necessary to support Mr. McCarthy against the majority of the Senate during the censure episode."[126] Max Lang's letter from Sterling, North Dakota, pleased Senator Young immensely. Lang mentioned that he supported Young's stance not to censure McCarthy. "As you would guess," Young responded, "I am receiving quite a few rather mean letters because of my vote against censuring McCarthy. It is a bit difficult to understand why so many people are so determined to destroy McCarthy."[127]

Willard E. Fraser of Billings, Montana, was pleased that his two senators, Mike Mansfield and James Murray, had voted to censure McCarthy based on the merits of the case, despite the partisan voting results.

"Wouldn't we be ashamed, out here in Montana," Fraser wrote, "if we were represented by a man like Senator Case of South Dakota, who apparently changes his opinion with each mail delivery?"[128] Vera Praast of Anaconda, Montana, was disappointed that her senators had voted to censure McCarthy. "I believe a great many Montana people favor Senator McCarthy," she wrote. "We want the Communists in jail. It is all too evident that the Communists are not too respectful to Americans whom they imprison and torture to death."[129]

Senators Case and Mundt of South Dakota faced harsher criticism at home over the censure vote. Mundt was never personally close to Eisenhower, and the hearings had further strained their relationship. But Mundt nevertheless wrote to the president, seeking his support for his upcoming 1954 election. "Your speech in Hollywood Bowl was a masterpiece, Mr. President, and several more talks in this fighting vein asking specifically for the return of a Republican Congress can help our mutual cause considerably."[130] Secretary of Agriculture Ezra Taft Benson was unpopular in the farming areas of the northern plains. Mundt urged the president to announce several farm programs without delay, such as a program to buy eggs for school lunches. "We need heavy Republican majorities in the farm areas to carry the Congress," Mundt warned.[131]

Mundt brought the vice president, Richard Nixon, into the state to campaign on his behalf. He prepared some talking points for Nixon, asking him to be especially careful of the one "ticklish" problem, the farm issue.[132] Mundt also brought Arizona senator Barry Goldwater to South Dakota to boost his political campaign, giving him the same talking points and warnings that he had given the vice president.[133] "I am deeply grateful to you for this splendid 'assist,'" Mundt told Goldwater, "and I know that you did our common cause a tremendous amount of good by your visit to South Dakota's Black Hills Country."[134] The Mundt campaign won easily, but the Republican ticket lost a tremendous amount of support that it had enjoyed during the 1952 election.

Case also suffered politically by trying to please everyone. People assumed that his change of view regarding the censure vote was politically motivated, although Case insisted that he was acting in accordance with his conscience after listening to the evidence. According to Case biographer Richard Chenoweth, "Case's activities on the Watkins Committee

. . . did not help his public image or political future. The pro-McCarthy people could not forgive him for supporting a condemnation of McCarthy, while the anti-McCarthyites saw Case hurting their cause."[135]

McCarthy died in 1957, only three years after his Senate condemnation. But from the void emerged the John Birch Society, an entire organization dedicated to denouncing Communists and anyone else who opposed its ultraconservative ideology.[136] Robert Welch founded the John Birch Society in 1958 to combat the perceived infiltration of subversives in the American government. The final objective of the John Birch Society, according to J. Allen Broyles writing in 1964, was to "root out all thought and leadership to the left of a distorted 'protectionist' Adam Smith in economics, Barry Goldwater in politics, Carl McIntire in religion, and the 'three R's' in education."[137] The leaders and members of the society saw their ideal as the only truly patriotic goal and regarded everyone who disagreed with this view as conscious or unconscious agents of international communism. The organization moved its headquarters from Benton, Massachusetts, to McCarthy's hometown of Appleton, Wisconsin, in tribute to a "true American hero."[138]

The John Birch Society was an orphan that few politicians would adopt. Citizens and politicians viewed it as a subversive, ultra-right-wing organization that worried more people than it attracted. Critics often labeled the group a Republican organization because of its conservative ideology, much to the embarrassment of the politicians of that party, who had repudiated the group. The society, in fact, was often harsher in its criticism of Republican politicians than of Democratic ones. It clung to a zealot ideology, not a political one. A map in the organization's headquarters indicated that considerable concentrations of supporters existed in Texas and southern California, with smaller concentrations in Phoenix, Wichita, and Chicago. But most states seemed to have a pin somewhere. A close inspection of South Dakota would probably have indicated that only one member of the John Birch Society lived there, although a number of constituents wrote to Senator Mundt, expressing their concern over the organization. A small but vocal contingent of the society lived in North Dakota and Montana.[139]

The John Birch Society was secretive about the numbers and names of members, so it is impossible to know exactly how widespread the organization was. The society boasted a national membership of more than 100,000, but others estimated that the true number was closer to 32,000.[140] The names of various coordinators were well known. Newspapers in Montana listed Vic Overcash, of the Montana Farmers Union debate, as the society's coordinator in Montana, Wyoming, and eastern Idaho. The organization named Overcash to the position in January 1962 and grew under his guidance. Democratic senator Lee Metcalf of Montana noted with some alarm that many of the new members that Overcash recruited were Democrats. "They have made considerable inroads among Democrats in our state," Metcalf said. "We are going to have to do what the Republicans are ultimately going to have to do: purge them from the party."[141]

The evidence suggests, however, that the society had few supporters on the northern plains. Montana's first meeting of the John Birch Society in June 1962 had more critics than members, though Overcash did his best to win converts. He showed a movie, gave a pointed speech about the danger to the nation from subversive forces, and even claimed that a Communist was serving in the Montana legislature. Overcash refused to identify the subversive, saying that "it was not the Society's purpose to name Reds but only to acquaint the public with the front organizations and connections speakers and officials had."[142] An unsigned letter to Lee Metcalf from a journalist summed up the meeting this way: "Overcash had prepared his answers to the obvious questions. I think, however, that the critical ones in the room were disgusted at the way Overcash tried to uphold [founder] Welch on his crazy ideas."[143]

Many Montanans were suspicious of the organization and wrote their senators to say so. The Flathead County Women's Club voted to request an investigation of the John Birch Society and publicly opposed the group. Cora E. Van Deusen was shocked at the number of prominent people that the organization named as Communists. "It seems as though anyone who is useful and serving their country to a very high degree gets the Communist tag," she wrote.[144] Barbara Hauge of Turner, Montana, brought the conflict closer to home, likening the society to fascism. "I think the lunatic fringe, which is fascism, poses as great a threat to our Democracy as does totalitarian communism because . . . the John Birch Society has the wealth of the rich and they camouflage themselves in the Bible and the Flag."[145]

North Dakota also had a contingent of society supporters focused around Bismarck, Grand Forks, Hazelton, and southeastern North Dakota. The number of members was a secret, according to Leo Landsberger, a former coordinator of Birch activities in the state. But the number of members was apparently growing during the early 1960s, if only by small amounts, as many North Dakotans adamantly opposed the organization.[146]

In 1964 an election pitted the John Birch Society against mainstream politics in North Dakota. John W. Scott, a wealthy farmer from Gilby and a banker in Grand Forks, ran as a Republican and received the backing of the John Birch Society as he sought to gain the congressional seat of Republican representative Hjalmer C. Nygaard, vacated upon his death. Scott campaigned through all twenty-three counties in the district, adopting the ideology of the Birchers as he attacked the United Nations, aid to agriculture and education, the sale of wheat to the Soviet Union, and the tax program. A Bircher managed his campaign, which had the slogan "Send John Scott to Congress and Barry Goldwater to the White House."[147] Republican Mark Andrews and Democrat John Hove opposed Scott, and Senator Young labeled the election a test of the society's strength. Goldwater endorsed Andrews not the Bircher Scott in the contest. Scott was soundly defeated in the election, garnering only 5,773 votes out of 92,536 cast. After Andrews won in a landslide, Young remarked: "Only a small minority has been making all the noise."[148]

The people of North Dakota clearly rejected the John Birch Society and its alarmist ideology in 1964, and the next election was a disaster for the organization. The John Birch Society in North Dakota supported a number of candidates in 1968. They were all candidates of the Taxpayers Republican Ticket, whose main purpose was to abolish the income tax. The most prominent candidate was Leo Landsberger, who was running for governor. He set up a three-day workshop for supporters held at an auditorium in Grand Forks that had seats available for 850 people after sending out 5,000 invitations. Only 30 people showed up.[149]

While the crusade against Communists seems to have permeated the American society in the early Cold War period, the evidence suggests that Communist hunting was not pervasive on the northern plains states. The Communist Party and the John Birch Society, representing the extreme left and right of the political spectrum, disintegrated.

Neither organization played a particularly pivotal role on the northern plains when the Cold War intensified. Many citizens in the region supported Senator Mundt's anticommunist legislation in 1948, while others applauded the trial and conviction of eleven Communist Party leaders in 1949. The significance of these events was diminished on the northern plains, however, where few citizens in the region even knew an active Communist. When the issue struck closer to home, as it did when Senator Bridges accused the Farmers Union of harboring Communists, people rose up in defense of the organization. Nearly everyone in the region knew a member of the Farmers Union in 1950. The Communist Party posed little threat on the northern plains, which is probably why right-wing organizations concerned with outing Communists found little support there.

The anticommunist period in America illuminated several conclusions. The first was that the state governments often emulated the federal example in controlling Communist subversion through loyalty oaths, investigation committees, and Communist-control laws. As evidenced in this chapter, however, the politicians on the northern Great Plains rarely enacted laws aimed at Communists with the same gusto as in other states; nor did the people demand that they do so. There were few Communists in the region, and residents saw subversives as a problem in major cities and not in local communities. Of course, politicians on the northern Great Plains did enact anticommunist laws when interested individuals and organizations thrust these bills upon state legislatures that could not avoid acting on them for political reasons, as happened in South Dakota with the loyalty oath. One department in Montana attempted to enact a loyalty oath but could not do so. A single state legislator there forced the creation of an investigative committee to eradicate subversives, though other committee members had the good sense to abandon the idea when FBI agents suggested that they were wasting their time. Montana also enacted a Communist-control law that was ineffective, as no Communist organization ever registered with the state government. The North Dakota state legislature passed no anticommunist laws. In sum, the people of the northern plains did not overreact to the situation. As North Dakota attorney general Wallace E. Warner cautioned in 1950: "In our efforts to attack communism at home and abroad, we must not become so overzealous that we indulge in witch-hunting and promiscuous name calling . . . nor transform America into a Fascist concentration camp."[150] Anticommunism, in the end, was another program developed at the federal level and enacted at the state and local level with varying degrees of success, reflecting the pragmatic approach of the northern plains people. Government officials also supported religious observance as a patriotic program, as discussed in the next chapter.

Chapter 2

One Nation, under God

The autumn evening was chilly, but no one complained as the audience members made their way into the Shrine Auditorium in Billings, Montana. Free admission to the evening's event ensured that each of the four thousand seats was filled. The main attraction that night was evangelist Merv Rosell, who came at the invitation of the Christ for Greater Billings Crusade, a conglomeration of city churches and religious organizations who paid all of the fees associated with his performance. Newspaper advertisements appeared in the weeks before Rosell's arrival, boasting that he had addressed crowds numbering 12,000 per night in Kansas City and 30,000 at a single meeting in Des Moines, Iowa. The show, originally scheduled for November 11–16, 1951, was held over for two days due to popular demand. The auditorium's business manager claimed that the November 18 show was the largest crowd ever assembled in the auditorium.[1] Rosell's message to the Montana crowd was dark but irresistible: he warned that "disaster lay ahead as five major crises confronted America." The problems, according to Rosell, included a century of bloody wars, the possibility of atomic attack, atheist and Communist subversion, disastrous economic poverty, and finally, a tidal wave of moral corruption. "Only Christianity has the answer to the problems of the world," the minister said.[2]

Rosell's message that faith in God would save humanity from communism was common during the early Cold War. Societal elites worried that Marxist ideology—which forbade the worship of God—might appeal to average Americans, who would spread the contagion throughout their communities. Political leaders, religious figures, journalists, and

even former Communists worked diligently to promote religious observance throughout America as a lever against "atheistic communism."
Marxism was more than a political ideology to American cultural leaders; it was a religion without a God on a collision course with American
spiritual values. The only defense against the godless Soviet philosophy
was an American campaign that focused on God and returned worship
to the center of American culture. Spiritual and political leaders organized their resources and mobilized a religious movement, the likes of
which the nation had never seen. This chapter examines the effort to
develop religious observance on the northern Great Plains in an attempt
to combat subversion.

Americans embraced religion more readily during the Cold War than
they did during the Great Depression or World War II. Cold Warriors
equated religion with patriotism, which did not happen in the wake of
other national crises. Between 1910 and 1920 American church membership was 43 percent. It remained steady or declined during the early
1930s but rose to 49 percent by 1940, as the Great Depression began
to subside.[3] Many Americans initially supported religious obedience
when the Great Depression hit, but churches did not have the resources
to meet the needs of everyone who required help. Disgusted, many
turned away from the church and toward the only other entity capable
of providing comfort and relief: the government. Likewise, people felt
little pressure to accept religion during World War II. Just 13 percent
of Americans reported going to church more often because of the war,
but 57 percent reported no increased religious interest in their communities.[4] Perhaps most significantly, President Roosevelt refused to
construct the conflict in religious terms to protect the wartime alliance
with Joseph Stalin, though many religious leaders considered communism far more offensive to American values than fascism, at least early
on.[5] Positive public opinion of the Soviet Union reached its zenith in
1943 but began to decline in 1944 and plummeted in 1945, as people realized the Soviets would control all of Eastern Europe. Once the Cold
War became reality, political and religious leaders did not hesitate to
turn the conflict into a religious crusade against communism, pitting
atheism against spiritualism. As evidence, 55 percent of Americans reported attending church in 1950, 62 percent in 1956, and 69 percent
in 1960.[6]

The federal government was instrumental in the effort to engage religion against communism. Most famously, the words "under God" appeared in the pledge of allegiance in 1954, at the direction of President Eisenhower. The idea can be traced to a 1951 national board meeting of the Knights of Columbus, a fraternal organization of the Catholic Church, which adopted a resolution requesting that they all add the words "under God" to the pledge normally recited at the opening of their local meetings. The national board called on the United States Congress to make the change official the following year. Additionally, leaders of the national board mailed letters with the same request to the president, vice president, and Speaker of the House. By the following March the issue had attracted national attention, prompting the Gallup organization to question Americans about the proposed change. Of those questioned, 70 percent favored the addition of "under God" to the pledge. The Knights of Columbus continued to endorse the idea. By the summer of 1953 the national board again reached out to the president but this time also forwarded the resolution to every member of the House and Senate. Not until the president's Presbyterian minister took up the cause in February 1954 did the measure finally gain the needed momentum. The Reverend George Docherty told his congregation, which included Eisenhower, that something was missing from the pledge. "Apart from the words 'United States of America,' the pledge could refer to any republic." Adding the words "under God" to the pledge, he argued, would differentiate America from the rest of the world. By June the Congress had introduced and passed the appropriate measures, forwarding the bill to the president, who signed it into law on June 14, 1954.[7] The term "In God We Trust" was added to all American money in 1956. When the phrase appeared on an eight–cent postage stamp, the president and secretary of state gave a public address honoring the occasion.[8]

The phrase "under God" had gained traction throughout the northern Great Plains and was used widely even before the change to the pledge of allegiance. The *Bismarck Tribune* noted the connection between political eras when it ran an article on the front page entitled "In 1951 as in 1776." In George Washington's own words was a caution, initially directed at the British but equally applicable to the Soviet Union: "The time is near at hand, which must probably determine whether Americans are to be freemen or slaves, . . . [or] whether their homes are to be pillaged and destroyed. The fate of unborn millions will now depend, under God, on the courage and conduct of the American people."[9] The mayor of Bismarck used the phrase when he proclaimed June 11, 1950, to be "Wake Up America Day" in that city and urged citizens to cooperate in making the event an inspiring affirmation of their faith in their heritage of freedom. In the official proclamation the mayor declared that "our citizens have found their greatest expression in our social, economic, and political institutions, under God."[10] Even Eisenhower used the words as the Garrison Dam project in North Dakota neared completion on June 11, 1953. The occasion was the closure ceremony for the dam's embankment. The president warned the Soviets: "Do not attack us except at your own peril because we are going to live, under God, as a free, secure people."[11] In another speech in 1953, this time from the White House, President Eisenhower commented on the Communists who arrested Stefan Cardinal Wyszynski in Poland: "Communist violations of the inalienable rights of man, under God, do not go unopposed."[12]

After the words "under God" were added to the pledge of allegiance in 1954, civic and political leaders on the northern Great Plains invoked the words to add emphasis to their speeches. In Pierre, South Dakota, the Daughters of the American Revolution (DAR) convention in 1958 adopted the theme "This Nation, under God."[13] The Right Reverend Phillip F. McNairy lamented that more money was spent on dog food in America than on Christian education. The speech was made in Mitchell, South Dakota, in 1960 at the 76th annual convocation of the Episcopal Church. "In a country where the people believe in loyalty, under God . . . I think more should be done with religion than is being done."[14] World War I veteran and American Legion official Walter W. Bernard gave a Veteran's Day Speech to the Butte Lions Club in Montana in 1956, in which he also invoked the phrase. "Yesterday," Bernard said, "the eleventh hour of the eleventh day of the eleventh month, we paused in solemn reverence to our hero dead, the gallant men and women who gave the last measure of their devotion, that the flag . . . might float, under God, forever free."[15]

Opposing communism and endorsing religion was popular in the 1950s, but Catholic opposition to communism dated back to 1846, when Pope Pius IX condemned "that infamous doctrine of so-called communism which is absolutely contrary to the natural law itself, and if once adopted would utterly destroy the rights, property, and possessions of all men, and even society itself."[16] Resistance continued unabated throughout the twentieth century, including a denunciation by Pope Pius XI in 1937, when he issued the encyclical *Divini Redemptoris*, which denounced communism for threatening the foundations of Christianity. His remarks were so scathing and his position was so well entrenched that President Roosevelt sent an emissary to Rome, pleading with the pope to soften the rhetoric against the Communists, lest his enthusiasm undermine the developing yet fragile alliance between America and the Soviet Union. Pope Pius XII assumed his role as pontiff in 1939. Events soon thrust him into the position of ardent anticommunist. After the war President Truman requested that he amplify the volume of his condemnation. Pope Pius XII needed no encouragement in denouncing the Soviets when they began persecuting Catholic officials in Eastern Europe immediately after the German surrender in 1945.

The first confrontation occurred in Poland, which Soviet infantry and armored divisions rolled through on their way to Berlin. Once the Soviets held Polish territory, they promised to allow the citizens there to construct the government of their choice. But the promise proved hollow when the Communists installed their own form of government. Poland was one of the most ardently Catholic nations on earth, and the people there did not submit readily to the atheistic ideology. To lead the faithful, the pope named Adam Stefan Sapieha as the cardinal of Krakow, with a mission to maintain the church in Poland. Sapieha had faced death many times as a leader of the Polish resistance to Nazi occupation during the war and had learned patience and resilience, traits that he would need in his assignment. The Soviets initiated antireligious propaganda, outlawed spiritual instruction in school, and occasionally even executed a Catholic official. They arrested Cardinal Wyszynski, the archbishop of Warsaw, in October 1953, when he reported the brutal torture of Catholic adherents. The Communists failed to weaken Polish resolve, however, and allowed the confrontation to transform into a stalemate.[17]

The second event in Eastern Europe that molded the battle between Soviet ideology and the church occurred in September 1946, with the arrest of Archbishop Aloysius Stepinac in Yugoslavia. Josip Broz Tito's police charged Stepinac with assisting the Nazis during the occupation. But Catholic leaders noted that Stepinac's arrest occurred at the same time as numerous other actions against religious figures and concluded that the charges were unsubstantiated. Stepinac was found guilty and sentenced to sixteen years in prison, a verdict that prompted the pope to excommunicate every Yugoslavian citizen involved in the trial. American Catholics were spurred to action: 140,000 Catholics staged a mass march in New Jersey in support of Stepinac. Undersecretary of State Dean Acheson expressed his concern over the arrest, while Catholic members of Congress attempted to pass a resolution demanding that the state department lodge a formal complaint.[18]

The motion failed to pass, but the trial of Hungarian Jozsef Cardinal Mindszenty transformed the Catholic offensive into an international alliance of religious factions. He was an outspoken critic of Communist atheism and staged an organized resistance to government attempts to nationalize all schools, including Catholic institutions. Mindszenty excommunicated every Hungarian involved in the plan and faced arrest just after Christmas 1948 for his opposition. He was tortured and sentenced to fifteen years in prison in another show trial, a verdict that generated international condemnation and united Catholics in their anticommunism. Twenty thousand Catholics staged a demonstration in Brooklyn to pray for Mindszenty's release. Lay organizations such as the Knights of Columbus and Catholic War Veterans endorsed rallies and demonstrations throughout the nation.[19]

The pope held a momentous consistory in February 1946. He named thirty-two new cardinals, many of whom were militant anticommunists, to lead in the burgeoning conflict. Several members of this new class of cardinals emerged onto the international scene and assumed important positions, as several critical confrontations with the Soviets propelled the Catholic Church to the position of international anticommunist watchdog. For decades following the initial crisis Catholic priests throughout the world reminded the international community of the crimes committed against their fellow Catholics and led their congregations in prayer for the conversion of Russia. American Catholics were only too happy to comply with the pope's denunciation of Soviet ideology and welcomed the opportunity to show their patriotism after more than a century of anti-Catholic persecution in America.[20]

Two American clergymen emerged to lead Catholic opposition to communism in the United States. The first was Archbishop Fulton J.

Sheen, who attacked the Soviets and their godlessness while scolding the Truman administration for its friendly relationship with the Kremlin. His radio program *The Catholic Hour* reached 4 million listeners through 334 radio stations.[21] Sheen was a preeminent intellectual in the Catholic Church and presided over a number of notable conversions of Communists. Louis F. Budenz was the editor of the Communist newspaper the *Daily Worker* and made the most public transformation under the guidance of Bishop Sheen in 1945. Budenz had often attacked Sheen in his Communist newspaper but eventually succumbed to Sheen's relentless appeal for him to return to his faith. Budenz recorded his spiritual journey in his book *This Is My Story* and began a new career as an anticommunist. He was joined by other notable former Communists such as Elizabeth Barkley, the notorious "spy queen" during the war, who also converted under Sheen's tutelage. Sheen baptized Barkley in 1948. Budenz and his wife, Margaret, served as her godparents.

The most famous conversion was of Whittaker Chambers, a Soviet spy working in the United States during the 1930s, who broke with Stalin in 1938 and eventually testified against other spies operating in America, most notably Alger Hiss. Chambers withdrew from society while he composed his autobiography, entitled simply *Witness*, published in 1952.[22]

The other American Catholic leader was Francis Cardinal Spellman, who attacked the Soviets for their persecution of Catholics around the world and was a personal friend of Cardinal Mindszenty. Spellman endorsed the demonstration of two thousand high school girls who formed a living rosary on the New York polo grounds to publicize the plight of Mindszenty. Spellman addressed a convention of military chaplains and lamented the imprisonment of Archbishop Aloysius Stepinac in Yugoslavia "by men themselves imprisoned and enslaved by atheistic communism." He advised the young chaplains to lead the battle against "the brutal bludgeon" of the Soviet hammer and sickle. Spellman raised money and built Archbishop Stepinac High School in White Plains, New York. He claimed that the Soviet treatment of Stepinac proved that America was fighting for its soul against "satanic Soviet sycophants."[23]

While the church hierarchy continued to battle communism throughout the nation, Catholic officials in Montana strode into the fray with determination and zeal. The Catholic Church has a long tradition in Montana and has always been the state's dominant religion. A federal census conducted in 1906 found that 74 percent of regular communicants in Montana were Catholics, exactly twice the national average.[24] One of the major reasons for the prominence of the Catholic religion was the large Irish population in the western half of the state, particularly in the mining regions around Butte and Anaconda. By 1900 approximately 12,000 immigrant and second-generation Irish lived in the county surrounding Butte, out of a population of just under 48,000. More than 90 percent of the men working the mines were Irish.[25]

If the miners were the flock in Montana, the shepherd was the Most Reverend Joseph M. Gilmore, bishop of the Diocese of Helena, who led Montana Catholics in their anticommunist efforts throughout the early Cold War period. Gilmore led the Diocese of Helena from 1936 until his death in 1962, a period that coincided with the height of the Cold War. When the Communists sentenced Jozsef Cardinal Mindszenty to prison in Hungary, Gilmore responded: "His only guilt, if guilt it be, is that of opposing Communists as he opposed Nazis in their efforts to destroy religion and freedoms in his native land."[26] He called on Catholics in the diocese to join a national prayer effort for the persecuted cardinal in 1949 and continued to lead his congregation in prayer for priests and other Catholics of the world and for the conversion of Russia throughout the 1950s.

Gilmore was born in New York City on March 22, 1893, the son of Irish immigrants. His father moved the family to Anaconda in 1898 to begin work as a smelter, but Gilmore left Montana to attend high school and college at St. Joseph's in Dubuque, Iowa. He graduated in 1911 with a bachelor's degree and then attended the seminary in Rome, where he earned a doctor of divinity degree in 1914. For the next three years he held the distinction of being the youngest doctor of divinity in the world. Gilmore required special dispensation from Pope Benedict XV for ordination, being only twenty-three when he was ready to join the priesthood in 1915. Church rules required candidates to have reached the age of twenty-four. Nonetheless, he was ordained and served in Montana as a priest in Whitehall and Butte, taught for a term as a professor at Carroll College, and served a period as chancellor of the Helena Diocese. His consecration as bishop of Helena in 1936 was a great achievement, as he was the first Montana priest to attain such a high position in the Catholic Church and was the first bishop consecrated in the state.[27]

Bishop Joseph Gilmore of the Diocese of Helena addressing a building fund dinner on October 7, 1955. Courtesy Diocese of Helena Archives, Image I.E.116.

Gilmore's leadership in Montana and the national effort to coerce spirituality led to a considerable growth in Catholicism within Montana, where Catholic resources strained to keep up with religious interest. Gilmore helped to build or renovate twenty new churches, twelve rectories, nine convents, three high schools, and various additions to hospital and college buildings during his twenty-six years as bishop of the Diocese of Helena. Most of these projects occurred during the Cold War. The highlight of this building effort took place on the campus of Carroll College, where Bishop Gilmore led a massive fund-raising effort that resulted in a number of new buildings in the 1950s. These new units included a new four-story science building, a minor seminary where young men began their education leading to the priesthood, a new dorm for female students, and a student center known as Carroll Commons.[28]

Gilmore frequently told his congregation that it was impossible to be a Christian and a Communist, because the Soviet ideology denied the primacy of God within the world, denied the belief that humankind was created in the likeness of God, and denied the moral law based on God's commandments. Perhaps most importantly, Gilmore charged, communism denied proper freedom in society and an orderly economic system. The greatest danger to the United States was the apathy with which many people approached the Communist menace. Gilmore suggested that the only real defense against the godless philosophy was a faith in God: "Our efforts to combat communism . . . derived from a belief in God and in the rights and dignity of man need spiritual motivation. Only then will we see that communism is intrinsically evil and that no believer in God may collaborate with it."[29]

Nothing served to unite the heritage of Irish Catholics more than the ritual gathering to pay homage to St. Patrick, the patron saint of Ireland. The faithful gathered at several celebrations throughout the state, but perhaps the most colorful fete was held at the Finlen Hotel in Butte, a Montana tradition since 1908. The Irish celebrated with traditional Irish food, drink, song, and dance and vibrant speeches that recognized the contributions of Irish Americans to their adopted nation. In one of the first gatherings in the postwar era, an immediate topic of conversation was the rise of international communism and Irish Catholic opposition to it. Father James P. O'Shea of St. Joseph's Catholic Parish in Butte played the important role of toastmaster at the holiday event in 1947. In his opening remarks he noted that the observance of St. Patrick's Day held more significance than ever before. "The world we know today," he said, "is a world of two great ideologies in human affairs. These ideologies are spearheaded on one hand by the teachings of St. Patrick and the other by principles contrary to Christian teachings of the great saint." O'Shea went on to tell his audience that the culture that St. Patrick brought to Ireland and then to the world was more important than ever before, as communism was spreading throughout the globe.[30]

The celebration the following year featured Father Emmitt P. O'Neill of Anaconda, who compared the teaching of St. Patrick with the teaching of Karl Marx. O'Neill said that both offered those who were suffering a vision for a better world, but communism aimed to seize their hearts, minds, and souls. "We must not overlook the splendor of the

Marxist vision . . . and we can only meet a vision with another, superior vision. Never was there a more terrible challenge facing men [than] the vision of Marx."[31]

St. Patrick's Day celebrations continued throughout the early Cold War period. Each speaker took the opportunity to extol the virtues of the blessed saint of the Emerald Isle, to promote the benefits of leading a Christian life, and to lament the influences of communism throughout the world. By the time Butte's faithful celebrated their fiftieth anniversary of St. Patrick's Day in 1958, the Communist menace dominated the discussion. One of the speakers that evening was John W. Mahan, senior vice commander of the Veterans of Foreign Wars and an attorney in Helena. Mahan discussed Irish immigration and reminded listeners that 4 million Irish immigrants had left their native soil and ventured to America, where their contributions to American conflicts helped preserve freedom. Thirteen signers of the Declaration of Independence were among the first immigrants to come to America, and thousands of their fellow Irish fought in the war for independence. Irish immigrants also fought in the War of 1812, and 410,000 first- or second-generation Irish immigrants fought to preserve the union in the Civil War. Innumerable Americans of Irish ancestry also fought in the Spanish-American War, World War I, World War II, and Korea. Then he spoke of the price of freedom: "We must . . . prepare our country for the battle against oppression and tyranny. We must be prepared militarily, economically, and morally." Mahan warned of the strength of the Russians and that the United States must stand up militarily to the nation that had chosen to destroy it. "The challenge that is directed to all Americans today," he said, "was one of the acceptance of the teaching of St. Patrick, the avoidance of indifference, and of cynicism. Here, on St. Patrick's Day in 1958, we see the greatest nation in the world struggling with the problems of both a foreign and domestic nature." The story of St. Patrick is one of the greatest stories ever told, Mahan continued, telling the audience that St. Patrick was among the foremost of the world's spiritual giants. "No man, save Christ, accomplished the wonderful things he did," Mahan said. "As a result of his preaching and miracles a whole nation was added to the fold of Christ, and it became a nation of saints and scholars."[32] Mahan undoubtedly hoped that a modern St. Patrick would find his way to the Soviet Union.

While the Irish brought the religion with them, others found it within the state. Native American Catholic traditions dated back to around 1820, when twenty-four Iroquois arrived in Montana. These men were in the employ of the Hudson Bay Company and had religious instruction from missionaries from the Society of Jesus in the East. These new missionaries settled near present-day Plains, Montana, and began their work with the local Flathead Tribe and established St. Mary's Mission at Stevensville. Catholic instruction continued in 1854 with the founding of the St. Ignatius Mission. One hundred years later the centennial celebration included a visit from Francis Cardinal Spellman, who delivered one of his rare sermons when he came to celebrate the historic occasion at the St. Ignatius Mission. Indians on horseback and dressed in traditional clothing greeted Spellman, Gilmore, and other dignitaries as they rode in a horse-drawn wagon to the valley where Jesuit missionaries had established the mission years earlier. This greeting was a reenactment of the meeting between Father Joseph Desmet, a Jesuit from St. Louis, and the Flathead Indians, who requested his help and established the mission there. The original log cabin church still stood at the site but included a larger church and an Indian school by the time Spellman arrived. As part of the centennial celebration, the Department of the Interior had authorized the Indians to take a buffalo in Yellowstone Park to help feed the gathering of nearly ten thousand members of the Salish Confederated Tribes, including the Flatheads, the Kootenais, and the Pend d'Oreilles. The observance included a traditional Catholic mass, followed by festivities throughout the weekend that incorporated Native American dances, a band concert, and an elaborate centennial pageant. Concluding the celebration was the Flatheads' traditional "burial of Christ," a long symbolic procession commemorating the passion of Christ.[33]

The centennial celebration of St. Ignatius came at a difficult time for Indians, as the federal government looked with suspicion on their ancient and communal culture and decided that it looked too "communistic." During the bitter winter of 1947–48 Congress cut funding to the Navajos in Arizona for this reason.[34] The story of Navajo suffering hit the front pages of newspapers across the nation. Public support for the Navajos forced the president to respond, but the idea to cut funding to the Indian nations gained momentum. In 1952 the House of Representatives called on the Bureau of Indian Affairs to publish a list of Indian tribes able to survive without government programs, resulting in a determination to cut funding to several states. Congress decreased funding to tribes living in ten more states the following year and set in motion complete termination of federal oversight of tribes.[35] The government worked to move Indians from their reservations to cities, where they could assimilate into urban culture and find work. Approximately 6,200 Indians of an estimated 245,000 reservation inhabitants had been moved to urban centers by the end of 1954. About 54 percent of those relocating came from reservations near Aberdeen, South Dakota; Billings, Montana; and Minneapolis, Minnesota.[36]

While Congress grumbled about Indians, Catholics nationwide devoted each May Day to observing Loyalty Day by attending church and praying for the conversion of Russia. The Catholic Church had called for prayers directed at the Soviets during the Russian Revolution in 1917, but the practice gained new importance with the deterioration of American and Soviet relations after World War II. Twenty thousand Catholics filled the Hollywood Bowl in 1948 to pray for the transformation of the Soviet state.[37] Prayers for the conversion of Russia also permeated Montana's Catholic community in the early Cold War period, when over a thousand Catholic students gathered in Butte for a statewide youth meeting in 1946. The students adopted a number of resolutions at the conclusion of the conference, including a call for the "intensification of Catholic action in homes, schools, and recreational worlds, the promotion of world peace, and the conversion of Russia." In fact communism was a recurring theme at the gathering. Bishop Gilmore warned the students that "Communistic inroads throughout the world provide a challenge for modern youth never before equaled and Catholic youth stand today like the Catholic Church, as a bulwark between the forces of communism and civilization."[38]

Catholics in Montana dedicated numerous masses throughout the Cold War era to the conversion of Russia. Students often took the lead in special ceremonies, as in the 1952 inaugural "Pilgrimage of Peace." Over a thousand Catholic students in Helena from elementary, middle, and high schools and from Carroll College met on Sunday, May 25, to participate in a procession to "Our Lady for Peace and the Conversion of Russia." Students marched from the college through nearby streets. Carroll College student Jack Klessens led the rosary. Students gave the response and then sang hymns after every fifth decade of the rosary. The May Queen, Barbara Peters, crowned the statue of the Virgin Mary with a floral wreath, after which Father Raymond Hunthausen gave the sermon. The following year over twelve hundred people took part in the May Day ceremony. The Catholic community in Montana continued to pray for the conversion of Russia, particularly on special occasions. Bishop Gilmore called for the weeks from September 13 to September 25, 1959, to be a "Crusade of Prayer" to coincide with the visit of Soviet premier Nikita Khrushchev to the United States. During Khrushchev's visit, every Montana diocese was instructed to offer a prayer at the end of each mass for the conversion of Russia and for peace in the world. "Another and clear occasion is given us to remember our fellow Catholics behind the Iron Curtain, whose freedom to worship God is so restricted, who suffer in prison or slave labor camps . . . who suffer torture and death rather than deny Christ," said Gilmore.[39]

Protestants were not going to be outdone by the Catholics. Historian Jon Lauck points to the powerful Protestant traditions in the Dakota Territory, which encompassed the future states of both North Dakota and South Dakota. The Christian church was one of the first buildings constructed in a territorial town. The many denominations often led to tension, especially between the relatively few Catholics and the numerous Protestant worshippers in those states. Residents cared enough about religion to dispute its proper interpretation. The settlers in the Dakota Territory came largely from the Midwest and the eastern seaboard or migrated from the Scandinavian nations and Germany, places renowned for their strict Protestant traditions and the tremendous influence of religious leaders. Some time had passed between the settlement era of Dakota Territory and the origins of the Cold War, but not enough to diminish the importance of the religious traditions there.[40]

Strict Protestant tradition and the presence of a forceful religious leadership were one reason why nomadic clergy received a warm welcome in the region. Few could trumpet the dangers of subversive communism to Americans better than evangelical ministers, and their message was immensely popular on the northern plains. They were experts at pointing out the flaws in individuals and in society at large and could break down a situation into its elements of good and evil, God versus Satan. Only a small portion of the population was evangelical in the 1930s, with many viewing the religious experience as divisive and rough. Many evangelicals sought to soften the delivery, if not the message, during World War II and to move the venues from tents on the outskirts of small town to arenas in major American cities. One of the most successful evangelical preachers in the new tradition was Charles Fuller, who was broadcasting his radio program to over 450 stations per week and had the most popular radio program in America by 1943. His wife read listeners' letters over the air, and his musical arrangement was more upbeat than people expected. Fuller and his wife were more like trusted friends than firebrands. Other evangelicals adapted to new technologies and presentation styles, making the religious experience mainstream.[41]

If the Fullers brought a new method to evangelicalism, no preacher could match the intensity or intelligence of Billy Graham. He was born on a North Carolina farm in 1918 and found religion through a traveling fundamentalist preacher at age sixteen. Graham graduated from Wheaton College in Illinois in 1934 and then served as president of several evangelical colleges in Minnesota. He built a remarkable career as an evangelical minister as he traveled throughout the nation and then throughout the world.[42] Graham became a national figure in 1949, when he scheduled a series of religious events in Los Angeles. His appeal to youth and his attack on communism caught the attention of newspaper magnate and militant anticommunist William Randolph Hearst. Hearst thought that Graham could significantly obstruct Communist efforts and sent a succinct message to his editors, telling them simply: "Puff Graham." From this point on, Graham's popularity enjoyed a steep trajectory: he appeared on the cover of *Life* magazine four times and the covers of *Newsweek* and *Look* six times each. He had a syndicated newspaper column that appeared in 125 newspapers and a weekly television program beginning in 1952 and regularly appeared on lists of most admired Americans. Billy Graham was a religious force of significance, especially in the early Cold War period, and his message proclaiming the dangers of communism was a significant theme throughout the era.[43]

Graham made anticommunism a popular topic for evangelical ministers who traveled the nation and the northern Great Plains. Jack Shuler was one such minister, who brought his revival to Sioux Falls, South Dakota. Officials originally scheduled his performance in the Coliseum annex, but his audience was so large each night that the managers moved his show to the main stage in the Coliseum itself. Attendance at the event was free, as churches in the city paid Shuler's fees. Over 40,000 people attended Shuler's revival over twelve days in 1950, an impressive number for a city with a population of 55,000 at that time.[44] His message was "Aimed at God Haters and Red Baiters—A Solar Plexus Blow to American Communists," his full-page advertisement proclaimed. He not only warned that the Communists sought to replace religion with communism but warned people to prepare their souls for the afterlife, lest atomic war catch people unprepared. "Complete human annihilation has been brought within the range of technical possibility," Shuler told his audience. He worked the crowd magnificently and enthusiastically, proclaiming that the "Day of the Lord" could face all humankind, as he thundered that the atomic bomb was likely the fulfillment of the biblical prophecy "the heavens shall pass away with a great noise, and the elements shall melt with fervent heat, and the earth also, and the works that are therein shall be burned up." Pointing to the ongoing development of the hydrogen bomb, Shuler quoted Professor Harold Urey, who said that he and all the scientists he knew were frightened. Shuler told his audience: "Folks, I am not frightened! God is still on his throne and He has a blueprint for the ages and His plans have always worked out." God will not destroy the world, Shuler said, if people follow His commandments and turn away from sin.[45]

The American Legion also demonstrated the perils of communism when it sponsored a double-page advertisement in the *Montana Standard* in March 1958 that asked in bold headlines: "Will You Be Free to Observe Easter in the Future?" Five bold responses followed:

NOT UNLESS You and other free Americans begin to understand and appreciate the benefits provided by God under the American system of self-government.

NOT UNLESS You and other free Americans awaken to the true meaning of Communism and understand that it is your enemy.

NOT UNLESS Your children and their educators quit swallowing the false, sugar-coated, one-sided description of vicious Communism supplied by dedicated Communist sympathizers.

NOT UNLESS Americans generally begin to understand that Communism is NOT just another political party.

NOT UNLESS Otherwise well-meaning Americans begin to understand that "academic freedom" without morality leads to national suicide.

The headline concluded: "Communism Is Out to Destroy You!" The rest of the considerable space was taken up with the transcript of an interview that members of the Committee on Un-American Activities of the House of Representatives had conducted with Dr. Frederick Schwarz, a popular speaker and minister who warned of communism and its devious methods for attracting followers.[46]

Schwarz was a surgeon and psychiatrist from Australia who abandoned his medical practice to spread the word of God and to warn of the Soviet peril. He was a renowned educator on Communist strategy, and his presentation underscored reasons why communism was incompatible with religious faith. He made his anticommunist crusade his life's work in 1952, when he met evangelist Billy Graham, who encouraged Schwarz to create an organization linking religion and anticommunism. The result was the Christian Anti-Communism Crusade.[47] Schwarz's message was incredibly powerful to the people of Montana. He returned to the state a number of times to deliver his warning. "Communism was a disease of the body because it has killed millions of bodies, it was a disease of the mind because it creates delusions, and it was a disease of the spirit because it denied God and morality."[48]

Schwarz presented his case to Montana crowds in the form of seven arguments. The first argument was that communism intended to conquer the world, which he substantiated by quoting various Communist leaders throughout the world. The second point was that Communists were in fact conquering the world: he pointed to their political and military victories. He predicted that within a generation 1 billion people would live under communism. His third argument was that Communists were conquering the world by program and timetable. He reminded crowds that the Communists subdued Eastern Europe, then Asia, and would concentrate on America next. Based on the predicted rate of conquest, Schwarz continued, communism would conquer the free world by 1973.[49] He illustrated the fourth point, that communism meant literal slavery and death, by painting a picture of life in the Soviet Union under Stalin and in Communist nations around the world. His fifth point was that most Americans were helping the Communists destroy the United States and American children by reacting to the Soviets in a "softheaded way," by not confronting aggression. His sixth point was that the dangers of communism imposed a personal responsibility on everyone to write congressional leaders and to vote for politicians who would force vigilance and action from the government. Finally, Schwarz said that there was no limit to what citizens could do to combat communism, citing the success of groups and individuals around the world who stood against communism.[50]

Though many evangelists explicitly connected religion with the fight against communism, others implicitly made the connection when they simply worked to spread the word of God. Popular evangelist Oral Roberts came to Bismarck, North Dakota, in November 1955 at the request of twenty-two ministers and their churches in Bismarck and Lemmon, South Dakota. He preached the gospel twice a day for four days, and crowds enthusiastically jammed Bismarck's Memorial Auditorium during each performance. Police and fire fighters had to turn away crowds of people at the start of each performance because the building ran out of seats. Hotels throughout North Dakota and in Canada reached maximum capacity during Roberts's visit, as people arrived from North Dakota, South Dakota, Iowa, Minnesota, Montana, and Wisconsin to hear the young evangelist. Roberts carried his message by visiting countless communities throughout the nation. His monthly magazine had 435,000 subscribers, his radio program was heard over a network of two hundred radio stations, and his television show was carried on sixty-three outlets. Roberts was popular because he billed himself as a "salvation-healing evangelist" who claimed that God worked through him to heal illness. The faithful came in wheelchairs, were carried, or hobbled into the building and filled out their prayer cards, asking Oral Roberts to heal them. About fifteen hundred people filled out cards that went to Roberts's staff before the first event in Bismarck. During the revival assistants read out the names of the few selected for the "healing line," where they could pray with Roberts, asking God to take away their maladies. The others were told that they would get into the healing line at another revival meeting that week.[51]

Evangelist Oral Roberts addressing a congregation. No date given. Courtesy Oral Roberts Evangelistic Association.

Roberts set a goal of winning 1 million souls for Christ by July 1, 1956, and continuing a conversion program that would save 1 million souls in each successive year. At some point during each program he would call to the crowd and ask that each person desiring eternal salvation come forward to the front of the auditorium to pray with Roberts. The crusade through North Dakota helped Roberts attain his goal. He averaged thirteen hundred converts per night in Bismarck, from crowds averaging around five thousand. Throughout the nation he averaged six hundred to seven hundred converts a night from crowds averaging fifteen thousand to twenty thousand. Staff members associated with the Roberts ministry said that they had never seen anything like the number of people in Bismarck who chose to dedicate their lives to God.[52]

Evangelists were popular on the northern plains as they reminded their listeners to beware of Communist ideology, but another powerful message was brought forth by the Black Hills Passion Play that depicted the crucifixion of Christ. Josef Meier brought the play to the United States from Germany in 1932 and hoped to find a natural amphitheater in which to present his play. Meier found the perfect location in Spearfish, South Dakota, in 1938 and spent $250,000 to build a massive stage and construct his headquarters. Spearfish also served as the home for the cast and crew. Meier was not only the producer but also the star, portraying Christ in the play. The company produced the play three times per week from June through August in South Dakota and then throughout the United States during the winter months. During his career, Meier portrayed Christ more than five thousand times over twenty-five years before audiences numbering over 10 million. Meier's family owned the play, and the role of Jesus had been in the Meier family for over seven generations. At the age of forty-eight he prepared to hand the role over to his nephew, age twenty, in 1951.[53]

Regardless of who was playing the leading role, the Passion Play was a huge hit throughout the northern plains. More than 7,500 residents of Bismarck saw the play over its four-day run in 1949.[54] Huron, South Dakota, residents set a single-day attendance record on September 16, 1953: 2,873 attended the matinee performance and 2,332 witnessed the evening show.[55] In fact the Passion Play continued to draw audiences in ever-increasing numbers throughout the early Cold War period as religion grew in importance in American society: 26,268 people saw the play in 1949, compared to the 44,578 people who saw the play a year later. As the decade drew to a close, over 79,558 people viewed the presentation in 1958.[56] To some people who saw the play, the spectacle was akin to a miracle. The *Billings Herald* called the enactment a "sermon as powerful and as deeply religious as if it were preached from the mightiest pulpit."[57] Meier's interpretation was so moving that some had difficulty separating the man from the role. After one performance members of the audience requested that Meier place his hands on a blind child. The surprised actor politely refused, feeling that it would be sacrilegious.[58]

While the national government was responsible for many of the programs encouraging religious observation during the Cold War,

Postcard depicting five Passion Play scenes. No date given. First performed at Luenen, Germany, in 1242, the Passion Play came to America and was performed for years in the Black Hills of South Dakota at Spearfish. Courtesy South Dakota State Historical Society.

many local leaders also encouraged spiritual reflection. The Reverend George E. Stickney of Billings told a local crowd of Rotarians just before Thanksgiving in 1953 that "Communism finds its most fertile soil among those who are hungry, and more than half the world will be hungry and a sizable fraction are starving."[59] He encouraged the crowd to share their many blessings with others. The Reverend Norman E. Brauer told the Bismarck, North Dakota, Rotarians in 1952: "Communism and Christianity are irreconcilable, as communism teaches a philosophy of hate, subjugation of individuals, and violence while Christianity teaches love, charity, and sanctity of the individual."[60] South Dakota governor Sigurd Anderson called for church bells to toll on July 4, 1951, and "asked that the day be commemorated by observing 'the sacred and spiritual foundations of our freedom.'"[61] The number of priests, ministers, and other religious leaders who talked about the dangers of communism with their congregations cannot be counted, but probably almost all of them did at one point or another. Today only a few newspaper articles tell the story, but many religious leaders undoubtedly warned against the evils of communism, although their warnings have been lost to history.

Devout congregations on the northern plains, however, were also enjoined to love their neighbors, a message that resonated with the friendly folk in the region. To illustrate this point, farmers and ranchers from South Dakota publicly welcomed bona fide Communists into their homes for meals and entertainment at the height of the Cold War in August 1955. The occasion was an international exchange program, as ten farmers from the United States visited the Soviet Union and ten Soviet farmers and agricultural specialists visited South Dakota and other states. The attitude of South Dakotans toward their guests was welcoming and gracious despite their ideological differences, and the Soviets were nothing if not well fed during their short stay in the state. South Dakotans were as ardently anticommunist as anyone in the nation, but neighborliness trumped political ideology on the northern Great Plains.

The Soviet delegation arrived in South Dakota and spent part of the first morning touring the agricultural research facilities at South Dakota State College in Brookings and the rest of the morning touring a cattle ranch and then several farms. At each of these stops the mission was overwhelmed with offers of food and coffee from the farm families and neighbors. The group had lunch with the Watertown Chamber of Commerce, visited another farm, found time for a picnic lunch at Clear Lake, and then stopped for haircuts in downtown Aberdeen. The Soviet delegation ate dinner with the Aberdeen Chamber of Commerce, where a local yet accomplished pianist performed Russian music for the visitors. William Yates, who had performed three times in the Soviet Union, climaxed the event with a rousing rendition of "The Star Spangled Banner," which brought the Soviets and Americans to their feet. A number of impromptu speeches followed the music, including remarks from Yuri Golubash, who told the crowd through a translator that "we will gain much from our impressions of American agriculture which later will be useful in our agriculture production." The final "speech" of the evening was a humorous affair. John Strohm, an American traveling with the Soviet delegation, rattled off some Russian words that he had learned only recently. Andrei Shevchenko translated for the crowd using newly learned English: "Hello my friends. Good mornink. Good day. Good evenink. Goodbye. Hookay." Shevchenko then added another new phrase, "Thank you from the bottom of my heart." The small gathering roared approval with a standing ovation.[62]

The Soviet delegation made its way to Huron—at the personal invitation of South Dakota's governor Joe Foss and flying in his official plane—to witness the Holiday on Ice show in the Huron Arena. The Americans were quite timid about introducing the Soviet delegation, fearing that the crowd might express its displeasure with the Soviets by booing the visitors. The Soviets thought that it would be disrespectful if the delegation was not introduced and wanted an introduction, so the announcer presented the party after the intermission, and the crowd responded with the utmost dignity. There was much applause, no unkind remarks or gestures, and great interest as members of the crowd craned their necks to get a better look at their guests. Once the show concluded, the Soviets and their American escorts made their way to George's Restaurant, a local establishment where some of the show's cast met up with the group. There the numerous photographers could not resist the temptation to stage a picture of one of the Russian men, with obvious delight, receiving a kiss on each check from two of the young female performers. This was an unusual occurrence, as the Soviets did not allow anyone to take pictures that would show the delegation in a negative light. They must have decided that the fun was harmless. Photographers got the photo out to the East Coast on the first available plane and put Huron in the national spotlight for several days.[63]

South Dakotans welcomed the Soviet visitors with dignity and respect, but they did not confuse patriotism with good manners. The Soviet farmers were deluged with offers of food, entertainment, and companionship as American farmers enthusiastically explained to them the ways in which they could improve agricultural productivity, thereby strengthening the Communist state, not weakening it. The people of the northern Great Plains considered their visitors' Marxist ideology abhorrent and remained determined to eradicate revolutionaries in their midst but saw no reason to be unfriendly to their guests. While most South Dakotans were interested in the delegation, or at least mildly curious to see what a Communist looked like, some could not help but draw comparisons between the Soviets and the local citizens. An editorial in the *Huronite and Daily Plainsman* pointed out that many of the local farmers who came out to greet the Soviets were ethnic Germans who had been born in Russia. Their ancestors had been enticed to live in Russia through popular government incentives during the eighteenth century. They moved to the United States when the Russians withdrew the enticements that brought them there. The exodus began at the end of the nineteenth century and continued throughout the 1930s. As the editor observed, the naturalized Americans and the Soviets were roughly the same age, both born in the same country, but vastly different. How many of the Soviet farmers, the editor wondered, wished that they could trade places with the Americans? The Soviets would no doubt be "much happier, freer, and affluent." Who among the Americans would trade places with a Soviet farmer?[64]

Religious observance continued to influence American society through the 1950s but lost influence as the immediate threat of Communist attack or subversion subsided and the nation addressed other issues in the early 1960s. By 1965 less than one-third of Americans thought that religion was still increasing its influence upon society.[65] If religious adherence declined among the population, however, it left an indelible imprint on the American landscape. Religion as a barrier to the spread of communism was a natural fit during the Cold War. Political conservatives still join religion and patriotism, suggesting that one is not complete without the other. Religion on its simplest level is the story of good versus evil, a situation with which Americans were all too familiar, viewing the postwar world as a confrontation between American democracy and Soviet communism. As the Soviets sought to dominate the world stage, some subversives were working behind the scenes to bring down America and its ideals. Government officials did not just fight with words against the encroaching danger: they responded with action. Proof of American supremacy was showcased in the Freedom Train, the Friendship Train, and the Crusade for Freedom, examined in the next chapter.

Chapter 3

Freedom Crusades

The Benevolent Protective Order of Elks, or Elks Club, had taken particular interest in Flag Day since President Woodrow Wilson initiated the celebration in 1916. The holiday assumed special significance as the Cold War intensified after World War II. In June 1950 the North Dakota Elks held an enormous convention in Bismarck in conjunction with Flag Day ceremonies on the capitol grounds. Four thousand Elks and spouses crowded onto the open spaces, one of the largest crowds to assemble in that location. The Bismarck Elks Band entertained the gathering for half an hour as they waited for the Flag Day ceremony to begin. At the appointed time the music fell silent. The members of the crowd bowed their heads, listening as the loudspeakers carried the words of the invocation across the grounds. The crowd looked up as the prayer concluded, waiting to hear the keynote speaker. I. E. Solberg, an instructor at Bismarck Junior College, spoke on the Elks national theme of "Wake Up America," with its warning of Communist aggression confronting Americans. Solberg referred to the Soviet belligerence: "Although in this 'modern age' all of the emphasis is placed on the many changes that are occurring, there are some things that will always be the same, such as love, beauty, and friendship." Solberg reminded the masses that the flag "is the emblem of our unity, our power, our thought, our purpose as a nation. It has no other character than that which we give it from generation to generation. It is the symbol of great events and of a great plan of life worked out by a great people."[1]

Entertainment and events continued that evening and into the following day when the Flag Day Parade began. Ten thousand spectators lined the streets of Bismarck to watch the exhibition, a considerable number in a city with a population of only eighteen thousand in 1950.[2] Sixty-five organizations made up the parade, including ten bands and thirty-three floats, much to the enjoyment of the assembled crowds. That evening U.S. vice president Alben W. Barkley delivered the closing remarks at a banquet with over one thousand people in attendance. "Now that American has become the leader of the free peoples of the world," Barkley said, "this country is obligated more than ever to make the rights and liberties this nation enjoys ever more universal." He called on all groups and organizations in the United States to fight to preserve their own democracy and freedoms: "No one who is not acquainted with the efforts that are being made to destroy these liberties can appreciate the intensity with which the assault is being made." As Barkley pointed out, "One third of the world's population is under the control of a form of government they did not choose and in which they have no voice." He urged: "The United States must continue to set the example of freedom and prove to the world the advantages of our way of life."[3]

The patriotism evident in this episode was common during the early Cold War period, when national organizations such as the Elks Club and federal officials warned of a Soviet Union bent on worldwide domination and demonstrated the ability to infiltrate and dominate weaker nations such as Iran, Greece, Turkey, China, South Korea, and others in the early Cold War era. Alger Hiss's perjury conviction amid accusations of spying for the Soviets in 1950 and the emergence of the Rosenberg spy case the same year seemed to confirm the existence of disloyal Americans working for the federal government and subverting national ideals. In response, the federal government and national civic organizations sponsored many programs to advance the positive traits of Americans and to promote American ideals: "Americanism." The idea was to stand for something: the democratic form of government guaranteed in the Constitution, the many freedoms defined in the Bill of Rights, and the love of an eternal God who loved the nation in return. National leaders developed these programs and planted seeds at the state and local level, where they sprouted and then blossomed. Americans enthusiastically embraced these programs, especially citizens living on the northern Great Plains.

The first example of a national program carried out at the state and local level was the American effort to ship an extra 100 million bushels of grain to the starving masses in Europe, in addition to the hundreds of millions of bushels already going there. President Truman asked the American public to save grain by forgoing meat twice a week, allowing the government to ship the grain to Europe. Another example of a program formulated nationally and applied regionally was the Friendship Train that crossed the country, collecting hundreds of boxcars full of donated food and clothing for the hungry people in Europe. The arrival of essential items was meant to undermine the influence of the Communist parties gaining momentum there. Yet another example involved the U.S. attorney general, who envisioned the Freedom Train that carried over one hundred of the nation's most precious documents to hundreds of American cities. Crowds across the northern plains met the train with unbridled enthusiasm and broke attendance records set by much larger cities. In another national venture called the Crusade for Freedom, a civilian organization—with the clandestine support of the Central Intelligence Agency (CIA)—supported a program to broadcast pro-American propaganda into Communist-controlled territory. Thousands of Americans throughout the nation and the northern plains contributed "truth dollars" to support the broadcasts and for a parallel campaign to purchase and hang a "Freedom Bell" that could be heard ringing throughout Communist-controlled East Berlin. Finally, a number of national organizations such as the Elks, the Eagles, the Veterans of Foreign Wars, the American Legion, and the Daughters of the American Revolution developed their own campaigns and pushed them to the local chapters for implementation.

Government officials designed a number of campaigns to combat communism, but President Truman first asked the American people to participate in a patriotic program during the early Cold War to help feed the starving people in Europe. The United States exported enormous quantities of grains to Europe in the years following the war, but experts projected that current shipments would fall short of the minimum requirements by 50 million bushels of grain in 1947 and encounter a similar deficit the following year. In Germany officials distributed food based on the type of work performed: those doing heavy labor received the most food. The old, sick, and those with less arduous work received far less in their food allotment. The average adult male in Germany was thirty pounds underweight, and the average German male in the

American zone of occupation weighed just 112 pounds.[4] President Truman knew that communism would make inroads into the communities of Europe unless he addressed the food shortages there, so he asked Boston executive Charles Luckman to head the Citizen's Food Committee that would help Americans take 100 million bushels of grain out of the American food system and send it to Europe. In response Luckman's committee devised a radical plan that took grain from all areas of the American food industry. The plan took effect on October 7, 1947, and included a sixty-day moratorium on the production of whiskey, while the bread industry set about creating smaller bread loaves and pies consisting of only one crust. In addition the committee asked the American public voluntarily to observe meatless Tuesdays—meaning no beef or pork— and poultryless Thursdays. Experts had testified before the committee that cattle matured on hay but finished on grains and that poultry consumed massive amounts of grain throughout their lives. The committee believed that reducing the demand for meat would reduce the number of animals, thus saving grain.[5]

Many farmers saw great opportunities in the European situation, as the northern Great Plains was one of the nation's greatest food producers. In fact demand for grain was so intense that even the record crops coming out of the fields demanded unprecedented prices on the grain exchanges. Wheat production in the United States had broken the 1 billion bushel mark only five times in history, including the 1915 crop and the four years leading up to the 1947 crop. While the United States set records in farm production, Senator Young of North Dakota noted that it would take years for Europe to come close to its prewar crop production levels, as nations there were short of machinery, fertilizer, and seed. Europe's decimation virtually guaranteed continued prosperity for Young's constituents. Additionally, Math Dahl, North Dakota commissioner of agriculture and labor, urged officials to buy excess farm horses and to round up wild horses from the western plains to convert into meat for Europe and profits for the northern plains. "Horses running wild on the western plains could be converted into good red meat animal protein to go with cereal starches offered by North Dakota wheat shipments," he said.[6] Dahl's plan was impractical due to shipping costs but showed the possibilities open to the agricultural industry.[7] European suffering translated into profits for the northern plains, which was not lost on the residents there. A poll released in March 1948 showed that 93 percent of North Dakotans favored the Marshall Plan and aid to Europe.[8]

While the idea to export horses to Europe was impractical, others came up with innovative ideas to help increase the amount of food available for shipment. President Truman called on the faculty members at all state colleges, and professors and extension agents convinced farmers to wage a war against rats as one way to help save grain. George I. Gilbertson was an extension agent in Brookings, South Dakota, who told an assembled group of farmers how to eliminate the rats that consumed or spoiled about 200 million bushels of grain each year, more than enough to make up President Truman's 100 million bushel shortfall. In Fargo, North Dakota, Dr. D. K. Christian demonstrated how to mix poison into two hundred pounds of horsemeat and then distribute the deadly concoction around a farm, while Montana extension agent C. W. Vaughn told farmers of a massive influx of rats invading northeastern and central Montana due to eradication efforts in neighboring states. Farmers in South Dakota noted that rats were not the only animals to help themselves to grain intended for human consumption and called for another pheasant season during the winter of 1947–48 to reduce grain losses there. The state legislature responded with special shooting permits available to any farmers who thought that the birds damaged their crops.[9]

The efforts paid off when Luckman confidently announced in early November that the goal of saving 100 million bushels of grain was within sight. He pointed to a nationwide poll in which 60 percent of Americans found it "easy" to comply with food sacrifices, while an additional 12 percent indicated that they observed the president's request even though they found it "difficult" to do so. While Luckman put a positive twist on the survey results, problems existed. For example, the decision to stop whiskey production put thousands of employees out of work for sixty days, and restaurants refused to deny patrons the foods they ordered even if it meant violating the president's appeal. Restaurant associations in Sioux Falls and Huron, South Dakota, and in Butte and Kalispell, Montana, specifically decreed that they would encourage customers to support the president's campaign but would nonetheless fill all orders as requested. "Mrs. Hay Seed" of Huron, South Dakota, summed up the problems with the grain-saving program when she sent a letter to the editor of her local paper, the *Daily Plainsman*. She pointed out that reducing the amount of meat consumed would not conserve grain but would inevitably have the opposite effect. If consumers reduced their demand for poultry, for example, farmers would have to feed their flocks for longer periods, thereby consuming more grain. Washington officials agreed with her assessment when they rescinded the poultryless Thursday request on November 8, after about a month in existence.[10] The food conservation campaign died out by Thanksgiving due to lack of support, and the committee officially ended the drive on January 7, 1948. But Luckman was able to save the required amount of grain through a more effective effort involving the Friendship Train.[11]

While the president's food conservation program met with mixed success, Luckman teamed up with a syndicated columnist and nominee for the Nobel Peace Prize, Drew Pearson, who envisioned a grassroots initiative to meet the needs of the starving continent. Pearson doubted the effectiveness of a program that called for people to take food off their plates but speculated that Americans would happily donate, collect, and transport food supplies directly to those who needed it. The idea occurred to Pearson as he was touring Europe in 1947, when he noticed that Communists received lavish praise for their donations of food to Western European countries. Pearson believed that America, with its agricultural and logistical strength, could easily surpass the Communists in bringing relief to the beleaguered nations. He announced his plan to form a Friendship Train on October 11, 1947, asking Americans to donate food from their homes, gardens, and fields for shipment to Europe. Charles Luckman and the Citizen's Food Committee organized their national resources and energized the program. A locomotive left Los Angeles on November 7 amid great fanfare and passed through eleven states, collecting assembled boxcars containing the donated food and supplies from all forty-eight states. The journey ended in New York on November 18, 1947, when the supplies made their way onto ships headed for Europe. The Friendship Train organizers hoped to amass eighty train cars full of food for Europe but collected over seven hundred. Railroad officials had to break down the boxcars into several trains, requiring more locomotives to move the items. Even so, monetary donations covered all of the costs associated with the train, including collections and delivery.[12]

Every state in the nation contributed to the Friendship Train, and the northern plains states were exceedingly generous. South Dakotans contributed over $130,000 worth of cash and crops for the train, including some twelve carloads of wheat and oats donated by farmers from that state. Although no precise numbers exist for North Dakota gifts, the people there probably contributed similar amounts. Special trains loaded with donated items left the state and traveled through South Dakota, picking up the boxcars there and joining up with the Friendship Train in Kansas. While North Dakota and South Dakota sent their donations south, Montana and other northwestern states—Oregon, Washington, Idaho, and the territory of Alaska—sent their contributions west to Seattle and then transferred their goods to the "Christmas Ship" that was supposed to reach Europe by the holidays. Montana governor Sam C. Ford commended his state and recounted Montana's contributions: "One city rallied to the cause with a 60,000-pound load of assorted foodstuffs. The people of another contributed 1,000 pounds of dry beans, from a third came a carload of wheat. A fourth gave twenty tons of flour. Another city gave three tons of flour and canned food."[13] The people on the northern plains came through in grand style for the destitute inhabitants of Europe.

A delegation from the northwestern states flew to Europe and toured German and Austrian cities, helping with food and clothing distribution and bearing other gifts. The Alaskan delegates brought salmon, the Idaho delegation brought potatoes, the Oregonians brought peas, the Washingtonians brought apples, and the Montanans brought bread made of Montana flour. Food reserves in Berlin were nearly exhausted when cargo from the Christmas Ship made its way to the city and saved the residents from near starvation. Berlin was in the Soviet zone of Germany, so all food into the city came by rail, truck, or barge. Americans had pledged 1,500 calories per person when they occupied their portion of the city, but consumption averaged just over 1,000 calories in the three years after the war.[14] The death rate was three times the birth rate, and health officials estimated that 70 percent of the city's residents had permanent disabilities. The growth of children between ten and fifteen was stunted permanently, all due to lack of food.[15] The city had only hunger and misery, until the cargo from the Christmas Ship alleviated suffering, if only temporarily. The mayor of Berlin sent a letter to Governor Ford, asking him "to convey publicly our gratitude to all donors of your country."[16] The mayor of Berlin also gave a commemorative china plate to Montana delegate Josef Sklower that now resides in the Montana Historical Society.[17]

Newspaper editors on the northern plains reported when food-laden ships reached ports in Europe, describing the appreciation of the hungry crowds and the ways in which Americans simultaneously promoted the advancement of humankind and retarded the influence of communism. Citizens on the northern plains read about the mayor of Florence, Italy, who greeted a food train with speeches, gratitude, and smiles, though he was a Communist. They also read about the Communist mayor in Milan, Italy, who refused to greet the food train there, about the train set ablaze by Communists in Paris, and about the ten thousand Sicilians who swarmed onto their train as soon as it reached the rail yards. The trains brought food to the hungry and political liability to the Communists.[18]

Most Europeans were thrilled to receive the generous contributions of food, clothing, and other supplies to help them through the tough winter months. The French were so grateful that they organized a "Merci Train" in 1948 to show their appreciation for the American generosity. Each of the forty-eight states in the union received a boxcar stuffed with a variety of donated gifts from the people of France. The boxcars were the "40 and 8 type," meaning that they could accommodate forty men and eight horses each. Huge crowds in North Dakota, South Dakota, and Montana turned out to watch volunteers unload the boxcars when they arrived in early 1949. The items came from French citizens and included dolls, pictures and photographs, books, and assorted trinkets. In South Dakota the most valuable gifts from the train went to museums, with the rest divided among nine cities and auctioned off. The proceeds from the auction went to help purchase a whirlpool bath for polio patients. The state historical society kept all of the gifts from the North Dakota train, and Montana officials distributed their gifts throughout the state. Each state on the northern plains still has the "Merci Train" boxcars, which are available for viewing. The Montana boxcar is located at the Fort William Henry Harrison in the state. The North Dakota boxcar is located at the Historical Society of North Dakota in Bismarck, and the South Dakota boxcar is located at the Dakotaland Museum at the State Fairgrounds in Huron.[19]

While the Friendship Train and Christmas Ship showed American generosity, U.S. Attorney General Thomas Clark worried as communism spread globally that the divisive American society he saw was unprepared for the coming battle. Partisan politics, divisions between business and labor, increased shortages of consumer goods, and rising inflation coupled with the decline in law and order divided the nation as the Soviet Union and its poisonous ideology seemed to be gaining strength. The American people needed to unite behind some movement to energize their patriotism, he thought, much as they did for World War II. The idea, as eventually agreed upon, was to send a train throughout all forty-eight states with a cargo of the most precious and historic American documents.[20]

William A. Coblenz, the assistant director of public information at the Justice Department, first developed the idea of the Freedom Train when he envisioned a single railcar with captured Nazi pictures and documents on one side and a depiction of American culture and values on the other. The idea grew and transformed under Clark until a "campaign to sell America to Americans" evolved.[21] Many government and business leaders supported the plan, agreeing that a nonprofit organization should take the lead and selecting the American Heritage Foundation (AHF) for this role. One of the first changes that the AHF leadership enacted was to discard the notion of including Nazi information and make the display purely American, with a more positive emphasis on Americanism. Debates ensued over the selection of documents and the definition of freedom. Republicans worried that the Democrats would use the Freedom Train to publicize liberal causes or, worse, as a campaign tool for the upcoming 1948 election. The AHF leaders sought to create a nonpartisan exhibit that specifically celebrated American freedom, expansion, and battlefield victories. Thousands of communities across the country continued to request a visit from the historic train even after officials finalized the schedule.[22]

From the time the Freedom Train made its initial appearance in Philadelphia, Pennsylvania, on September 16, 1947, it mesmerized the nation's citizens. A bottle of champagne broken across the locomotive's nose completed the christening ceremony, followed by a number of prayers and speeches. Attorney General Clark delivered one of the stirring messages, insisting: "Unless America shares its freedom with all nations, there will soon be no freedom for anyone in the broad reaches of the world." Slamming his fist on the lectern, he emphasized to the crowd: "All of us must be free or none of us are free!"[23] When the train left on September 19 for Atlantic City, New Jersey, it embarked on a 33,000-mile trip to over three hundred American cities. A staff of thirty maintained the red, white, and blue train. An honor guard of thirty marines protected the documents at all times, including two of the marines who had helped raise the flag over Mount Suribachi on Iwo Jima. The major attraction included three train cars of artifacts plus a lounge car, a baggage car, and sleeping quarters for the staff. The visitors' area was air conditioned and had a custom fire suppression system. As patrons entered the display area, they encountered the oldest documents first, including Christopher Columbus's 1493 description of a new continent. Citizens could view the Mayflower Compact, the Declaration of Independence, Thomas Paine's pamphlet entitled *Common Sense*, a letter from General Washington describing conditions in Valley Forge, the Constitution, the Gettysburg Address, and the surrender documents from Germany and Japan that essentially ended World War II, just to name a few.[24]

The Freedom Train visited Montana as the first of the northern plains states, stopping in Missoula on April 15, 1948, followed by visits to Butte on April 16, Helena on April 17, Great Falls on April 18, and Billings on April 20. Governor Ford prepared the people of Montana for the visit beginning in September 1947. The AHF asked each community to prepare a "Rededication Week" of patriotic festivities for the week before the visit, concluding with the train's visit. Each day consisted of special events that included parades, speeches, community dinners, or other events.[25] As the governor stated: "In this day of totalitarian threat to American liberties, it is most significant that we in America will be able to unroll the pages of history and see for ourselves the documents which are the foundation of our form of government."[26]

Excitement intensified throughout the state as many Montana residents planned to travel to one of the locations where the Freedom Train would stop. The Inter-Mountain Transportation Company, a bus company that operated in numerous Montana communities, warned people not to count on riding a bus to one of the host cities due to tremendous demand. Overwhelming requests for information worried company officers that too many people would count on the buses for transportation, leaving many stranded. Local police advised citizens to leave their cars at home, as school buses and other chartered vehicles crowded the

downtown city streets. State and local police officers, army and navy re-
servists, and even the local Boy Scouts assisted with traffic control when
the train arrived in each city. Officials asked visitors to stand two abreast
as they walked through the train to ensure that the maximum number
of citizens got inside. Unfortunately, in every city in which the train
stopped, large numbers of people never got onto the train due to capacity constraints. Many people could not see the original documents, so
several businesses throughout the state displayed these important documents for their customers. They were copies, of course, but the gesture
was important.[27]

Enthusiastic crowds turned out when the train pulled into Missoula.
One particular item held special significance for the residents there.
When marines struggled to capture the island of Iwo Jima in 1945, a
transport ship named the USS *Missoula* carried an American flag. Navy
officials took the flag from the transport and gave it to the six marines
who eventually raised the flag over Mount Suribachi, giving photographers an opportunity to shoot the picture that has inspired generations
of Americans. The Freedom Train carried the flag raised on Iwo Jima,
but that was actually the second flag-raising on the mountaintop that
morning. Earlier that day four marines, including Louis C. Charlo, a
Flathead Indian from Missoula, raised the first American flag on Mount
Suribachi and then unceremoniously folded it up again, guarding the
area for two hours before those six famous marines arrived and raised the
renowned second flag. Charlo died six days later, though his body did
not return to Montana for burial until several years after his death, about
the same time the Freedom Train arrived in the city. This gave crowds an
additional reason to visit the traveling exhibit.[28]

In Butte crowds exceeded all expectations. A near-record 10,146 citizens got onto the train to view the documents, only 42 shy of the record
west of the Mississippi River of 10,188 set in Spokane. This was far short
of the official record of 13,222 visitors set in Paterson, New Jersey, but an
impressive showing nonetheless. Officials in Butte turned away hundreds
waiting in line when they stopped allowing visitors to board the train at
10 P.M. From the time the doors opened that morning at 10 until closing,
lines of spectators wound around downtown city blocks, awaiting their
opportunity to board the train and view the historic items. Adding to
the multitude were numerous school-aged children who, because area

schools closed in support of this event, made up a large percentage of the crowd. Perhaps the highlight of the tour for Montanans was when officials tapped fifteen-year-old Donald Hardesty as the 1,500,000th visitor to the train. Train officials recognized every half-millionth visitor for a special award, but Hardesty knew nothing of the honor as he and his two classmates prepared to view the train's contents in Butte. Nearby a marine in the train's entryway clicked his mechanical counter, consulted his clipboard, and then detained the young man. The Freedom Train's director, Walter H. S. O'Brien, and the commander of the marines aboard the train, Lieutenant Colonel Robert Scott, came forward and congratulated Hardesty. The two distinguished men gave Hardesty and his companions a guided tour through the train and then presented him with a copy of the book *Heritage and Freedom*, containing the official story of the Freedom Train and a description of the documents it contained. Both O'Brien and Scott signed the book for Hardesty. When asked to recall the most memorable document he had seen, Hardesty was hard pressed but after some thought settled on the Declaration of Independence.[29]

Visitors in Helena and Great Falls also enjoyed seeing the documents. Some 8,769 residents of Helena viewed the train's exhibit, following a detailed rededication week. Events included Women's Day, Veterans' Day, Religious Day, Labor and Management Day, the "Bench and Bar day" that recognized aspects of American law, Youth Day, Civic Organizations Day, and then Train Day on Saturday. Thousands of Great Falls residents viewed a special item when the train opened its doors to the public on April 19, 1948. They saw the surrender documents of the U.S. Marine capitulation on Wake Island, bearing the signature of a former Great Falls resident. Major General Lawson H. M. Sanderson was in charge of the island when the war started and directed its defense, though he eventually surrendered the island to the Japanese after a prolonged battle. Sanderson spent his youth playing baseball for Great Falls in the state league and was a star football player at the state university.[30]

The last Montana city where the Freedom Train stopped was Billings, where the citizens responded with overwhelming enthusiasm. Months before the train arrived, ninety of the city's churches, schools, civic and service clubs, labor organizations, and fraternal groups pledged their support for the week-long celebration. The "Rededication Week" consisted of Billings Day, Veterans Day, Industry Day, Labor's Day, School's Day, Women's Day, and Freedom of Religion Day. Undoubtedly, the highlight of the week was the parade the day before the train arrived. A short ceremony kicked off the parade, in which members of the naval reserve officiated at the flag raising and the city band played the national anthem. The parade began at the conclusion of Mrs. Clark I. Israel's speech. She likened the arrival of the Freedom Train to Paul Revere's ride, saying that the train symbolized a "cry to Americans to wake up and look at what we have."[31] Numerous organizations took part in the parade while planes from the 702nd Very Heavy Bombardment Squadron flew in formation at two thousand feet. When the train finally opened its doors the next day, the enthusiastic crowd could not wait to view the train's cargo. When the doors closed twelve hours later, some 10,109 Billings residents had viewed the documents on the train.[32]

The Freedom Train left Montana and arrived in Rapid City, South Dakota, on April 22, 1948, when the exhibit drew the largest crowd ever assembled in the city and set an attendance record for communities west of the Mississippi River, beating out such urban centers as Spokane, Seattle, San Diego, San Francisco, and Los Angeles. That day 10,425 patrons went through the train, as residents from every town west of the Missouri River in South Dakota viewed the Freedom Train documents. Each school in the Black Hills canceled classes to allow students a chance to visit the train, and thousands of adults throughout the region descended upon the town in the midst of an unseasonable heat wave.[33] Officials admitted people into the train's display area beginning at 10 A.M., but the line stretched for blocks as thousands of citizens waited in the sweltering heat. Three people fainted from sunstroke, and medical personnel from the nearby air base provided assistance to those in need. A short while later a violent thunderstorm enveloped the town, but no one sought shelter—people stubbornly stayed in line to see the train's historic cargo. That afternoon a doctor from the local air base hospital brought thirty disabled veterans to the exhibit, hoping that train administrators would allow the veterans to jump the line and get inside more quickly. The officer in charge of the train did not want to upset those people already in line after their hardships, but Rapid City mayor Fred Dusek assured him that the people of the Black Hills would not deny the disabled veterans this opportunity. The mayor was right: the waiting crowd

Crowds waiting to enter the Freedom Train in Rapid City, South Dakota, April 22, 1948. Courtesy National Archives and Records Administration.

applauded the veterans as they made their way onto the platform and into the train, often with the assistance of those waiting in line. To show his appreciation to the train's crew for visiting Rapid City, Mayor Dusek organized three separate tours for the train personnel to visit Mount Rushmore, also known as the Shrine of Democracy. Both the crew and the citizens of western South Dakota realized that the figures displayed on Mount Rushmore had written some of the documents preserved inside the train.[34] Those citizens who viewed the historic documents that day undoubtedly left the Freedom Train with an immense feeling of patriotism and faith in democracy, which was exactly the federal government's intent when initiating the campaign.

The capital city of Pierre was the smallest community where the train stopped, though South Dakotans crowded the streets, restaurants, hotels, and lines stretched for blocks to see the display. The crowd that turned out that day numbered 10,299 visitors, which also broke the Spokane attendance mark but fell just short of breaking the Rapid City record.[35]

One of the guests who viewed the exhibit in Pierre was Sarah Summersdale, who turned ninety-nine the day before the train arrived. She held the distinction of being the only granddaughter of a soldier from the American Revolution to view the contents of the Freedom Train.[36]

The Freedom Train left South Dakota and made its way through North Dakota, stopping first in Bismarck. Nearly nine thousand people made their way through the train, but one of them would not have gotten inside if not for the benevolence of train officials. A. W. Cuddington, a Canadian from Saskatchewan, chartered a plane to fly him to Bismarck, where he could view the historic documents. He waited in line for hours, but his pressing schedule meant that he had to view the train's cargo soon or leave. Cuddington explained his situation at KFYR radio station, which contacted train officials. They let Cuddington into the train once they learned that he was a veteran of the last war, helping him keep his scheduled appointment.[37]

The train left Bismarck and traveled to Minot, North Dakota, where a record-setting crowd waited. Nearly twenty thousand North Dakotans, the largest crowd ever assembled in the city, came to view to historic documents. One official reviewed the guest book and noted that hardly any community from the northwest portion of the state was without representation. Many people waited in line for up to five hours to get inside the train, and perhaps half the people who wanted to board the train never did so. Officials finished counting all of the visitors in Minot and announced that the small city had broken the single-day attendance record of 10,425 visitors previously set in Rapid City. The old record fell when Minot established a new record of 10,907 individuals who visited the Freedom Train before it left for its new destination.[38]

Jamestown, North Dakota, turned out an impressive crowd, with 8,785 people passing through the train. What the small city lacked in size, it made up for in vitality. A dedication ceremony greeted the train as state representatives gave short statements, testifying to the solemnity of the occasion. North Dakota attorney general Nels Johnson told the assembled crowd that "in order to keep our freedom every citizen must take an active part in local and state affairs; he or she must know the problems and help solve them; serve willingly in public offices; take an active part in law enforcement and participate in civic organizations."[39] Following the speeches, the newly crowned "Miss Freedom" assisted with the next portion of the ceremony. Mary Taylor, a student at Jamestown College, won the coveted title and cut the red, white, and blue ribbon to signify the opening of the train to the public. She led the procession of dignitaries to the city's armory, helping to prepare for other events that day. While people waited their turn to enter the train, ten bands from the region entertained the visitors throughout the day.[40]

Another record crowd awaited the train when it made its way to the final two stops in North Dakota. Edging out Minot by a mere eighteen visitors, Fargo set the new record for the most people to visit the train west of the Mississippi in a single day: 10,925 people viewed its contents.[41] Mrs. Albert Birch of Fargo had a personal interest in seeing the historic items. One of the documents contained the signature of her grandmother, Matilda Joslyn Gage. Gage was an important activist and a good friend of Elizabeth Cady Stanton and Susan B. Anthony, the famous founders of the National Women's Suffrage Association. The three women had signed a petition endorsing women's rights in 1873 and forwarded the document to Congress. Although the legislative body failed to act on the appeal, it was nonetheless an important piece of American history. Gage's granddaughter had met Anthony several times and received a book from her with the inscription: "with hope that you may equal her [Gage] and do a great work for women and humanity."[42] The train then left Fargo and made its way to Grand Forks, where another large crowd awaited it. The train's director, Walter O'Brien, was so impressed with the turnout in North Dakota that he suggested unofficially that the state probably had the distinction of having the greatest proportion of its citizens view the train's contents.[43]

The Freedom Train left North Dakota, made its way to Minnesota and Wisconsin, then returned to South Dakota to visit Watertown on May 11 and Sioux Falls on May 12, 1948, wrapping up its venture through the northern plains. In Watertown, thirteen-year-old local Boy Scout Dick Stone took particular pride in making sure that ninety-year-old O. H. Tarbell was the first resident to enter the train and then acted as her escort while she viewed the historic documents. As Stone reasoned, Tarbell was the first female settler in Codington County and should be the first visitor on the train. The youth had presented the case weeks earlier to city officials, who issued two special passes after agreeing that the idea had merit.[44]

The crowd in Sioux Falls was smaller than in some cities, but people there were just as eager to see the train. Officially 9,543 citizens made their way through the train, with crowds thinning out by late afternoon until it took only a few minutes of waiting in line to see the items. Thirteen-year-old Irene Morrill was taking no chances on whether she would make it inside the train: she and several friends lined up at 4:30 A.M. in order to ensure their entrance to the exhibit. As part of the "Rededication Week" that officials planned for Sioux Falls, a formation of B-29 bombers simulated a bombing run on the city, as crowds waited to enter the train. Lieutenant Colonel Joe Foss, Medal of Honor winner and pilot during World War II and future governor of the state, led the "defense" of Sioux Falls, as he and fifteen fellow pilots drove their fighter planes through the bomber formation, certainly "downing" most if not all of the "Soviet" attackers.[45]

Both the Friendship Train and the Freedom Train were enormously effective in fighting communism: they combined patriotism with action, and people could see their achievements making a difference. The Friendship Train helped the federal government to accumulate much-needed food and other items for Europe, and the Freedom Train brought a better understanding of the nation and its government to American citizens. These measures inspired patriotic and pro-American feelings both at home and abroad.

While the two trains crossed the nation and battled communism in late 1947, the National Security Council instructed the director of the CIA to conduct covert psychological operations against the Soviet Union. CIA officials knew that one way to meet this requirement was to enable radio stations to carry messages from defecting citizens that criticized the Communist way of life and praised democracy. These voices ostensibly should be independent of the U.S. government and not tied directly to any American agency. The CIA had initially suggested using the Voice of America (VOA) program, but this idea had a number of drawbacks. For example, the VOA was an American production, funded by Congress, and its program directors could not directly criticize the Soviet system, its leaders, or its people. Government officials envisioned something quite different called Radio Free Europe that was not encumbered by regulations. George Kennan, State Department employee and Cold War strategist, proposed that a group of trusted private citizens—under the control of the CIA—act as a front organization for Radio Free Europe. The idea caught on with those who had the authority to turn the proposal into reality. The clandestine organization took the name of the National Committee for Free Europe (NCFE), holding its first meeting in May 1949. The list of directors and officers included future CIA director Allen Dulles and future president Dwight D. Eisenhower, *Reader's Digest* owner Dewitt Wallace, publisher Henry Luce, and others.[46]

The NCFE took over a much smaller project in Berlin started just after the war, designed to broadcast radio programs only into the American sector of the city. This small project became a behemoth. Project leaders assembled equipment, a technical crew, and broadcasters in Munich, Germany, and produced the program's first transmission on July 4, 1950. The objective was to broadcast news and information from the free zone of Germany into the occupied zones behind Communist borders. By late 1950 the organization had assembled a number of journalists specializing in different languages, who interviewed defectors and exiles for stories and information to use against the Communists. Listening to the broadcasts could mean imprisonment or even death for those behind the Iron Curtain, but thousands of people in Communist nations tuned in every night to listen to the programming. Although most of the funding for Radio Free Europe came secretly from the CIA, the NCFE devised the "Crusade for Freedom" to hide the CIA funding and to tap into American pocketbooks and people's antipathy toward communism. Project directors labeled each dollar collected a "truth dollar" that could finance one minute of broadcast time directed at Communist lies.[47]

American military hero General Lucius Clay agreed to lend his name and support to the endeavor. The board of directors quickly named him to head the project, while a professional advertising company helped with the promotion and fund-raising. The advertising committee felt that it needed a symbol to excite the American people and to assist in fund-raising, a combination that led to the "Freedom Bell" initiative. President Eisenhower received the credit for the idea when he announced the campaign on Labor Day in 1950. The idea was to give a Liberty Bell to the free sector of Berlin. Its ringing would resound a dozen miles into the Communist zone of Eastern Europe. Artisans cast the bell in England. It weighed twelve tons when it came out of the giant molds but lost two tons in the 400-hour tuning process. Crusade for Freedom officials brought the bell to New York City and paraded it through the streets. There people could see the bell's inscription of Lincoln's words from the Gettysburg Address: "That this world, under God, shall have a new birth of freedom."[48]

The citizens on the northern plains contributed enthusiastically to the Freedom Bell Campaign, which consisted of collecting donations and having people sign the Freedom Scrolls eventually encapsulated within the bell structure in Berlin. Fifty thousand Montanans contributed financially to the project and signed the scroll. Citizens who could not sign the Freedom Scroll at one of the local centers had the option of mailing a form to the Freedom Bell headquarters, where officials added the sender's name to a Freedom Scroll. Butte had a "lights on" night: interested citizens could leave their porch light on and Boy Scouts, Girl Scouts, or Campfire Girls would stop by seeking pledges and signatures on the Freedom Scrolls. Similar campaigns took place throughout the state and the nation. The first plane leaving the United States carried the names of 13,186 Montana citizens, with the other names reaching Berlin on other Freedom Planes.[49]

North Dakota officials set up a state Crusade for Freedom headquarters in the Association of Commerce offices in Bismarck to coordinate activities. The directors of the Association of Commerce donated the space and cooperation because "they believe a campaign will do much to alert the people of this state to the dangers they face . . . and to remind them that our way of life . . . is immeasurably better than any other —ism practiced on the face of the globe."[50] Working in the Crusade for Freedom offices was a state general chair, an executive state chair, a Bismarck City chair, and an office assistant. The objective was to have fifty thousand North Dakotans sign the Freedom Scrolls by having faculty, staff, and students from three hundred high schools sign the Freedom Scrolls in addition to local adults. Booths were set up in banks, civic organizations, and other venues around the state seeking signatures and dollars.[51]

South Dakotans also supported the Crusade for Freedom. Governor George T. Mickelson was the honorary chair of the state's campaign effort, but the real work went to James H. Lemmon of Lemmon, South Dakota, who explained: "This crusade offers every American a chance to play a personal part in a great moral crusade for freedom, faith, and peace throughout the earth." He invited citizens to sign the Freedom Scrolls available across the state, including the state fair booth, where South Dakotans displayed a small replica of the Freedom Bell. When the fair ended, the bell went to the state capitol grounds, where citizens waited to hear it ring.[52]

The original Freedom Bell visited sixteen American cities after leaving New York City and then made its way to Berlin, where it hung within the bell tower at the municipal building. Almost half a million people gathered to watch the installation and the dedication ceremonies on October 24, 1950. General Clay gave a short speech, then at 11:03 P.M. in Berlin pressed the button that started the bell ringing. Half a world away, members of city departments, schools, churches, businesses, and individuals took up whatever bell they had and rang it for five minutes to ring simultaneously with the Freedom Bell in Berlin to show their support.[53] The replica bell in Pierre, South Dakota, rang for the first time on October 24, 1950, at the same moment the Freedom Bell in Berlin rang for the first time, as citizens in every town on the northern plains also participated in the event. The *Daily Argus Leader* called the effort a "separate, private means of psychological warfare."[54]

The effort to fund Radio Free Europe continued throughout the nation during the 1950s using a number of innovative techniques. Bing Crosby and his four sons organized the "Youth Crusade with the Crosbys," where the family asked each young person listening to donate three cents to liberate Europe, about the cost of three sticks of gum. Actor Ronald Reagan was an enthusiastic supporter of the program, and General Dwight Eisenhower kicked off each fund-raising season at the end of October with a speech. The closest the northern plains came to celebrity endorsement was from political leaders; governors and congressional leaders gave their names and their support to the effort. Nationally the Fraternal Order of Eagles advised its chapters to launch balloon campaigns to raise awareness about Radio Free Europe. *Reader's Digest* supported essay contests about the benefits of Radio Free Europe, and winners traveled to Germany to read their essay over the airwaves at the Radio Free Europe broadcasting station. Eleven-year-old Joseph Landenfeld of Mitchell, South Dakota, won a complete set of *Encyclopedia Britannica* from the state's Crusade for Freedom committee for writing the best essay in the state by completing the phrase "I believe the most important thing people behind the Iron Curtain should know is." The NCFE followed up the Freedom Bell project with the Crusade for Freedom Motorcade. Committee members persuaded the Ford Motor Company to donate forty-eight new pickup trucks and Chevrolet donated a like number of station wagons, sending them across the country to raise awareness and funds. The trucks looked identical, with a common paint scheme and a Crusade for Freedom logo. Each carried a replica of the Freedom Bell, a Radio Free Europe transmitter, and an image of an "arrow of truth" penetrating a replica of the Iron Curtain. The Chevrolet cars, also painted identically, carried two loudspeakers so that citizens could hear actual broadcasts that had gone over the Radio Free Europe airwaves.[55]

Citizens throughout the northern plains readily endorsed the Crusade for Freedom Motorcade. Advance teams from the NCFE preceded each motorcade appearance to ensure that sufficient excitement surrounded the event. Often cities would sponsor parades or some other celebration to raise support and increase the likelihood that people would contribute to the cause. When the motorcade arrived in Billings, the mayor announced the beginning of "Freedom Crusade Week," organized well in advance. The two-car motorcade in each state made its way to nearly every city throughout the region in the fall of 1951, often visiting several cities in a single day. At the conclusion of the motorcade's visit, local leaders would often imitate the "Winds of Freedom" initiative by filling balloons with helium and releasing them, often with messages for those who found the balloons.[56]

The Winds of Freedom project was another Radio Free Europe initiative carried out between 1951 and 1956. These volunteers used balloons to float over the borders of Communist countries and disperse messages to people trapped inside. Weather balloons were readily available through military channels at this time and were often filled with anticommunist propaganda or messages of encouragement from citizens in democratic nations and then sent into Eastern Europe. In some cases specially designed balloons would float up to thirty thousand feet and burst, dispersing a cargo of leaflets over a wide range of Communist territory.[57]

While balloon barrages were an effective and relatively inexpensive method of disrupting Communist society, they were also an effective

Crusade for Freedom Motorcade in front of the state capitol building, Helena, Montana. (*Left to right*) Sergeant Paul Wirick, Jr.; Montana attorney general (and future U.S. congressman) Arnold Olsen; Howard Ellsworth, State Crusade for Freedom chair; Walter H. Marshall, coordinator. No date given. Courtesy Montana Historical Society Research Center Photograph Archives, Helena, Montana.

way of raising awareness about the Crusade for Freedom in the United States. Patty Collins of Bismarck, North Dakota, was an eighth grader when she suggested that she and her classmates should send valentines and money to the Crusade for Freedom instead of exchanging valentines with each other and name the project "Valentines for Freedom." The idea came to fruition two years later, in 1955, when the Crusade for Freedom headquarters agreed to send the valentines into Communist-controlled territory through their balloon barrage. The Fraternal Order of Eagles agreed to help the young girl locally by sponsoring a contest for the best valentine made in the city, which created a large number of valentines headed to Europe. Eagles officials announced the winner on February 12, Lincoln's birthday, and after a short ceremony launched a number of their own balloons to raise awareness for the Crusade for

Freedom. They launched twenty-one "Freedom Balloons" with various cargo, including a Freedom Scroll, contribution envelopes for the Crusade for Freedom, and a number of postcards that asked whoever found them to mail them back to their origin in Bismarck. One of the returned cards came from Britton, South Dakota, 153 miles from Bismarck.[58]

While many balloons landed in South Dakota, a number also took off from there, including a fifty-foot-tall plastic balloon operated by Ed Yost, a twenty-five-year veteran of ballooning. He set out from Joe Foss Field in Sioux Falls as a crowd of one thousand stood by. Yost intended to fly to the East Coast and bring attention to the Crusade for Freedom at the same time. He had four radio stations in Sioux Falls operating a marathon for each minute he held the balloon aloft, hoping to garner dollars for the project as the balloon traversed the continent. The gondola held radio equipment with which Yost planned to broadcast his position and messages from each governor as he crossed into new states. Yost's flight ended, however, when 150 pounds of ice formed on the balloon, forcing him down near Amboy, Minnesota. He saw the lights of a farm from the sky and aimed toward it, finding Mr. and Mrs. Robert Lawson still awake. Mrs. Lawson made a hot meal for Yost before offering him a spare bed for the night.[59]

Balloons undoubtedly played an enormous role in bringing attention to the Crusade for Freedom, imitating a real endeavor to deliver messages through the Iron Curtain, but they were not the only events. Many residents on the northern plains gained an awareness of the Crusade for Freedom through the ingenious proceedings of other citizens. First prize for the best noncommercial float in the Montana State Fair Parade of 1951 went to the American Legion's float, with the Crusade for Freedom theme. Newspapers throughout the region donated space to run ads and raise awareness for the campaign. Probably the greatest publicity event was when leaders in the North Dakota Crusade for Freedom sponsored a visit by the supreme allied commander in Europe, General Alfred M. Gruenther. The general visited the North Dakota state capitol in 1959 and gave a speech at the House chamber in which he explained the dangers of communism and celebrated the work of Radio Free Europe and those trying to assist with that endeavor. Seating capacity was the only limiting factor for the general's speech. Speakers were placed through the capitol grounds for those who could not fit inside the chamber.[60]

The general was a fervent supporter of the Crusade for Freedom, meeting many from the North Dakota organization at his headquarters when volunteers visited Europe to view the Communist border and to see the difference that their contributions made. Harvard Noble of Mitchell, South Dakota, was one such official. He left for Europe in 1959 to examine the Radio Free Europe facilities after two years as the state's head of fund-raising for the organization. When the officials returned from Europe, their personal stories helped to raise more funds to finance the operation for another year.[61]

The Crusade for Freedom financially supported Radio Free Europe until the end of the 1950s, when sources revealed that the CIA was secretly funneling funds to the enterprise and the value of the project came into doubt. No one is certain why radio personality and syndicated columnist Fulton Lewis, Jr., launched the attacks that he did, but his battle began in late 1957. In October of that year Fulton ran a column entitled "Your R.F.E. 'Truth' Dollars" that explained the involvement of the CIA and argued that Radio Free Europe's broadcasts were glorifying Tito and his form of communism rather than lionizing Western democracy. He also insinuated that the Crusade for Freedom had experienced financial irregularities. Lewis continued his attack through 1958, causing members of Congress to seek clarification of the CIA's role in the organization and resulting in a wholesale abandonment of the project by the public. Corporate donors, always the backbone of the project, dried up completely. Lewis had abandoned his attacks by 1960, but the executive committee decided on a name change for the program in light of the CIA revelations, changing it from the Crusade for Freedom to the Radio Free Europe Fund.[62] The CIA continued to fund the program into the late 1960s, but it never regained the enthusiasm or crowds that it had in the 1950s.

The Crusade for Freedom lost support, but other endeavors remained popular. Civic organizations throughout America also pushed patriotic activities down to the state and local levels. Many of these groups used the phrase "under God," which was popular at a time when President Eisenhower changed the pledge of allegiance. Representatives from sixty national organizations, with a combined membership of 50 million members, met in New York City in January 1956, to form a united front against worldwide communism. The American Legion's national commander, George N. Craig, invited all loyal Americans to join the fight. Many civic groups answered the challenge, carried on a public fight against communism, and supported many patriotic endeavors.[63] It is not surprising that the northern plains, which had the highest participation in civic clubs in the nation, had some of the most effective civic organizations attacking communism. Nationally the average number of club meetings attended per year varied from four in Nevada to a high of eleven in North Dakota and South Dakota. Professor Robert Putnam uses the term "social capital" to describe the phenomenon of people forming resilient bonds with one another, strengthened by a sense of loyalty and obligation to the group.[64] People from the region rallied against the empty promises of the Soviet ideology in hordes.

The American Legion called on Congress to outlaw the Communist Party in the early 1950s and sponsored the "Back to God" program in 1953, using religion as a lever against Communist subversion. The objective of the American Legion was somewhat different from those of other patriotic organizations that stood for Americanism and patriotism: the American Legion sought to root out and expose subversives. It even had a subcommittee that published a list of hundreds of suspected revolutionary organizations and publications. The American Legion deputized itself as the watchdog of loyalty throughout America and had local posts carry out "I am an American Day" that depicted the value of American citizenship and government. Additionally, local American Legion posts pressured state and local government leaders to require government employees to sign loyalty oaths, a measure that offended many who had to sign the oaths.[65]

The Fraternal Order of Eagles supported the Crusade for Freedom and the Benevolent Protective Order of Elks endorsed Flag Day, while other civic organizations also pushed national programs down to the state and local levels. For example, May 1 was usually a holiday simply abandoned to the Communists every year, but May Day became Loyalty Day throughout the United States, with parades, speeches, dinners, and dances that enabled citizens to demonstrate their patriotism and counter the Communist holiday. The Veterans of Foreign Wars (VFW) took the lead in re-creating the holiday. Interest waned after the Red Scare subsided in the 1920s but came roaring back in 1947, when veterans competed with Communists for the streets of New York City for their respective parades. The holiday had gone national by 1950, when the

VFW mobilized its posts to join the holiday effort. By 1952 at least forty-four states participated in Loyalty Day festivities. Congress passed a bill that the president signed into law in April 1955, marking May 1 of that year as Loyalty Day throughout America. The president asked all citizens to reaffirm their loyalty to the nation and to display their American flag. Throughout the United States Loyalty Day was formulaic, consisting of speeches followed by parades that routinely included veterans, civic groups, churches, government agencies, scouts, and schoolchildren. Loyalty Day became a command performance for state and local officials, when attendance at public events was virtually mandatory.[66]

Northern plains governors and city mayors proclaimed May 1, or the closest Saturday or Sunday to it, as Loyalty Day. In 1954 North Dakota governor Norman Brunsdale asked the state's residents to view Loyalty Day as a day "for open and avowed rededication to the things that made America great."[67] North Dakota had been observing Loyalty Day since 1950, and South Dakota also had a tradition of observing this holiday. In 1956 South Dakota governor Joe Foss asked that "every man, woman, and child in this state to join in a demonstration of his or her undivided allegiance to the government of the United States and the ideals which it defends and preserves."[68] Montana had a slogan for its Loyalty Day observance in 1955: "Loyalty Means Liberty." The VFW encouraged people to attend church as part of their celebration, and high schools held essay contests throughout the state.[69]

Women were critical to the success of many civic organizations on the northern plains. A 1959 article from the *Daily Republic* pointed out that the Nineteenth Amendment just forty years earlier gave women the right to vote after a long struggle. The paper described the protracted battle and concluded: "Under God, the people rule. Women are people too."[70] After World War I demonstration clubs replaced the suffragist movement. They were exactly what the name implied: women in rural areas taught others how to bake bread, can food for preservation, make a fireless cooker, and any number of other survival skills. As the years progressed, however, many women became more community minded, and the simple demonstrations gave way to other activities. The organizations became involved in hospital planning committees, organizing recreational centers, acting in community pageants, and other worthwhile endeavors. After World War II some women's organizations took up the study of world economics and international relations, which led to group participation in patriotic events. Three-fourths of rural South Dakota women were involved with these clubs in 1949.[71]

Women's groups often promoted patriotism, warned of the dangers of communism, and invoked religion in many of their activities. Montana governor J. Hugo Aronson proclaimed the week of October 11 to 17, 1953, to be "National Business Woman's Week" in the state. The members of the Helena Business and Professional Women's Club kicked off the week-long celebration by attending church. Fifteen hundred women throughout the state belonged to the business organization. Patriotism and religion remained the cornerstone of the group. According to one official, "Members pledge themselves to a firm stand for freedom and democracy and against all totalitarian and anti-democratic forces which seek to destroy the dignity and freedom of the individual." Additionally, members of the club agreed, "a firm, positive program must be adopted to strengthen the ramparts of our republic and to reaffirm our faith in a government, under God."[72]

Many women's organizations came to life in the early 1950s, and most of them promoted Americanism. Syndicated writer George Sokolsky titled a 1952 column "Aroused Women Form Grass-Roots Clubs." He mentioned the Freedom Club, organized in Los Angeles but spreading throughout the nation. The object of the group was to "spread aggressive Americanism at home." The club credo made the mission of the organization clear: "I believe in Freedom under God—that man has certain unalienable rights, and that among them are life, liberty, and the pursuit of happiness." One of the main attractions of this club, Sokolsky noted, was that it had avoided partisanship, an achievement unmatched by most groups.[73]

The Freedom Club in Helena was part of the national drive for activities promoting Americanism at home. The guest speaker at the Freedom Club's first meeting was Dean Chaffin, Speaker of the Montana House of Representatives, who informed the assembled guests about legislative procedure and the ways in which democracy worked. Later in the evening club organizers explained that the only requirement to join the Freedom Club was to agree with the basic values of Americanism, based loosely on the Declaration of Independence and the Bill of Rights, and to adopt "Freedom under God" as an important personal principle. The individual also swore a "rejection of anti-freedom, the anti-God force of communism and collectivism, and to pass on to their children a United States of America with new economic strength and moral vitality." The Helena club was a completely female-run organization but invited men to attend meetings.[74]

The Daughters of the American Revolution (DAR) was another national group with female leadership, whose stated purpose was to build social conscience and an appreciation of our inherited freedom. The women attempted to meet this goal through a number of national committees and contests. Perhaps most importantly, the national organization pushed its local chapters to connect with minority groups. The DAR had thirteen chapters in Montana, with the Oro Fino chapter organized in 1903, only thirteen years after the first meeting in Newark, New Jersey. The Montana DAR worked closely with Indian tribes within the state, trying to provide care and education, particularly on issues of citizenship. The national organization sponsored St. Mary's High School for Indian Girls at Springfield, South Dakota, and Bacone College in Oklahoma, organized for Indian students. "The DAR feels that it is necessary to extend opportunities or assistance to all who have not become assimilated in American traditions . . . and understand the blessings of liberty," as one newspaper reported the DAR's objectives.[75] Local DAR organizations in North Dakota, South Dakota, and Montana all supported the St. Mary's school and promoted patriotism and other civic projects throughout the early Cold War era.

The DAR also promoted Americanism through contests, including a national "Good Citizen" competition carried out on a statewide basis. The challenge was only open to high school senior girls from an accredited high school, and students in each school voted for their top three choices. The faculty and administration picked the final candidate, who competed on a statewide basis for the top award. There was no national winner. Criteria for selection included possession of the four qualities for good citizenship: dependability, service, leadership, and patriotism. In 1950, for example, seventeen girls from North Dakota competed for the title of DAR Good Citizen. Evelyn Kaisershot was the ultimate winner. She missed the opportunity to travel to Washington, D.C., as the DAR had discontinued the practice of sending "Pilgrims" to the capital in 1948, but received a $100 savings bond instead.[76]

These programs designed at the national level and carried out at the local level resulted in many newspaper articles, but the efforts of local clubs and organizations that hosted dinners, dances, organized celebrations, or sponsored speakers in the fight against communism have been lost to history. The number was undoubtedly great. A few examples developed and carried out at the local level have survived and merit further examination. One case in North Dakota was a "takeover" of Bismarck Junior College in 1954, when students demonstrated what it would be like to live under communism. Instructors were "arrested" on trumped-up charges and then herded into the student lounge to await trial. The instructors received a two-hour coffee break while student "Communists" gave classes in party-line ideology. Bismarck Junior College was instrumental in leading the fight against communism when the school created a "Freedom Shrine" of important national documents in 1956, including the Declaration of Independence, the Bill of Rights, the Emancipation Proclamation, and many others. The shrine was the object of a formal dedication ceremony that included the college band and choir. Lieutenant General William H. Arnold, commander of 5th Army in Chicago, gave the dedication remarks.[77]

All of these events, whether conceived at the national, state, or local levels, gave people a sense of direction in an uncertain world. But these displays waned as the early Cold War era ended. The 1960s brought a host of new concerns, as the grandiose displays of patriotism competed with antigovernment demonstrators.[78] During the late 1940s and the 1950s, however, these events mattered. The Freedom Train and Friendship Train crossed the nation at the same time, bringing with them America's best qualities of charity on one hand and triumph on the other. The Crusade for Freedom campaign brought hope to the nation, allowing average citizens to participate in some small way in the battle against communism. In whatever capacity the national government asked the people of the nation and the northern plains to serve, they did so. Often the government was not asking for difficult commitments of time or service. It asked the public to carry out the simple tasks of citizenship, such as paying attention to important issues, safeguarding the national identity, and showing support for the many events created at the national level and implemented locally.

Chapter 4

Civil Defense

Wall Street Journal staff writer Daniel M. Burnham noted in 1961 that it would take a serious threat to get people concerned about nuclear war in Montana. "If fighting actually broke out in Berlin," noted Great Falls mayor William Swanberg, "you'd see a lot more people digging in."[1] The air force had surrounded the city with nuclear missile silos, and Malmstrom Air Force Base (AFB) lay just to the east, making Great Falls a prominent target for a Soviet nuclear attack, but a surprising number of people seemed unconcerned with the possibility. "Everybody thinks we will go to war, but nobody seems to care," noted John Tanovitch, a resident of the city. One of the local physicians reported: "Nobody wants to cross the gap between believing war will come and what it could mean to them personally if it did come." Burnham observed that people in the city seemed unconcerned that federal civil defense authorities had labeled Great Falls a top target area. "After ten years of listening to the sirens blowing and reading dull pamphlets, people just don't get worked up anymore," one resident declared.[2] The idea that war would come to Great Falls required too much a suspension of disbelief, and civil defense was not a high priority.

Citizens on the northern plains generally did not engage in civil defense measures. A number of contemporary authors, journalists, and public leaders identified the public as the primary reason why civil defense measures were a failure. Federal leaders tried to engage the population, but civil defense failed at the state and local level. Though some called the citizens apathetic, this label is somewhat problematic. They certainly must have cared about a nuclear attack, but their fears or concerns simply did not translate into action. There were several complex reasons for this. Citizens did not believe that an enemy attack would impact them, could not justify the expense of a fallout shelter, or did not want to live through such an ordeal. Additionally, citizens received confusing and often contradictory messages from community and national leaders. These leaders explained that nuclear war was akin to Armageddon, wiping out all life on the planet, but citizens could live through it and go on to lead happy, healthy lives. Large number of officials tried, and failed, to get citizens to energize civil defense measures. This chapter explores the federal government's effort to activate a civil defense program and the failure to persuade citizens to construct private fallout shelters or engage in other defensive measures in the early Cold War period through 1961 (civil defense in 1962 and the Cuban Missile Crisis are examined in chapter 6).

Civilians had been vulnerable to bombing attacks since the Germans first bombed Paris in 1914, only eleven years after the Wright brothers had first taken flight. Bombing and navigational techniques and aircraft performance continued to advance between the wars, leading national leaders to consider the implications of bombing civilians. Antagonists in World War II initially tried to avoid harming innocent civilians and then recognized the value of specifically targeting civilian populations as the practice of "total war" became better understood and applied. During the Battle of Britain in 1940 and 1941 the Germans had killed over 60,000 civilians and destroyed 2 million homes in the nine months of the campaign. The British began a sustained bombing campaign of German military, industrial, and residential sites throughout the rest of the war, killing an estimated 600,000 German civilians in the process of destroying 131 cities and towns. Japan suffered throughout the war and not solely due to the atomic bombs dropped on Hiroshima and Nagasaki. The allied forces destroyed over a hundred Japanese cities and towns through a coordinated and sustained bombing campaign, killing more than 1 million civilians.[3] Aerial bombing of civilians thus was a standard tactic employed during times of conflict, and Soviet strategists would likely take advantage of it should the Cold War ever turn hot.

Civil defense planners began working shortly after World War II, formulating contingency plans to protect American citizens at home in case of attack. The survival plan during the Cold War has gone by many designations: including "Run or Dig" (or more descriptively "Run Like

Hell") and "Duck and Cover." These terms describe the various phases that national and regional planners intended to use to ensure the survival of the American people. The "Run" appellation refers to the strategy of fleeing a city prior to a Soviet attack, where plenty of advanced warning seemed likely. Significantly, the national government partially justified the American highway system through the argument that Americans needed well-constructed routes out of urban areas. "Dig" referred to the realization that citizens could never evacuate major cities fast enough to outrun a Soviet attack, especially once the missile age caught up with the Cold War in the late 1950s. Government officials encouraged people to find a public fallout shelter within the city or dig their own in their backyards.[4]

President Truman established the first federal civil defense organization with the passage of the Civil Defense Act of 1950. The act provided for the Federal Civil Defense Administration (FCDA), an organization that provided planning and organizing activities and produced numerous booklets and films that informed citizens of ways in which they could prepare for and survive a nuclear war. Most of these media depicted white, middle-class families waiting in their home fallout shelters for an attack to subside or students taking refuge under their schoolroom desks. Truman greatly expanded the defense budget while in office, but he did not intend to subsidize a national civil defense program. The actual cost of early civil defense was a state and local matter. All vehicles, equipment, and shelter space came from these governments, virtually ensuring that little was done due to budget constraints.[5]

Citizens also disregarded civil defense in the 1950s because President Eisenhower attempted to defuse atomic tension. Historian Ira Chernus argues that Eisenhower wanted to be seen as a man of peace and sought to reduce the possibility of war. Eisenhower, the supreme allied commander of World War II and the ultimate soldier and hero to the nation, made clear to America's foes that the United States would respond to aggression around the world with any means necessary. Eisenhower the military strategist may have been willing to use nuclear weapons in war, but Eisenhower the president knew that such a war was unthinkable and tried to forestall such a possibility early in his presidency. He appeared before the General Assembly of the United Nations in 1953 and delivered his "Atoms for Peace" oration. Eisenhower proposed that the

United States, the United Kingdom, and the Soviet Union would make joint contributions from their stockpiles of nuclear material to an International Atomic Energy Commission, set up under the leadership of the United Nations. Following the contributions, scientists from all over the world would study ways to use atomic energy for peaceful means. "Thus," Eisenhower reasoned, "the contributing powers would be dedicating some of their strength to serve the needs rather than the fears of mankind."[6]

The world will never know what might have happened with Eisenhower's Atoms for Peace proposal. The Soviets rejected Eisenhower's offer. The Atoms for Peace idea ushered in a new way to contemplate nuclear energy that involved not mass destruction but significant opportunity.[7] To illustrate the possibilities of atomic power, Eisenhower and the Atomic Energy Commission sought to alleviate Americans' fear of it. The technology promised inexpensive and abundant power to feed America's expanding appetite for fuel, and an education program was necessary to show citizens the possibilities. The Atomic Energy Commission sponsored a roving education program that made its way around the United States in a bus, reaching major cities and the northern plains, specifically Bismarck in North Dakota, throughout the late 1950s.[8]

There were plenty of reasons throughout the Cold War to assume that a nuclear war was not only possible but probable. The Soviets exploded their first nuclear device in 1949, detonated a hydrogen bomb in 1953, and launched the first satellite, known as *Sputnik*, in 1957, ushering in the age of intercontinental ballistic missiles. If a nation could build a rocket big enough to propel a satellite into orbit, it could replace the innocuous payload with a nuclear device. President Eisenhower left little alternative to nuclear war in dealing with any military crisis when he drastically cut defense spending, relying on nuclear weapons and an enormous air force to deliver atomic bombs. This plan left small room for negotiation; it was an all-or-nothing proposition. Even more frightening, President John F. Kennedy pledged to defend Berlin with atomic weapons in 1961. The United States and the Soviet Union nearly exchanged nuclear missiles during the Cuban Missile Crisis in 1962.[9]

The American nuclear arsenal grew under Eisenhower's administration, when the number of nuclear weapons and the rapid development of aircraft capable of delivering those devices to their targets occupied the

Atomic Energy Commission Atoms for Peace Mobile Unit that visited North Dakota, July 30, 1958. The Atomic Energy Commission sent a bus to travel the nation, explaining to citizens that atomic energy could be harnessed and put to peaceful use. Courtesy State Historical Society of North Dakota, Item 0080-box2-file15-01.

thoughts of millions of Americans. At the same time, several branches of the American military establishment initiated crash programs to develop nuclear missiles, leading to an array of land- and sea-based offensive nuclear weapons. The Soviets launched their own nuclear arms programs. Eisenhower understood that the advent of nuclear weapons meant that war could no longer be an option of international relations; survival of nations depended on there being no war at all. To that end President Eisenhower ordered that military targets were the only viable option in case of nuclear war, in an effort to reduce the number of casualties. Robert McNamara, the secretary of defense throughout most of the 1960s, is credited with the development of the nuclear strategy know as Mutually Assured Destruction (MAD) and took the argument to the next level after the Cuban Missile Crisis in 1962. Instead of avoiding civilian casualties, he argued that each side must target cities with massive civilian populations in order to cause the maximum number of casualties. Given the size of American cities and the explosive power of atomic weapons, a nuclear war could mean the end of the industrialized world. MAD assumed that neither side would start a nuclear war if it could not be sure of surviving it.[10]

MAD was a product of the 1960s, but in the 1950s the outcome of a nuclear war was far less predictable. The government told citizens that they could easily survive a nuclear war if they took the proper precautions. Civil defense authorities worked hard to educate the public. They created "Bert the Turtle" in the 1950s, a popular cartoon character who told schoolchildren and adults the ways in which they could protect themselves in the event of nuclear war. The federal government printed over 20 million cartoon booklets with civil defense warnings and over 55 million wallet-sized cards with the same information. State and federal civil defense organizations published pamphlets with information on the effects of a nuclear blast and the defense against it, while newspapers and magazines carried articles showing citizens how to construct bomb shelters and stock them with the necessary provisions. Even with all the information available, few people actually followed through with these preparations.[11]

State and local governments did little with civil defense initiatives in the early Cold War era, even though Americans seemed to understand that nuclear war was a distinct possibility. A Gallup Poll in July 1953 showed that 56 percent of Americans thought there was either a good or a fair chance that their community would be hit with atomic bombs.[12] Another Gallup Poll in June 1956 showed that 63 percent of the population thought the Soviets would use the hydrogen bomb against the United States in the event of another war.[13] If knowledge of the nuclear threat was widespread, reaction in the form of civil defense preparation was muted. At the time of the 1953 poll, in which a majority of Americans thought an atomic bomb might hit their community, only 4 percent of those polled said that they were doing any work in a civil defense program.[14] During the height of the Berlin Crisis in 1961, only 7 percent of the population said that they had made any plans to prepare their homes in case of nuclear attack.[15]

Significantly, Americans considered fallout shelters a government responsibility. A 1956 Gallup Poll showed that 64 percent of those surveyed approved of a plan that would require every man and woman to contribute an average of one hour per week in civil defense work.[16] Only 4 percent of the population was actively engaged in civil defense, however, which meant that the government would have to mandate civil defense participation, which never came to pass. Another Gallup Poll in 1960 showed that 71 percent favored a law that would require each community to build public fallout shelters.[17] The citizens and the government seemed to disagree significantly as to responsibilities for protection against fallout.

Despite the many sound reasons to engage in civil defense activities in 1956, even the Federal Civil Defense Administration (FCDA) concluded that civil defense was a flop. Scientists and professionals hired to evaluate civil defense in America concluded that the FCDA was a "boondoggle." America had no civil defense. Congress was dragging its feet in appropriating money, and the federal government pushed all real responsibility to the state and city level. America spent $35 billion on military defense, but only a fraction of 1 percent of that on civil defense in 1956.[18]

Though little was actually done on an individual or governmental basis, advocates of a national shelter plan emerged in large numbers in the late 1950s. They became more energetic in their quest for governmental action that would take the lead in protecting all of America's citizens. National magazines ran articles with drawings depicting the design and implementation strategies of a national fallout shelter program, including an article in *Life* magazine on March 18, 1957. This article showed a cut-away drawing of a series of tubes running under major metropolitan areas connecting buildings to one another, which would also provide underground shelter in case of nuclear war. The major theme that many authors proposed at this time was a dedicated shelter program, specifically designed and built to save humanity. The national fallout shelter idea had two problems. First, it was extremely expensive, with estimated costs running into the tens of billions of dollars. The other problem was that nearly half of the people did not think that there was a real possibility of attack. A spokesperson for the House Military Operations Subcommittee stated in 1957: "The supreme irony of civil defense in the U.S. is that the American people . . . refuse to accept the distasteful facts of reality simply because they are distasteful."[19]

The first real impetus for a national shelter program, albeit a private one, came in 1959. New York governor Nelson Rockefeller brought Central Intelligence Agency director Allen Dulles to a meeting of forty-five

(*Left to right*) State civil defense director Major General Homer E. Jensen, Leonard Swanson (owner of the home where a shelter was constructed), and Rapid City civil defense director Douglas Van Eyclebosch examining fallout shelter models, March 1960. These were on display in business places for week before the dedication of the Swanson shelter and then in the garage adjoining the Swanson home during the day of the dedication. Courtesy South Dakota State Historical Society.

governors and gave them a classified briefing on Soviet objectives. Dulles remarked: "The evidence is overwhelming, that the Soviets intend to use nuclear blackmail as a major weapon to promote their objective—namely, to spread communism throughout the world."[20] Dulles and Rockefeller advised the governors to take the lead in getting their citizens to build fallout shelters. A nationwide system of private shelters would block Soviet intentions and save millions of lives in the event of war. Governor Rockefeller later championed the idea that the government should provide shelter space for the American public but dropped his stance because of the opposition from his own state legislature.[21]

If government and community leaders decried citizens' apathy toward building fallout shelters, they were uncertain about the effectiveness of these structures. General Curtis LeMay, head of the Strategic Air

Command, opposed the suggestion that the government invest heavily in public fallout shelters. "You can't fight a war with shelters," he insisted. "I think you'd get more deterrence by buying more weapons."[22] It is little wonder that citizens were confused about using fallout shelters: opinions toward them ranged from "immoral and cowardly" to "the last chance for civilization."[23] It seems that everyone had an opinion. One journalist argued against a national shelter plan because it would encourage the Soviets to attack before it was built, while others argued that shelters would guarantee the survival of most of the American population should nuclear war occur. Some argued that Americans would not or should not even want to live through such a catastrophe. Still others protested the construction of shelters based on their cost. The issue was nothing if not unsettled.[24]

In some instances the very leaders who dispensed civil defense warnings ignored their own lessons. A 1961 article in the *Montana Standard-Post* reported the results of an unnamed magazine survey, which humorously reported that people all over the country were in a mad rush not to build fallout shelters. More seriously, only five of the twenty-seven governors who responded to the poll had gubernatorial fallout shelters. Of the twenty-two heads of state civil defense organizations that responded, only seven had fallout shelters in or near their homes. The report continued: "The prevailing attitude is one of fatalism. Americans seem more pessimistic about the chances of survival than do their scientists and government officials who say that millions could be saved through protective measure." One of those scientists was Dr. Edward Teller, known as the father of the hydrogen bomb, who advised that 90 percent of the Americans could be saved through the construction of a home shelter. Notably, Dr. Teller did not have a fallout shelter in his home either.[25] If the fallout shelter program depended upon a timely reporting system that announced an imminent attack, many cities were in trouble: no suitable reporting system existed. Of the 258 largest cities in the United States, only 134 had adequate siren systems. Seven state capitals had no outdoor warning system whatsoever. Even if citizens in these cities had fallout shelters, they would probably never know of an attack in time to use them.[26]

The national director of the civil defense program, Val Peterson, added to the confusion when he stated in 1957 that 40 to 50 percent of the population would die in the event of a nuclear attack even with the best possible system of shelters in place. Peterson recommended that the U.S. government subsidize the construction of shelters but advised that the public should not put too much faith in them. He did not claim, as he testified before a House government operations subcommittee, that fallout shelters were the ultimate answer to civil defense. Just as important as shelters, Peterson maintained, was construction of new factories underground or built into mountains and rocks. Citizens were understandably confused about the value of fallout shelters when hearing this or similar testimony.[27]

The public's resistance to an underground survival mentality is clear: only about fifteen hundred homes in thirty American states contained private fallout shelters by 1960.[28] The public rejected shelters for a number of reasons. First, they were costly, and most people did not have the disposable income required to meet the expense. In addition, the shelter would shield occupants from fallout but not from blast or heat. Although a few critical events pushed Americans toward building a shelter, situations that did spark an interest in shelters such as the Berlin Crisis and the Cuban Missile Crisis were quickly and peacefully resolved. Perhaps the main reason shelters never really caught on was moral. Some people wondered whether life would be worth living after an attack or whether Americans should really burrow into the earth to guarantee survival, "rather like cowards" as one observer stated.[29]

When Eisenhower left office in January 1961, his budget reflected a request for $100 million in civil defense funds and the beginning of federalization of the civil defense process. Concern for civilian populations moved Eisenhower to initiate several programs under the largest civil defense budget to date. First, new federal buildings must provide fallout shelter protection. States would receive federal funding to renovate certain buildings, allowing them to serve as shelters as well. Additionally, federal dollars would match state and local civil defense funds, allowing local governments to begin effective civil defense programs.[30]

In 1961 Eisenhower also ordered a comprehensive examination of all federal buildings that citizens could use for fallout shelters. Corps of Engineers officials expanded this inspection to include all buildings in the country, including churches, businesses, and other properties.[31] But substantive changes in civil defense planning and implementation came when President Kennedy took office in early 1961. He outlined a request to Congress for over $300 million for civil defense funds to provide shelters for the population. Kennedy reiterated the deterrence theory in his speech to Congress, saying that an overwhelming response to nuclear attack meant destruction of the Soviet Union as the best defense. But deterrence "assumes the rational calculations by rational men. And the history of this planet . . . is sufficient to remind us of the possibilities of an irrational attack . . . which cannot be either foreseen or deterred."[32]

Significantly, no critical event during the 1950s solidified Cold War fear. Only the Berlin Crisis of 1961 brought the Cold War home, when Soviet premier Nikita Khrushchev threatened to turn Berlin over to the East German government and force the allies out of the city by the end of the year. Kennedy responded that the United States would not abandon the city and if necessary would defend its interests with nuclear weapons. As the Berlin Crisis intensified, Kennedy requested an additional $200 million in civil defense funds, primarily to identify, mark, and stock existing buildings for use as fallout shelters. Kennedy's immediate goal was to provide shelter space for the one-fourth of the American population located in urban centers. Citizens, however, still doubted the seriousness of nuclear war. When pollsters asked American citizens in 1961 if they would rather fight an all-out nuclear war or live under communism, 81 percent of respondents opted for nuclear war.[33]

Some people undoubtedly must have had a genuine fear of a Soviet attack, but a large segment of the population took no precautions and had no interest in learning how to survive a nuclear war. Burnham, the journalist from the *Wall Street Journal*, cited four reasons why this was the case. First, people simply did not believe that a nuclear exchange was likely; they could not imagine it. Second, other Montanans believed that war would not affect them directly even if it did come. Still others did not want to live through such a war if it came: what was the sense in emerging into a post-attack world? Finally, people simply wanted civil defense authorities to make all the preparations, leaving ordinary citizens to go about their daily lives.[34]

The federal government continued to develop civil defense plans and encouraged the states to adopt them, but the states lagged behind in these efforts. Governor Fred Aandahl created the North Dakota Civil Defense Council in August 1950 and charged the organization with creating plans to aid counties and larger cities in the event of attack or emergency. The council consisted of the governor acting as chair, the state attorney general, the secretary of agriculture, the state adjutant general, and twelve other members appointed by the governor. Aandahl named Brigadier General Heber L. Edwards, the state adjutant general, to head the organization in daily civil defense planning.[35] State civil defense authorities determined in December 1950 that both Bismarck and Fargo were likely targets in case of attack. Edwards used this to press the state legislature for civil defense appropriations. According to former lieutenant governor Lloyd Omdahl, federal civil defense planners who came to North Dakota were not convinced of the vulnerability of Fargo and Bismarck in case of attack. These federal officials established a separate civil defense planning committee in North Dakota, of which Omdahl was a member, and determined that Bismarck and Fargo were not strategic targets. In what Omdahl called the "Bismarck-Fargo Axis," political pressure mounted to include the two cities in defense planning, which the committee eventually did.[36]

Appropriations were slow, as many officials and citizens doubted that North Dakota was even a target for the Soviets. Most believed that an attack would target strategic centers outside the state, such as government buildings, military bases, or shipping and transportation centers. This indifference to Soviet attack plagued the state for years. The governor replaced Edwards as head of the state's civil defense organization in 1955, appointing Lieutenant Colonel Noel F. Tharalson, a soldier with over forty-two years of state and federal service in the United States Army.[37]

Tharalson admitted that his position as the head of civil defense in North Dakota was the most frustrating job he had ever held. "Apathy within the state will have to be overcome before any real program can evolve," he declared. "If you talk to North Dakotans about the possibility of bombing raids, they'll laugh and turn their backs. They just won't believe that an enemy bomber would bother with the wide open spaces around the state."[38] Tharalson attempted to draw attention to the problems of civil defense in North Dakota and called a meeting of the North Dakota Civil Defense Council in 1955, the first meeting in four years.[39]

South Dakota faced many of the same problems in 1955: the head of the state's civil defense program called his job a continual fight against local apathy. An air force general told R. P. Harmon, the state's civil defense leader, that the skies over North Dakota and South Dakota might be the battleground of World War III. Harmon tried to get the citizens of South Dakota to prepare for a nuclear threat, with little success. "People don't realize where science has carried us," he said. "Today, men are flying airplanes which travel faster than a bullet fired from a .45 caliber pistol. The rockets these planes carry travel three times as fast as bullets."[40] Harmon pressed the point that South Dakota occupied an important position in the Cold War: enemy planes would traverse air corridors over the state, to be met by American fighters. He noted that people in sparsely settled farm areas did not get alarmed over the possibility of bombs falling so far from an industrial target but argued that crippled bombers could jettison their cargos on any city or could bomb the air force base near Rapid City. "If people could hear the things told to us by civil defense and military leaders, [the people of South Dakota] would know it could happen here," he lamented.[41]

Given the Soviet threat, Tharalson and others concerned with nuclear war worked tirelessly to prepare North Dakota for the unthinkable. Each county had an organized civil defense plan by 1960 that included basic facts about atomic explosions, likely target areas, radioactive fallout information, and steps to survive such an ordeal. The counties containing larger cities even published locations of fallout shelters in the pamphlets, made available to citizens throughout the area. The state also produced a comprehensive plan to assist residents in case of nuclear attack, published in a booklet entitled *How You Will Survive.* The booklet included information on using root cellars and basements as short-term fallout shelters against thermonuclear attack and listed ways to decontaminate people, animals, and vehicles from deadly radiation. As the booklet explained, after a nuclear explosion people could emerge from their shelters, report in an orderly fashion to processing centers to receive food and supplies, and begin rebuilding their lives. The booklet was not realistic—no center with stockpiles of food and medication for the citizens existed—but the plan helped convince people that they could survive a nuclear event.

Omdahl left the survival project committee in 1959, when the official state strategy was to evacuate potential target areas, otherwise known as "Run." Shortly thereafter the official policy turned to "Dig." Once the missile era negated any realistic chance of early warning, the strategy became one of hunkering down in shelters, waiting for the attack to conclude, and then emerging from shelters with the intent of rebuilding the

How to build a fallout shelter. The attractive interior of this basement family fallout shelter includes a fourteen-day shelter food supply that may be stored indefinitely, a battery-operated radio, auxiliary light sources, a two-week supply of water, and first aid, sanitary, and other miscellaneous supplies and equipment, ca. 1957. Courtesy National Archives, photo no. 311-D-15-7.

nation. Omdahl had a more realistic reason for changing from "Run" to "Dig": each of the major cities had colleges where students drove unreliable automobiles. A percentage of the large numbers of "junkers" on the road would have broken down, clogging the evacuation routes. The transition from evacuation to fallout shelters meant that the state needed to identify as many potential shelters as possible.[42]

Fargo resident Don Bachmeier recalls that his father built new homes in Bismarck in the early 1960s. He knew that six had fallout shelters. In each case the owners went to great length to disguise the existence of the shelter. In one house the thick concrete patio flooring also served as the ceiling of the shelter, and builders hid the air vent for the shelter in the family barbeque pit. The total number of fallout shelters built during the Cold War is notoriously vague. People built shelters in secret for one basic reason: they did not want others showing up outside the shelter, begging for space in time of emergency. Many owners admitted that they kept a gun in the shelter to keep out neighbors. Lloyd Omdahl recalled a story about a church congregation that built a fallout shelter for the pastor and his family in South Dakota, sparking quite a discussion about who else might use the facility. Many other shelters certainly existed within the state, the plans for which were not difficult to obtain. North Dakota State University published plans for constructing a fallout shelter in 1963, still available on the Internet.[43]

A number of examples suggest that the nuclear era in North Dakota was an object of humor but also offered commercial opportunities. Trinity Builders in Bismarck urged customers to have their homes "Atomasticated" in 1953, which was nothing more than a protective coating that was pressure sealed directly onto an existing exterior wall.[44] It was probably more effective against moisture than against nuclear blast. The *Bismarck Capital* ran a headline that read: "Sure Sign of Atomic Age." The article noted that Sears Roebuck and Company had Geiger counters for sale. This was not a civil defense measure but a commercial venture: the sign that accompanied the products announced that the government would pay a $1,000 bonus to anyone who discovered a new deposit of uranium.[45]

South Dakota officials began preparing for a nuclear event as early as 1950, when governor George T. Mickelson named R. P. Harmon as the state director of civil defense. Harmon published the first comprehensive plan for the state in August of that year. In the introduction he called the plan a kind of an insurance policy: nobody wanted to use it, but it was there nonetheless for emergencies. Calling the document a plan is too generous. It gave general guidance but was vague, leaving much of the work and planning to individual cities.[46]

Harmon followed up this initial report with another in 1952, letting the governor and state legislature know the status of civil defense preparations within the state. Significantly, the new report cited the realization that South Dakota was probably on the ingress route of Soviet bombers making their way into the United States and concentrated on explaining communications systems and early warning networks that connected state agencies, including Ground Observer Corps units, mobile civil defense units, radio stations, ham radio communications systems, and

Fallout shelter constructed at the Leonard Swanson home at Rapid City, March 1960. The couple had to allow others to view the shelter in their home for one year to encourage people to build their own. Courtesy South Dakota State Historical Society.

telephone communications. The plan also included a number of volunteer organizations, such as the "Flying Farmers," consisting largely of crop dusters, available to transport doctors and firefighters throughout the state. In sum, the plan addressed the actions taken and did not attempt to provide more clear guidance in the event of emergency.[47]

Governor Joe Foss, Marine Corps pilot and Medal of Honor winner from World War II, ordered another update to the state plan in 1958. The revision concentrated on survivability during nuclear war. It outlined the assumption that the Soviets would use nuclear weapons within the state and the necessary countermeasures to reduce casualties. The plan listed the suspected targets, which included Ellsworth Air Force Base (AFB) in Rapid City, the state capitol in Pierre, the city of Sioux Falls (because of its large population and airport facilities), the ordnance depot at Igloo, and Sioux City, Iowa, which is close to South Dakota.[48]

Despite these warnings, Rapid City had only two fallout shelters in the community at the end of the 1950s.[49] To build support for a shelter program there, the state Office of Civil and Defense Mobilization authorized the payment and construction of a fallout shelter in the home of Mr. and Mrs. Leonard Swanson for the sum of $747 in March 1960. In return they had to open their home for one year so that others in the community could see the shelter and consider building a shelter of their own. Government officials endorsed the idea of shelters as an individual responsibility.[50] Governor Ralph Herseth gave a short speech at the dedication ceremony held in the home a few days after crews completed construction. "I trust that every family in South Dakota will realize the gravity of our vulnerability," he said, "and will take steps to provide shelter in case of emergency."[51]

With government endorsement, it seemed that Rapid City finally had the impetus to begin a sustained, if not booming, fallout shelter industry. In early 1962 F. R. "Bud" Stewart decided to cash in on the burgeoning business and started a fallout shelter construction firm. Rapid City was home to 159 missile sites in addition to the huge air base there, and Stewart knew that it was a strategic Soviet target in desperate need of fallout shelters. During the few months when he was engaged in the fallout shelter business, he lost a substantial amount of money and nearly went bankrupt. He got out of shelter construction just in time to save his business but blamed the failure of the shelter program on the national government. Stewart could not understand why the government would spend half a trillion dollars per decade to prepare for war but did virtually nothing to protect its people.[52]

In 1961 another government official tried to encourage South Dakotans to build fallout shelters. Colonel Frank A. Neuman, M.D., chief of the Office of Nuclear Warfare Instruction, came from Brooke Army Medical Center in Texas to address officials at a symposium held at the University of South Dakota. The purpose of the gathering was to discuss emergency preparation, disaster planning, and care of mass casualties. Attending the conference were two hundred doctors, nurses, hospital administrators, city officials, police officers, firefighters, and civil defense officials. Neuman began his discussion by asking how many people in attendance had a one-car garage. Many raised their hands in response. When he asked how many had a two-car garage, a few hands went up into the air. He then asked how many people had a fallout shelter. Not one hand was raised. Of all these people most likely to invest in a fallout shelter or to even see the value of one in the city, not a single person at the conference that day had a fallout shelter.[53]

The effort to build more fallout shelters experienced a short triumph nationally as Americans began to take the nuclear threat more seriously in the early 1960s and built over two hundred thousand home fallout shelters between 1960 and 1965.[54] Huron, South Dakota, is one of the few success stories in the region, but progress was slow. In 1955 officials tried to encourage citizens to take civil defense seriously, but some Huron residents expressed their true feelings toward civil defense when they published their own plan in the local paper. The plan was simple and inexpensive and called only for the creation of a large neon sign north of the city. The billboard, clearly visible to any invading Soviet pilot and in Russian, would declare that the next town was Huron, which was not a strategic target. Try Rapid City, three hundred miles to the west, the sign would helpfully suggest.[55] Momentum began to shift by 1961, as Beadle County, where Huron is located, hired a full-time civil defense director. I. O. Hagen preached survival and spread his gospel of fallout shelter protection to the point that interest in family shelters grew and people believed that they could live through a nuclear war.[56] Through Hagen's efforts, the community developed several fallout shelters that could shield about half of its citizens and created a portable hospital for use in emergencies.[57]

Montana also had a number of determined civil defense directors. Hugh K. Potter, state civil defense director of Montana, wrote to his Washington representatives as early as 1953, requesting more aid from the federal government. Potter also asked that his representatives support legislation to increase aid for civil defense programs and to acquire vehicles and equipment from other government agencies. Montana experienced the same shortage of operating funds from which most states suffered. Civil defense was usually a low-priority item that did not receive adequate or sustained funding.[58] The Montana Civil Defense Program had few shelter spaces available in case of emergency, but Cole Sullivan, director of civil defense in Butte, wrote to Montana senator James Murray, requesting funds to convert mines to fallout shelters in 1957. Montana, Sullivan pointed out, was required to provide care for a minimum of five hundred thousand refugees from the west coast in case of attack, according to the federal plan. "Thus, I would like to point out that many of these underground workings could be and should be used to store a tremendous amount of non-perishable food items," he wrote. Sullivan noted one more benefit: "This would accomplish a great deal towards relieving the unemployment situation in Butte."[59] Throughout the 1950s Montana's civil defense effort suffered from lack of funds. Montana never even published a comprehensive statewide civil defense plan; most people in the state depended upon publications produced by the federal government.[60]

Little had changed in Montana by 1960 except the name of the state's civil defense director. Robert Keyes had been adjutant general for the Montana National Guard for ten years before taking the position vacated by Potter. He confronted the same challenges from the apathetic public that other states faced. After attending a civil defense symposium in California, Keyes was quite shaken. "We have a pretty hard time convincing the public that an attack can come," he noted, though the federal government had designated Billings, Helena, Butte, Anaconda, Glasgow, Missoula, Columbia Falls, and Great Falls as target areas. "According to the estimates, we may have as little as fifteen minutes warning that an attack may come, and twenty-seven minutes at most," Keyes added. He acknowledged that it was not much time, but it was enough for a family to find their way into a fallout shelter, provided they had one. "With some citizens," Keyes said, "and in some cities, apathy is nothing short of amazing. They just don't think it can happen." He continued to vocalize his frustrations, lamenting that 20 percent of Montana counties had no civil defense plan whatsoever and that less than half of all Montana counties with written plans were doing anything with them. Sheriff Roy Stewart, the civil defense chair for Billings, agreed with Keyes. "We can work out a plan and get it adopted, but try and find anyone who will do the work that has to be done—they just don't see any urgency for it."[61]

Two months after attending the California symposium, Keyes spoke to the heads of all Montana government departments, telling them that more needed to be done in terms of civil defense. He pointed out the target areas within the state and counseled them on the harmful effects of fallout. Only 50 percent of harmful fallout would be stopped by the average home on the first floor, he told them, while 10 percent would still get into the average basement. Fully 99 percent of all fallout would be kept out of a fallout shelter, which could be constructed inside an existing basement for about $200. The biggest problem, Keyes noted, was the lack of funds with which to organize the civil defense program. The government spent $250 per person nationally on military defense. In Montana, Keyes observed, the state spent an average of three cents per person per year on civil defense. As the only full-time civil defense employee within the state, he noted that there was simply too much for one person to do.[62]

Keyes obtained funding in October 1959 to build a sample fallout shelter in Billings to demonstrate the simplicity and effectiveness of a shelter system to other residents. The home, or more accurately the backyard, of M. E. Evanson was chosen as the site for the demonstration shelter and was one of over one hundred shelters built throughout the United States at government expense to convince people to build their own shelters. To facilitate this, the shelter was open and available for public viewing, offering information regarding the construction of home shelters.[63]

Keyes continued to drive home the point of civil defense over the next several years. He managed to recruit at least one civil defense director from each of Montana's counties and invited them to a yearly conference at the state capital. At the conference in 1961 Montana governor Donald Nutter told the gathering: "It's time to stop listening to reports of how many megatons are in Russian bombs and start filling sandbags. It's time for action." Nutter conceded that recent events such as the Berlin Crisis had heightened awareness of civil defense but noted that the awareness was short-lived. "We must be prepared whether it is for tomorrow or three years from now. I know many of you face apathy in your hometowns, but it is being overcome," he insisted. The governor's main point was that the state, and by extension the counties, needed a plan of action. "Where are school children going to go in a matter of minutes? What will happen to clerks and shoppers in stores? What about people in hospitals, and those in old people's homes?" Money was not the issue, Nutter insisted, as county directors accomplished more in the last eight months with no money than in the last eight years. Planning, he persisted, was the key to getting through an emergency.[64]

Mayor Vern Griffith of Butte took advantage of the momentum generated by the statewide civil defense assembly and had a civil defense meeting for his community on the same day. "We do not want to be alarmist," he said, "but we must be realistic. No one knows when and if we are going to be faced with the question of survival."[65] After his introduction Griffith turned the meeting over to Cole Sullivan, county director of civil defense. He and a number of other civil defense officials gave status reports on various projects for which they were responsible. Most notably, the county had made great progress in providing fallout shelter space for many of Butte's citizens by procuring sites in the Big Butte and St. John grade schools and in the Butte Brewery Company building, and officials were surveying more sites. Additionally, volunteers were working hard to assemble the components of a portable hospital, which would be housed in the civic center when completed. Sullivan concluded the meeting by saying: "We're not trying to frighten people, but there is no doubt the public has been apathetic to the possibilities." He continued: "Unless we prepare to survive, we'll not win if the day should come that the Soviet Union should decide that there will be a holocaust. Time may be running out."[66]

The civil defense effort during the Cold War was a disjointed federal attempt to provide safety and security for citizens at the state and local level, but no coherent plan ever emerged. The major issue was money, and ways to pay for a truly effective program were elusive. One of the major problems was the mixed messages that the government sent to people. On the one hand, government officials warned people to prepare for nuclear emergencies and told them that they could survive; on the other hand, other officials warned that atomic war would wipe out the planet. Although the federal government gave civil defense greater support in the early 1960s, the effort did not ever really take hold with the public. Civil defense, never a popular subject, lost momentum after the Cuban Missile Crisis. Other topics became more important, such as civil rights and the Vietnam War. If anything, the public rejected civil defense as a justification for continuing the Cold War with the Soviet Union, as antinuclear demonstrations became more popular. During the Reagan presidency communities such as Grand Forks, North Dakota, even refused to participate in civil defense alerts because they were unrealistic and were devoted to promoting the illusion of protection during nuclear war. Plains people continued to consider civil defense a federal responsibility and rarely responded through their own efforts or resources.[67]

Although the public largely dismissed civil defense and fallout shelter construction, citizens were patriotic during the early Cold War period. To show their support and patriotism, many citizens joined the U.S. military, ready to serve in defense of their nation. Military service was not a viable option for many citizens, however, who still felt the desire to serve their nation. Many citizens volunteered for the Ground Observer Corps (GOC), an organization directed by the air force, employed at the local level to watch American skies throughout the 1950s, searching for Soviet airplanes that might try to cross the United States border and drop atomic bombs on American cities. While individuals did not embrace civil defense in general, they turned out in large numbers supporting the GOC and worked together for the benefit of all.

Chapter 5

The Ground Observer Corps

"**A**ircraft Flash," Jane Prohosky calmly stated into the telephone handset. Within seconds, the receiver crackled: "Air Defense, go ahead." Prohosky continued: "Two aircraft, very high, heading west, Golf Alpha Five Zero Black." This transmission did not take place during wartime and was not between professional soldiers. Prohosky was a volunteer at the Ground Observer Corps (GOC) post in Grant, Montana, in 1954 and was calling her counterpart at air force headquarters in Helena. The GOC was charged with searching the skies for Soviet aircraft that might try to cross into the United States to bomb American cities or other strategic sites at the height of the Cold War in the 1950s. The air force directed this civilian organization, giving people the opportunity to serve their country and aid in its defense when few effective radar systems existed. While the organization served a military function in the defense of America, it was also another opportunity for the federal government to enact a program at the state and local level to engender patriotism.[1]

The GOC was an opportunity for citizens on the northern plains, where the front lines of the Cold War began in the 1950s. These states occupied a strategic position geographically. The volunteers who stood ready to alert their fellow citizens of approaching danger were a diverse cross-section of society from across the social and economic spectrum. They ranged in background from Boy and Girl Scouts to hardened criminals serving time in the nation's prisons, from newly arrived immigrants to the Daughters of the American Revolution, from Indians to members of the U.S. military, and from Hollywood stars to homemakers. The volunteers were as different as any group could be, but they served unselfishly from 1952 to 1959, every minute of the day, watching the skies.[2] They stood watch both night and day, summer and winter, prepared to warn that an enemy force was approaching and threatening the nation's security. Civil defense and the hunt for Communists did not generally interest citizens on a local level, but the GOC called for local and national cooperation and had an active agenda. As noted, Americans generally did not build personal fallout shelters, but they were willing to work collectively in their communities to promote security.[3] In addition the civil defense programs on the northern plains were underfunded and generally unorganized, whereas the air force generously funded certain aspects of the Ground Observer Corps, paying for the telephone system of each GOC post, award ceremonies, and other special events. Local civic organizations helped to fund other operating costs.

While the story of the GOC is not well known, it offers an extraordinary insight into the mind-set of average Americans at the height of the Cold War. Historians have overlooked the topic, and the public has forgotten the effort. Thanks to several magazines and newspapers of the era and the air force magazine *Aircraft Flash*, which captured the monthly accomplishments of the volunteers, their story is not lost.

The Cold War began in earnest during the late 1940s, and many feared a Soviet attack in the 1950s. The Soviets had more than a thousand bombers and three thousand troop transport aircraft stationed at new air bases in northern and eastern Siberia, ready to strike the United States through several routes. U.S. military officials understood that the Soviets could launch an attack over the Pacific Ocean and strike the west coast or fly over the North Pole, targeting the northern portion of the United States and perhaps Alaska. These planes could drop nuclear bombs or paratroopers, depending upon their mission.[4] The topic of a Soviet air invasion was especially sensitive to the citizens on the northern plains, who knew that the safety of the rest of the nation might depend upon the diligence of these GOC volunteers who lived and operated on the periphery of the nation's northern boundary. Though small in population, the states of the northern plains organized their meager resources and carried out a highly successful sky-watching campaign that was of immeasurable assistance to the government.[5]

Ironically, the Americans put an exhaustive effort into the detection of Soviet aircraft at a time when the Soviets had few if any heavy bomber aircraft that could reach American soil. The Soviets had an incredibly small bomber force throughout World War II: only ninety-three planes constructed and no more than thirty bombers available at one time. The American and British forces could muster over one thousand planes in a single raid. Stalin had imprisoned most of the bomber designers during the purges in the late 1930s, depriving Soviet generals of the option of strategic bombing for lack of suitable aircraft. At the end of World War II the Soviets effectively had no long-range strategic air capability and had to build their Cold War bomber force from scratch.[6]

When the Soviets set about the Herculean task of building a formidable air force, their first problem was the lack of a suitable design. Fate seemed to offer a solution when three intact B-29s landed in the Soviet Union after suffering damage while on a bombing mission over Japan. American officials asked for the planes back, a request that the Soviets ignored. The planes made their way to the aircraft design center in the heart of the Soviet Union for testing. Eventually the Soviets completely copied the planes and ordered massive production for their strategic bomber force. The Korean War had shown the vulnerability of propeller-driven bombers by the end of 1951, and American forces largely withdrew them from daylight operations. While the Americans pulled the B-29 from service, the Soviet copy of the same plane rolled off assembly lines and became the backbone of the Soviet strategic bomber forces for the rest of the decade. The Soviets produced 847 copies of the B-29, while the Americans produced the B-36 and the B-47, far superior aircraft that used jet propulsion, not propellers. The Soviet planes also lacked the range to bomb any American target outside of Alaska, even with refueling operation in midair. If the Soviets launched a one-way suicide mission, the planes could reach only the northwestern portion of the United States until the end of the decade, when new aircraft with greater capabilities emerged.[7]

Despite this lack of capabilities, the Soviet Union was a closed society. Little information regarding Soviet force structure was available in the West, leading to a policy of fervent preparation for the worst-case scenario. Military planners prepared for Soviet strikes and settled on three defensive measures to combat the possibility of attack. First, an array of radar systems could track incoming bombers or troop transports, though few operational radar systems existed by 1952. Second, the air force maintained fighter aircraft on a high state of alert, routinely patrolling American skies, ready to intercept any Soviet plane that ventured into American airspace. As a final measure, the United States Army stood ready with anti-aircraft weapons, including first-generation surface-to-air missiles. But each system had fundamental problems. The sky was a vast area to survey, and enemy planes could easily enter U.S. airspace without American pilots ever seeing them. Additionally, surface-to-air missiles could not detect aircraft, only shoot them down once their position was known. Finally, radar technology at this time was rather primitive.[8]

Radar was the most problematic of these options, as low-flying aircraft were invisible to radar. The small number of radar systems created holes in the radar coverage, meaning that Soviet planes could pass through the early warning net undetected. In analyzing the problem the secretary of the air force remarked: "Radar is not completely effective in spotting low-flying aircraft, and it is not completely immune to jamming by enemy counter-radar."[9] The air force relied on hundreds of thousands of volunteers of the Ground Observation Corps to bridge this gap, watching the skies at remote observation posts and reporting aircraft sightings to air force administrators for evaluation.

Military officials formed the GOC during World War II but disbanded it at the end of the conflict. Air force general Ennis C. Whitehead, responsible for the defense of North America during the early Cold War period, officially reconstituted the GOC in February 1952, though civil defense officials had organized hundreds of posts during a test phase before the official start time. The air force initially estimated that it required 160,000 volunteers to operate the 8,000 observation sites throughout the American north. This plan encompassed only thirty northern states prior to 1955, but the increasing popularity of the program and reliance on the GOC to supplement radar coverage led the air force to establish GOC stations in all of the lower forty-eight states and Alaska that year. Just before the air force disbanded the GOC in early 1959, some 350,000 active observers stood watch at 16,000 observation posts throughout the United States.[10]

Observers occupied old buildings, rooftops, or observation towers and scanned the sky for low-flying aircraft. Volunteers tried to identify any aircraft spotted and then called their headquarters via commercial telephone line and reported specific information regarding type of aircraft and heading. At each air force headquarters, known as a Filter Center (FC), officials consolidated information. Aircraft that observers could not positively identify as friendly required the nearest air base to scramble jets, meet the unidentified aircraft, and confirm their identity. The observers served an important role, ensuring that only friendly aircraft occupied American airspace. As General James W. McCauley, an air force official charged with continental defense, reiterated in 1953: "If the skywatchers help alert the Air Defense Command of just one plane carrying just one atom bomb, that alone would justify the work of the GOC."[11]

Community cooperation was essential to the success of the GOC on the northern Great Plains. Volunteers came from each community, but civic groups often supported the GOC with financial contributions and served as a likely pool of additional volunteers. The Badlands Chapter of the Daughters of the American Revolution (DAR) supported the local GOC post in Dickinson, North Dakota, helping to pay the utility bills, and many members of the DAR served with the local GOC post. The American Legion Auxiliary in Flaxton, North Dakota, received a check for fifteen dollars from the DAR in recognition of its support for the best civil defense program. This award came as little surprise to the members of the American Legion Auxiliary and the GOC post they supported: Viola Potter was the president of both organizations, and her dedication and enthusiasm were evident regardless of where she worked.[12]

For many communities, it was a matter of pride to build an observation post out of donated funds, labor, and materials and then operate the site with volunteers. The air force paid for the telephones and the cost of the calls, but the volunteers paid for the observation towers, their furnishings, and all utilities. It was amazing that some posts operated at all. New Hradec, North Dakota, a town with 35 residents, accomplished what seemed impossible by establishing an observation post that required a staff of 100 members. Residents recruited volunteers from outlying areas and swelled the ranks of observers to 125.[13]

Other posts consisted of a single family, with one member home at all times to perform spotting duties. Mr. and Mrs. Ely Wright and their daughter established a post in their home in Haynes, North Dakota. In just over eighteen months they averaged 1,260 hours of sky watching per month. Mrs. L. A. Blattner and Mrs. G. O'Callaghan lived twenty miles away in opposite directions from the FC in Bismarck, North Dakota, one to the north and one to the west. Both contacted the GOC to offer assistance. The FC established observation posts at each home, and the two women placed in the top ten of North Dakota's most active observation posts every month, proving that community effort was important, but not necessary, to make significant contributions to national defense. While Blattner and Callaghan watched from their homes, Marvin Skie and his large family kept watch from the top of their silo at their family farm in Lennox, South Dakota, operating the post on a 24-hour basis.[14]

Hundreds of thousands of volunteers kept watch around the nation. With so many people involved, a few strange events were bound to occur. One example of this was the GOC post operated on the ranch of Mr. and Mrs. Harold Goldhahn in Geraldine, Montana. Apparently their television set was an active sky watcher, as the reception got fuzzy every time an airplane passed over. Turning off the set made little difference, as the antenna would vibrate noticeably. The Goldhahns were irritated at first but later noted that the phenomenon made their aircraft-spotting duties much easier, leading to their rating of "highly effective" from the Helena FC.[15]

The antenna was effective but not as enthusiastic as Pudgy, a small dog owned by Mrs. Wilkeen of Billings, Montana. Pudgy used to accompany her to a GOC post in town, where he showed no real interest in spotting aircraft. When the post moved to Wilkeen's home in 1954, Pudgy displayed a real talent for it. He could detect an airplane long before his human companion. If she was inside, Pudgy raced to the front door, where he would bark furiously until she came out to identify the aircraft. Once an aircraft was identified, Pudgy would follow her inside and wait while she reported the aircraft to the FC. Pudgy spotted seventy-seven aircraft and one balloon in July 1956 alone, making him one of the most prolific volunteers for the Billings GOC.[16]

Air force officials asked members of the Harry Allen family as early as 1949 to watch for unidentified flying objects (UFOs) in Montana, but whether that meant Soviet planes or extraterrestrial objects is not clear. Flying saucers were a popular phenomenon in the 1950s, and many citizens reported their strange sightings to military and police agencies. The government was interested in knowing what flew over American airspace, so it made sense to report unusual activity through the proper channels. The Allen family ranch occupied a strategic location in a sparsely populated area of Pipestone, Montana, so they could spot either Soviet bombers or UFOs. GOC observers reported at least one unidentified craft over Montana in 1956: a GOC team called the air force to report bright lights over Kalispell one dark night. One observer reported that she observed a bright light that could not be mistaken for a star: it was too bright and too large. Malmstrom Air Force Base in Great Falls scrambled five jets to intercept the object but apparently never did. Two other planes joined the search from Spokane, Washington, as the jets searched throughout the night, finding nothing unusual.[17]

Though observation posts could function with one family taking turns reporting aircraft, it made sense to staff others with many volunteers, which were often in short supply. The air force set an objective of recruiting 1 million volunteers to staff existing, newly constructed, and future posts in 1955. Radio broadcasts helped to recruit new people to the organization, as did ice cream socials held at the filter centers and observation posts. Minot, North Dakota, staged a "bombing raid" when a local pilot dropped balloons over the city with requests for help. Each balloon carried a free ticket to see *Invasion USA*, a popular movie viewed throughout the country that illustrated what might happen if Soviet bombers struck an American city. Ronald Tennil of Redfield, South Dakota, had produced a number of films on the subject of safety and decided to put his talent to work for the Ground Observer Corps. His film *Golf Quebec Two Five Black*, the air force designation of the post in Redfield, was quite successful recruiting volunteers. Volunteers in Kalispell, Montana, opted for another method of finding volunteers. They closed off the four streets of the town's main intersection, taking the time to explain the GOC to those trapped in the traffic jam. Citizens there must have exercised incredible patience: 155 residents agreed to volunteer their time.[18]

Other creative ideas for raising awareness of GOC needs were beauty pageants, where an FC or GOC queen was crowned, and floats in Independence Day or Veteran's Day parades. National newspapers and magazines also helped in the recruitment effort. An advertisement in

Billboard soliciting volunteers for the Ground Observer Corps. No date given. Units spent almost as much time recruiting volunteers as they did watching the sky. Courtesy Duke University Library and the Outdoor Advertising Association of America.

Newsweek depicted three observers at an observation post looking at the sky with the caption: "Another town is safer tonight because these trained civilian members of the Ground Observer Corps are scanning the skies to warn against possible enemy attack." The paragraph went on to proclaim that many towns did not have such protection and encouraged concerned citizens to volunteer for the GOC.[19]

North Dakota publications brought the issue closer to home. The *Golden Valley News* printed a drawing of a Soviet soldier conducting an orchestra with musical notes floating by. The caption read: "Do the Russian leaders really want peace or to lull us into a sense of false security?" The *Minot Daily News* carried an advertisement that read: "WARNING: Russian War Planes in a Single Raid Could Attack All of the Most Critical U.S. Targets Leaving Millions Wounded or Dead." Each notice also contained several paragraphs proclaiming that the Soviets possessed a considerable number of bombers and nuclear weapons that could wreak havoc upon the American population. The message was that the U.S. States military was on alert and working hard, but the nation needed GOC volunteers.[20]

Women were an important part of GOC operations. In fact over 65 percent of all GOC volunteers were women. In the 1950s women were not encouraged to find employment outside the home, and family expectations weighed heavily on a woman's career choice. Many women throughout the northern Great Plains wanted to volunteer their time in support of the nation—if not in the military, then somewhere else. Women had many reasons for joining the GOC, but two consistent themes emerged. First, many women lost loved ones in World War I, World War II, or the Korean War and wished to serve as their relatives and friends had. Second, many women simply felt the need to serve their country for the same patriotic reasons that men served in the military. The GOC was a respectable alternative to military service. Women on the northern plains served in a variety of positions, including being post commanders and leading training sessions on aircraft reporting and recognition.[21]

Throughout the region many of the volunteers at GOC posts were veterans of the nation's wars, including the observers at the Little Bighorn Battlefield National Monument in Montana. Seven veterans of three American wars, all of whom lived and worked on the battlefield grounds, kept watch for enemy aircraft throughout each night, while other volunteers kept watch during the day. In Columbia Falls, Montana, forty veterans at the State Soldiers' Home, some of whom saw action in the Spanish-American War in 1898, organized a GOC post. The post operated from 6 A.M. to 8 P.M. daily and occupied a strategic location, less than fifty miles from the Canadian border. The veterans were meticulous in their tracking, sometimes reporting dozens of aircraft in a single day.[22]

Teenagers, particularly the Boy Scouts and the Girl Scouts, performed admirably as GOC volunteers, watching the skies, recruiting new volunteers, or building GOC observation posts. John Sullivan was a Boy Scout who served with the GOC in Bismarck, North Dakota. He recalled that it was great fun for the scouts to go out and spot airplanes. Bill Lardy volunteered with the GOC for more practical reasons. He remembers that it was enjoyable to get out of study hall and spot airplanes at the post on his school's roof and perhaps sneak a cigarette when no one was looking. Lardy was one of the students from Sentinel Butte High School in North Dakota who volunteered his time during the school day, spotting aircraft after he completed his work. At night the school principal and the district superintendent took over the aircraft-spotting duties from their homes, with the help of their families. The Junior History Club and the Optimist Club from a local high school in Sioux Falls, South Dakota, volunteered their time at the FC after school and on weekends.[23]

Sparse population on the northern plains presented a formidable hindrance for air force officials, but innovative citizens solved the problem. The J. Neils Lumber Company and the National Forest Service maintained ranger stations and fire watch towers throughout Montana, giving the GOC a number of posts with little organizational effort or cost. Most rangers and firewatchers reported that they enjoyed the additional duty, because watching the forest could get monotonous at times. As one U.S. forestry official put it, "We are glad to be of service to our air defense system. Skywatching fits perfectly into our fire lookout program since both are designed to provide protection against destructive enemies."[24]

The Stoltze Land and Lumber Company operated lumber camps in the western portion of Montana and had a number of vehicles with powerful radios that observers could use to call reports to dispatchers at the company headquarters, who forwarded the information to the FC. Workers from the Nodak Rural Electric Co-Op, who ranged throughout North Dakota performing their duties, used a similar process, calling reports to clerks at the company headquarters, who forwarded the information to the FC. Workers of the Milwaukee Railroad in South Dakota, who traveled up and down the tracks fifteen miles east and west of McIntosh, used their radios to report aircraft to their station agent, who in turn called the Rapid City Filter Center.[25]

The GOC was effective throughout the northern Great Plains because of volunteers like those at the post in Divide, Montana. They complained to officials that their skills were getting rusty in 1955, as they had not called in an aircraft in over a month. A few days later a flight of thirteen aircraft flew low over the post: the air force had specifically requested the changed flight plan in order to accommodate the observers. As early as 1953 the air force began testing GOC readiness when officials sent two B-25 bombers over western North Dakota to see how many GOC posts would spot the planes. Over twenty-four posts reported the aircraft to higher headquarters. Officials could rest assured that GOC readiness in the region was at a high level, as volunteers stood ready to raise the alarm if Soviet planes ventured near.[26]

The enthusiasm with which volunteers reported aircraft to the FCs was evident in September 1955, when Air Defense Command launched a surprise evaluation. A low-altitude detection mission, flown by a KB-29 from the 407th Air Refueling Squadron, left Malmstrom AFB to test the effectiveness of the GOC, proving that an enemy bomber would have had trouble penetrating American airspace. The Cut Bank, Montana, GOC post reported the aircraft first, followed by a succession of posts along the northern frontier as the plane meandered above the plains. The final objective of the flight was to simulate a bombing mission in Fargo, but a jet fighter from the North Dakota Air National Guard spoiled the attack on Hector Field in Fargo, North Dakota, "shooting it down" after receiving the GOC warning. Had the test aircraft been a Soviet bomber, the Air Defense Command could have destroyed it at any point along its 2,000-mile route.[27]

The GOC attracted the best talent from the local communities, including residents who had only recently arrived in this country. "I know what it means to lose my country—don't lose yours," advised Julius Szakats, who worked in the FC in Sioux Falls, South Dakota. Szakats was born in Budapest, Hungary, and was the son of a Hungarian Supreme Court justice. International tensions forced his family to flee their home in 1940. His family spent five years in a displaced persons camp in Germany before making their way to the United States. Amy Grablander, also of South Dakota, met her husband while he served with the U.S. military in England during World War II. Grablander and her parents served as civil defense wardens in her home country, a skill that followed her across the Atlantic. She worked as an observer at the Mission, South Dakota, post, while her mother remained active in Britain's Civil Defense program.[28]

A number of Indian tribes participated in the GOC, "doing as much for their country as if they were in the Air Force," observed one government official.[29] Members of the Blackfeet Tribe in Montana staffed several GOC posts, including one at a school on their reservation known as the Star School. Phillip Sellew, whose father was one of General George

Armstrong Custer's scouts at the Battle of the Little Bighorn and managed to escape the battlefield alive, was the advisor to the students and worked as a special officer of the Blackfeet Tribe. Two adult observers, Audrey and Estella White Grass, assisted the students in their observation duties. The post operated around the clock, with students, teachers, government officials, and other members of the tribe acting as spotters, earning the post laudatory comments from the air force. Chippewa Indians from the Turtle Mountain reservation in North Dakota were active as plane spotters, while another reservation school was active as a GOC post. Mr. Manahan, principal of the school on the Lower Brule Reservation in South Dakota and supervisor of the post, reported that students and tribal members not only served their country but also learned other important lessons. Many members of the tribe had never used a telephone before the post went into operation.[30]

Throughout the United States one of the benefits of having citizens staffing an official post with a wide view of the surrounding countryside was the assistance that they could give in time of emergency. Observers in Grant, Montana, saw a giant aircraft, a B-47 that was helplessly lost and kept circling the area. When volunteers at the local GOC post called the FC to report the problem, the air force dispatched interceptor aircraft to lead the bomber to Malmstrom Air Force Base. Without the GOC assistance, the bomber might have crashed, killing the crew and perhaps other citizens on the ground, to say nothing of damage to or loss of the expensive aircraft. When an aircraft did crash outside of Miles City, Montana, the observer on duty, George Crapo, called the FC and gave a detailed account of the event, noting that the plane had crashed in a freshly plowed field outside of town. Rescue personnel responded quickly, pulling the passengers and crew, all of whom escaped injury, from the wreckage. When another jet fighter crashed near Regent, North Dakota, in May 1954, quick-thinking volunteers at the local GOC post reported the incident to the air force, which immediately dispatched rescue personnel, who found the pilot unharmed.[31]

Severe weather conditions were another circumstance in which the GOC played an important role. When a tornado hit Fargo, North Dakota, on June 20, 1957, the GOC reported the formation of the funnel clouds to civil defense authorities, who sounded the alarm in the city. Citizens had the opportunity to take shelter, although ten died because of the twister and the town sustained millions of dollars in damage. The storm tore the roof off the FC. Heavy rain damaged the inside of the building. The battery-operated telephones remained one of the only remaining communication methods within Fargo, as the storm had taken down lines and damaged the telephone system infrastructure. Had it not been for the volunteers of the GOC warning the community of the approaching storm, the number of casualties could have been much higher. In the aftermath the volunteers used their phones to coordinate relief efforts.[32]

The national, state, and local government officials, as well as air force representatives, were lavish in their praise of the GOC and organized a number of events to recognize the volunteers. In February 1955 civic leaders in Mobridge, South Dakota, organized a "Recognition Day" for residents who had taken part in the GOC program. Events included a fly-over by F-86D jet fighters from Ellsworth Air Force Base, displays and movies in the city auditorium, and a dinner sponsored by the Mobridge Chamber of Commerce for all members of the GOC. South Dakota's civil defense director R. P. Harmon and Major Lester Garrigues, the South Dakota GOC coordinator, presented outstanding volunteers with certificates of recognition. The air force gave awards liberally to those who had earned them. Volunteers could earn "wings" for various qualifications and badges with bars attached to them for every 250 hours of voluntary service. A similar celebration took place in Fargo, North Dakota, on March 23, 1957, when the FC unveiled its new plotting board, prompting the mayor to proclaim the day "Ground Observer Corps Day."[33]

Major General William F. Dean, the highest-ranking prisoner of the Korean War and deputy commander of Sixth Army following the conflict, visited the Helena, Montana, FC in 1955 to show his appreciation for the volunteers' effort. "It is a pleasure to meet people working in such an important aspect of civil defense," he remarked. "I am very proud to have you people behind me."[34] This was high praise from a man who understood sacrifice and teamwork, but Dean knew that it was important to let people know that the government appreciated their contributions. Perhaps the greatest show of appreciation that the government could give to the volunteers was the opportunity to watch the detonation of a nuclear bomb. Six GOC volunteers from the northern Great Plains, two

Mrs. C. M. Chapman (*holding flag*) and assistant chief observer Mrs. James Lennox (*holding halyard*) raising the American flag over their Ground Observer Corps post in Missoula, October 7, 1956. Courtesy M. Margaret Owen, Archives & Special Collections, Maureen and Mike Mansfield Library, University of Montana–Missoula, Image 569(III)1.

from each state, were guests of the military as it exploded an atomic device at Yucca Flat, Nevada. The trip was a reward for a job well done but served as a reminder to the volunteers of just how devastating a Soviet attack would be.[35]

While individuals performed splendidly throughout the northern plains states, their parent organizations also reflected the worthy efforts of the volunteers. The FC in Sioux Falls, South Dakota, was the envy of many other organizations for its community involvement. The "Sioux Falls Plan," as it was called, incorporated a legally constituted board of citizens known as the "Advisory Board of the Civilian Ground Observer Corps." This organization included representatives from virtually every civic, fraternal, and patriotic organization within the city, thirty-one organizations in all. The board served to strengthen the ties between the volunteers and the community, enabling a more effective recruiting program and a potential source of financial assistance. Colonel Broun Mayall, director of civilian air defense for the air force, remarked: "It gives others in the present GOC area something to shoot at. Your plan is being recommended to, and copied by, other communities."[36]

The Billings FC also had an incredible relationship with the local community in general and two large organizations in particular. On the weekend of October 30 and 31, 1954, a celebration dubbed "Operation Lifesaver" kicked off in the Montana city, involving Frontier Airlines, the 29th Air Division (Defense), and the Billings FC. The celebration brought the three organizations together for a weekend of festivities. The air division agreed to make all safety provisions available to Frontier Airlines, including radar and the GOC. As the highlight of the affair Frontier Airlines christened a new DC-3 passenger aircraft as the "Sunliner–Billings Filter Center." The three Operation Lifesaver participants invited the local residents to join the celebration. An estimated twenty thousand of the city's forty-five thousand citizens crowded into the local airport to participate in the weekend's events. The gathering highlighted the conjunction of military, volunteer, and business interests for a common cause.[37]

North Dakota also hosted an outstanding organization, leading the air force to recognize the post in Drake, North Dakota, as the GOC Post of the Month in August 1955, a highly coveted award. Although the town claimed a population of only 650, the community launched a massive recruiting drive for volunteers and worked with local business and civic leaders to acquire a new observation post. The post originally operated on the roof of the local theater, requiring volunteers to climb over seventy feet of stairs. Many, especially the elderly, had trouble negotiating the steps, leading to the effort to construct a new post. When a number of disparate groups raised the money, the volunteers acquired land for a new site and built a new post. The Bismarck FC highly encouraged Drake's selection for the high honor.[38]

The GOC provided a unique opportunity during a time of intense international friction. Not all those who wanted to preserve freedom had to serve in uniform during the Cold War, but the opportunity to assist the GOC gave many citizens a sense of pride in serving their country. Radar improvements gradually reduced the reliance upon civilian volunteers by 1958 and eliminated the requirement for a 24-hour alert.[39] The growing scope and efficiency of new radar systems gave officials the assurance that they could detect an enemy strike before it reached the United States. Specifically, the Distant Early Warning (DEW) Line across the arctic and its extension through ships and airplanes into the Atlantic and Pacific Oceans, coupled with a similar line across the midpoint of Canada called the Pine Tree Line, provided the United States with a technological alternative to human detection efforts. Furthermore, technological advances in jet aircraft made it possible for bombers to fly higher and faster than humans could detect them, allowing the air force to relieve GOC volunteers of the surveillance burden. Finally, the new Semi-Automatic Ground Environment (SAGE) System, an early computer-based communication system, transmitted aircraft plots from a remote outpost to air force installations almost instantaneously, making human communications outmoded. The air force was entering a new phase of war planning, relying on technology to counter any invasion threat.[40]

Lieutenant General Joseph H. Atkinson, the air defense commander responsible for the GOC and its deactivation, wrote a personal letter to each of the GOC post supervisors with this tribute:

You have borne these duties well and faithfully, and have provided invaluable assistance to the air defense of our country. We will be forever grateful for your sacrifices. A most significant aspect of your work in the GOC is that it shows what free and independent people can accomplish through voluntary association and spiritual unity in the cause of the nation's security. I salute and commend all volunteers for a job well done. The Air Force, the Air Defense Command and, indeed, all American citizens owe you a great debt of gratitude for helping the air defense system deter aggression. I hope that the Air Force will continue to merit the confidence and support you have so generously given it in the past.[41]

The purpose of the GOC was to detect, identify, and then report enemy airplanes invading American airspace. The Soviet Union never attacked the United States, so the GOC never fulfilled its ultimate mission. GOC officials might argue, however, that the Soviets never attacked the United States because they knew that the GOC was standing watch. The intent was never to win a war but to prevent one from occurring. In this sense the GOC was highly successful.[42] Authorities disbanded the GOC in early 1959, while numerous closure ceremonies throughout the nation marked the end of the GOC's proud tradition.

The Ground Observer Corps was one of the few highly successful civil defense programs to come out of Washington and play an important role at the state and local level. The difference between this civil defense program and others, however, was that the air force provided people with a mission that required them to watch the sky, provided training and some resources to fulfill their mission, and recognized the individual contributions of its members. Other civil defense programs could not offer the same benefits. Those volunteers who covered their shifts at the local GOC center were part of a larger effort to save the rest of the nation, not just their local communities. While most people would not construct a fallout shelter for their own survival, they would donate their time and energy to defend others as part of a larger effort.

The GOC on the northern plains served on the front lines of the Cold War, ready to provide early warning to the rest of the nation in case of emergency. Volunteers there also lent assistance to numerous commercial and military aircraft, sometimes calling for rescue teams when a plane went down. Volunteers also responded to innumerable natural disasters, from issuing tornado warnings to providing communications during floods. They reported fires and issued other warnings, in all instances saving human life and valuable property. Thousands of volunteers from diverse backgrounds and economic circumstances gave freely of their time and talent during the time of the GOC, from 1952 to 1959, ready to lend assistance. Most importantly, the GOC provided these ordinary citizens with the opportunity to serve their country, giving people on the northern plains the feeling that they could fight back against an unseen enemy. As John Milton, the blind poet, once stated: "They also serve, who only stand and wait."[43]

Chapter 6

The Cuban Missile Crisis

Students at the University of North Dakota were stunned when President Kennedy informed the nation that the Soviets had placed nuclear missiles on the island of Cuba, demanded that the Soviets withdraw the weapons, and outlined his plan to quarantine the island. Crowds gathered around every television set on campus, and administrators noted that no one spoke during the president's address. Only after the speech did anyone discuss the story. Some tried to make light of the situation, referring to their draft status. As some sixty people gathered around a television in a Fargo hotel lobby business came to a standstill. "You could have heard a pin drop, it was that quiet," said a local businessperson.[1] The reaction was also subdued in Helena, Montana, where patrons in a tavern called the Last Chance Gulch watched the president's announcement. As one patron noted, "Everyone stopped drinking. Everyone stopped talking. Even the band fell silent." The shock soon gave way to gallows humor, as one weather forecaster predicted: "Lows tomorrow in the 40s, highs could reach 4,800 degrees."[2] As historian Alice George has noted, "For a precarious week in 1962, all Americans got a taste of life on death row."[3]

The Cuban Missile Crisis in 1962 was an alarming event in America's history, as John F. Kennedy and his staff attempted to manage a situation that threatened to spiral out of control. The Soviet Union had placed nuclear missiles in Cuba, an island nation only ninety miles from the Florida coast, and President Kennedy and his administration were determined to get them out. The problems lay in the method selected to remove the missiles. Pushing the Soviets too hard by resorting to a military solution greatly increased the likelihood that the Soviets would launch a preemptive strike on the United States. If Kennedy appeared too weak, then the Soviets might try to take advantage of the situation, forcing him to resolve the issue through military strength. Underlying all of these problems was the vulnerability of Berlin, a tempting prize for the Soviets that Kennedy had promised to defend with nuclear weapons if necessary.

Nuclear war seemed imminent, and the population was woefully unprepared. As chapter 4 points out, citizens did not spend the 1950s preparing for nuclear confrontation with the Soviet Union. American backyards had no abundance of fallout shelters. Most citizens did not embrace civil defense measures before the crisis. Civil defense officials did not prepare the populace for atomic war because no coordinated effort to provide fallout shelters for American citizens had been made during the previous decade. Indeed only the Berlin Crisis in July 1961 gave any impetus to a national civil defense plan, when President Kennedy initiated a comprehensive fallout shelter program. The plan was not complete by the time the Soviets put missiles in Cuba in 1962. It seems that the Soviets caught the United States in the middle of establishing a shelter program. The states on the northern plains—North Dakota, South Dakota, and Montana—were not prepared for a nuclear crisis.[4]

Many historians have attempted to ascertain why Soviet premier Nikita Khrushchev put missiles into Cuba at all. Some have argued that Khrushchev sent the missiles to Cuba because he lacked long-range missiles in significant quantities. Medium-range missiles he had in abundance, so why not "throw a hedgehog at Uncle Sam's pants," he asked in April 1962. The simple answer is that Khrushchev wanted to spread revolution throughout the Latin American countries. The United States could hardly object to the missiles, Khrushchev argued, as England, Italy, and Turkey all had American missiles aimed at the Soviet Union.[5]

The situation was serious, as the United States would not tolerate Soviet nuclear weapons in the Western Hemisphere. The question was how to get rid of them without provoking a nuclear war. Advisors urged the president to reveal nothing to the American public until his staff settled upon a course of action. Kennedy's advisors presented several options, including an airstrike, an invasion, or a combination of the two. Eventually aides raised another alternative: a quarantine that restricted Soviet ships from approaching Cuba. While quarantine was not an act of war, a blockade was. Kennedy's careful choice of words was an attempt to resolve the confrontation without an exchange of missiles.[6]

When the administration settled on the quarantine idea, many military officials and presidential advisors were skeptical. Most of Kennedy's advisors favored a decisive military response, despite the obvious consequences of a Soviet attack on Berlin that would surely follow an attack on a Soviet ally. Quarantine offered the best chance to avoid military confrontation, allowing the Soviets to withdraw peaceably. Eventually a consensus for quarantine developed among the president's staff. Kennedy went on live nationwide television to inform the people of the critical situation on October 22, 1962, six days after photographs had revealed the existence of the missiles. The president accepted the least aggressive action, quarantine, but insisted that the Soviet Union withdraw the missiles.[7]

The situation was indeed grave; the United States and the Soviet Union had nuclear weapons on a high state of alert. The crux of Kennedy's speech was the quarantine, which many saw as a blockade and thus an act of war. The administration claimed that the quarantine dated back to a 1947 legal concept known as the Inter-American Treaty of Reciprocal Assistance used in the Caribbean. Professor Harry Tomasek, a professor in the political science department at the University of North Dakota, checked some his resources and did not find the word "quarantine" mentioned. He said that the word insinuated a blockade, which was an act of war.[8]

Thousands of citizens across the nation expressed their support for President Kennedy's action, although many believed that it was coming somewhat belatedly. "He ought to have spoken up earlier" was a common reaction in numerous on-the-street interviews in New York.[9] Others expressed their feelings through a number of demonstrations that developed throughout the nation in response to Kennedy's announcement. The Student Peace Union, headquartered in Chicago, called upon its fifteen thousand members to march on Washington to protest Kennedy's blockade within the week. The group described itself as anticommunist but favored peaceful solutions to international problems. Members organized a number of other protests throughout the nation, including in Columbus and Cleveland in Ohio; Austin and Houston in Texas; Seattle, Washington; Berkeley, California; and Miami, Florida.

The organization's chapter at the University of Minnesota demonstrated against Kennedy's plan and confronted other students belonging to the Campus Republican Association and the Young Americans for Freedom. The conflict nearly resulted in a riot as three thousand students clashed and shouted at each other. Elsewhere fifteen Cuban sympathizers battled over two thousand Kennedy supporters on the Indiana University campus, resulting in taunting and fistfights until police broke up the melee.[10]

Women Strike for Peace, an organization dedicated to the elimination of nuclear weapons, protested in front of the United Nations building in New York City. The crowd, numbering some six hundred women, demanded that the United Nations settle the international dispute between the United States and the Soviet Union. New York City police commissioner Michael J. Murphy banned any protests in the Times Square area because they would draw too many people and obstruct traffic. The decision outraged numerous organizations, some of which had formed in response to the crisis. Vincent Lee, director of the Fair Play for Cuba Committee, was outraged. He informed the commissioner that committee members had already distributed over twelve thousand pamphlets announcing a demonstration in the area. Lee was successful in moving the demonstration to another area in the city.[11]

No mass demonstrations were held on the northern plains in the wake of Kennedy's announcement, but the test of nerves was evident as people tried to make sense of the situation. A number of citizens throughout the northern plains called local authorities to determine ways in which people could survive in the event of nuclear war. All the states redoubled their civil defense efforts. For the most part, however, residents simply supported the president. A number of people put out their American flags. The mayor of Williston, North Dakota, proclaimed the day after Kennedy's speech "U.S. Day," while the mayor of Minot, North Dakota, urged citizens to take part in a program at the local college highlighting the seventeenth anniversary of the United Nations. A number of newspapers reported the reactions of local citizens, all of whom expressed overwhelming support for President Kennedy's chosen course of action.[12]

Citizens in South Dakota also supported Kennedy's stance on Cuba. James Kreelman of Sioux Falls remarked: "I thought his talk was excellent. We have been getting pushed around too much."[13] Sentiment in

Montana was similar. As Wayne Montgomery stated, "President Kennedy spoke the words all America has been waiting to hear—fateful words, to be sure, but firm and purposeful."[14] Americans on the northern plains faced the threat of nuclear war, but they stood up to aggression and supported the president rather than worrying about their own safety.

The crisis offered communities the opportunity to test their civil defense plans, and state and local programs across the nation came up short. Communities tested their civil defense sirens to ensure that they could warn citizens should the need arise. Seven of nineteen sirens failed to sound in Olathe, Kansas, prompting civil defense director William A. Barker to note: "It told us what we needed to know—our degree of preparedness. I guess you could say it is not too satisfactory."[15] The civil defense sirens in Harrisburg, Pennsylvania, worked just fine: a demolition crew accidentally set off a siren after blasting a concrete structure in the Pennsylvania rail yards, igniting a panic in the city. Within minutes hundreds of people jammed the phone lines calling the local police stations, newspapers, and radio and television stations, requesting information. It took more than an hour to silence the siren, adding to the confusion.[16] Citizens in San Antonio, Texas, had a scare when the city's air raid siren accidentally sounded at the height of the missile crisis. "This place went plumb haywire," reported Harold Markeil, who was the alarm operator within the city. "Fire, police, and civil defense dispatchers were flooded with calls."[17] City manager Jack Shelly added to the confusion: he had announced that they would not test the siren, lest citizens become unnecessarily concerned.

An article in North Dakota's *Grand Forks Herald* on October 28, 1962, reminded citizens that the whistle at the Northern States Power Plant also served as the city's civil defense warning. Citizens should tune in to the radio if they heard the alarm, the article noted. Another article in the same paper reported that the Northern States Power Company would sound the whistle at noon the following Monday, signaling the start of the Potato Festival, an annual event each autumn; it was not a civil defense warning. Citizens in Grand Forks must have read both articles, because no confusion was reported. Officials in Sioux Falls did not need to worry about turning sirens on or off; they did not have one in the city. The city government had allocated $5,000 toward a system the year before, expecting matching funds from the federal officials. But

Civil defense officials marking a fallout shelter in North Dakota. Coinciden-
tally, this photo was taken on October 19, 1962, three days before President
Kennedy's announcement that the Soviets had placed nuclear missiles in Cuba.
Courtesy State Historical Society of North Dakota, 0080-box1-file10-06.

an adequate system would cost more than $30,000, and the city had not
yet purchased one at the time of the crisis.[18]

Officials in Miles City, Montana, published the civil defense plan in
the local paper. Should an emergency occur, a long and continuous blast
of the fire alarm would alert citizens to the danger. The article instructed
people to tune in to the local radio station and listen for emergency

warnings. School authorities would release children and send them home, warning parents not to drive to pick them up, as the large number of automobiles would snarl traffic when emergency vehicles might need freedom to maneuver. The article suggested that parents should arrange for children to stay with friends or relatives in town if they lived a long distance from school. The message also warned that authorities would reserve telephones for emergencies only and instructed citizens to take refuge in basements or other appropriate structures and to have food, water, medical supplies, and radios in their shelters.[19]

The impetus for a national civil defense plan had taken root only the year before, when President Kennedy publicly announced that the United States would use nuclear weapons if necessary to prevent the Soviet Union from taking over all of Berlin. Allied leaders had partitioned the city after World War II into Soviet, British, and American sectors. Soviet leaders since then had worked to evict the democratic nations. Kennedy outlined America's unwavering support for Berlin in a speech on July 26, 1961, in which he also advocated a massive increase in fallout shelter construction and conversion of existing structures into shelters. Kennedy wanted shelters to save lives. Interestingly, he also called for a handy gadget that plugged into any household outlet, designed to emit a loud buzzing noise in case of attack. Local power companies, which manipulated the electrical current, would activate the buzzer.[20]

Aside from the possibility of nuclear war, a number of people on the northern Great Plains did not think that Kennedy's Berlin speech went far enough in recognizing the need to stop Communist aggression worldwide. Catherine Coffin of Aberdeen, South Dakota, wrote to South Dakota senator Karl Mundt, pointing out that she opposed the measures in Kennedy's speech, which placed the United States in a largely defensive posture in dealing with the Soviets. "Are we never to quit this cowardly, disgusting bargaining, threatening, and giving in to Communists?" she asked. "If we are to fight Russia, let's fight to win. We can only hope to win a nuclear war since Communist countries outnumber us population-wise."[21] The way the crisis progressed in October 1962, Catherine Coffin might have gotten her wish for a nuclear war.

National civil defense officials invited a group of governors to Washington, D.C., to discuss protection issues at the start of the missile crisis. National and state leaders realized that America was woefully unprepared to survive a nuclear war. A speedy solution was necessary. Leaders developed a six-point program designed to buy time and meet over-whelming shortages with the limited resources. The key point that the governors agreed upon was to lower standards for shelter space to enable millions of people to find cover from radioactive fallout. North Dakota, South Dakota, and Montana all lacked a comprehensive plan that in-cluded fallout shelters stocked with essential items. Most of the fallout shelters were not even marked as such; expedited programs during the crisis led officials to mark known shelters, though most lacked food and medicine stockpiles. None of the states had enough shelter space for all citizens.[22]

Governor William Guy of North Dakota and several other senior governors from around the nation met with President Kennedy during the governor's conference. In private Kennedy urged the governors to implement new and detailed civil defense plans to bolster their state's readiness. "Kennedy was worried," Guy recalled, "and urged us to go home and get ready."[23] Upon his return from Washington, Guy urged department heads to improve the state's civil defense capabilities. He also called for a statewide practice civil defense alert. "This directive does not stem from information on the condition of our foreign relations which is not available to the public," he proclaimed. "It is simply a realistic ap-proach to our responsibilities as a state government."[24] The exercise was only for state officials and did not involve the public. North Dakota was the only state to hold a civil defense exercise in the region, though it was largely for show and to bolster public morale.[25]

The state civil defense director, Colonel R. W. Carlson, reported pub-licly that the state's civil defense program showed no major weaknesses during the crisis. But nineteen counties in North Dakota had no com-munity shelters with a capacity to accommodate fifty or more citizens, twenty-five counties had five or fewer shelters, and only eleven coun-ties had six or more. Not having shelters for all citizens apparently was not a major weakness. The statement was obviously for public morale. Carlson's report on the civil defense exercise illustrated this point: he remarked that the alert showed a "one hundred percent improvement" over the previous year. The alert largely consisted of checking batteries in equipment and a communications exercise that included three simulated nuclear attacks within the state, designed to test the state's ability to report such an incident. He noted that the state needed more personnel trained in handling messages.[26]

North Dakota governor William Guy (*center*) inspecting the National Guard and Civil Defense Headquarters in Bismarck. No date given. Courtesy State Historical Society of North Dakota, Item C1536.

The Williston City Commission in North Dakota also expressed an interest in stepping up civil defense programs within the city as the crisis gained momentum. Frank Markham, the civil defense director for the community, admitted that he was not completely sure how the civil defense system worked but was busy reading appropriate manuals. Civil defense directors frequently worked on projects other than civil defense during this era. The federal government often paid a portion of the salaries of civil defense directors to ensure that communities had someone to lead those initiatives, but these administrators often found themselves distracted by daily business needs. Back in Williston, Markham suggested that the city purchase a civil defense warning siren, the cost of which the state would share. Within the week Markham had visited the state headquarters and received a briefing on the North Dakota Civil Defense Plan. State officials suggested that the civil defense director should have an office, phone, and maps of the city in case of emergency, which he obviously did not have. The Williston commission agreed that this was a good idea and made the motion to approve the request before moving on to other business such as fixing community sidewalks and purchasing a new snowplow.[27]

The lack of civil defense planning is also evident in the small number of fallout shelters available. Williston only had room in its community shelters for about one thousand people. According to L. C. Levitt, the Williams County civil defense director, this number was far short of the required space for the populace. Officials rented about a dozen buildings to meet requirements, each of which could accommodate fifty to over three hundred people, and the Williston city government worked hard to bring the buildings up to standard. Levitt reported that he had received numerous inquiries from the local population regarding shelters. "Get people scared and they will get interested," he remarked. Citizens in Grand Forks began asking crucial questions about their survival, writing and calling civil defense authorities for information. Officials reported that people should keep several days' worth of food and water on hand and should listen to their radios for information in an emergency. One concerned citizen was relieved to hear that she could bring her cats to a fallout shelter.[28]

The situation was similar in Bismarck, where the city lacked the required number of fallout shelters for the population. Only about one-third of Bismarck citizens could have found shelter space, leading officials to lease buildings that they could quickly convert to fallout shelters for some nine thousand additional people. The owners of the buildings received no payment for the leases, contributing the buildings for free. Each shelter building in Williams County was clearly marked as a shelter, with the maximum number of occupants indicated, though there were no instructions on what officials would do once a building was full. Officials encouraged citizens to construct shelters in their homes to ensure that they would find adequate space.[29]

That North Dakota had any shelters at all was attributable to far-sighted civil defense officials who started to identify shelters long before the Cuban crisis. Additionally, the Kennedy administration had encouraged state and local governments to identify buildings to use as shelters and bring them up to code in a short time, making more shelter space available for citizens. Unfortunately, most shelters in North Dakota were not marked as such, leaving people to wonder where the shelters were.

The Corps of Engineers spent the crisis marking fallout shelters through-out the plains with the yellow and black signs that became familiar, although many of the buildings had no food, water, or other supplies.[30]

Officials in South Dakota also recognized the need to identify build-ings to serve as fallout shelters. Rapid City authorities were aware that their city was far short of the required fallout shelter space for their resi-dents and had begun the chore of leasing and stocking new buildings. One of the major issues was that the government buildings identified as fallout shelters were only large enough to accommodate the government employees that worked in them. Officials recommended that citizens stay home and establish shelters there.[31] Citizens in Sturgis had little idea how to respond to the situation. City authorities held a town meeting to discuss evacuation and communications plans, showed films on emer-gency procedures, and urged local merchants to stock and display items that customers might need in time of emergency. Additionally, officials identified fallout shelters in the meeting and explained how to find them, though no one mentioned food and other provisions. School officials at Black Hills Teachers College conducted a civil defense drill at the height of the crisis and noted some disturbing issues. Officials moved the fe-male students to the swimming pool and the male students to the heat-ing tunnels located beneath the campus. None of the students had food or water, and the air in the tunnels became stale after a short period. The men could not wait to get out of the tunnels, throwing the entire plan into question. Only the children from the day-care center seemed prepared, as they carried food and blankets to the locker room in the gymnasium.[32]

After the president's speech announcing the presence of missiles in Cuba, the Hughes County Civil Defense Unit in Pierre, South Dakota, went on 24-hour alert, checking shelters within the city and conducting communications exercises. The city had recently completed a survey of fallout shelters. Although the buildings lacked food, water, or medicine, civil defense director James Mulloy noted that the city had identified space for over twenty thousand residents in addition to the three hun-dred spaces in the Hughes County Courthouse, which had some emer-gency supplies.[33]

Sioux Falls authorities apparently had everything under control. The county civil defense coordinator, Carl Quisenberry, admitted: "We're just standing by, waiting," even though the city lacked sufficient shelter space for all residents. He noted that "very little had been done on shelter building in the Sioux Falls area in recent months."[34] Quisenberry and his organization had received no special orders from either state or national offices, so Sioux Falls civil defense officials answered the phones, speaking with citizens who called seeking information. Many residents wanted to know if the city had adequate shelters and if the facilities contained enough food and water, while others simply wanted to know what was going on or wanted to offer assistance. Exactly what Quisenberry told callers is unclear.[35]

Officials in Montana were justifiably critical of their preparation. Montana governor Tim Babcock ordered the Montana National Guard to active duty to help get the state ready for an emergency in the days following the president's speech. Babcock's decision to activate the guard came after a short briefing from civil defense authorities, who noted that nearly half of the state's fifty-six counties had failed to carry out a mandate from the state legislature to make adequate civil defense preparations. Under the governor's order, the National Guard would help prepare the state in four major areas: establishing an effective shelter program, communications, warning systems, and a radiological program for forecasting and detecting radioactive fallout.[36]

Although half of Montana was woefully unprepared for emergencies, the governor said that overall the state was in good shape, a dubious claim at best. The state had a central coordination center, and the state-wide communications system was working, but state civil defense director Robert A. Keyes stated that Butte was the only Montana city that had responded in any meaningful way to the public fallout shelter program. The week before Kennedy's speech the state spent two days briefing local officials on civil defense, when only half the counties sent representatives to the meetings. To remedy the situation Keyes ordered an intensification of state efforts in civil defense. "Some counties had emergency supplies stored," he said, "but others didn't take civil defense seriously—until now."[37] Beyond the obvious preparation issues, officials identified only 328 buildings throughout the state for use as fallout shelters, enough to hold about one hundred thousand citizens, only a fraction of the total number. The shelter program, Keyes noted, was far from completed, but a stepped-up program was underway.[38]

Civil defense shelter supplies for 50 persons: 10 water drums, 1 sanitation kit 5K-IV, 1 medical kit "A," 1 shelter radiation kit, 10 cases survival biscuits. Dimensions 36" × 72" × 3' 7". Official U.S. Army Photo released by Dept. of Defense Washington, D.C., November 1, 1962. Courtesy South Dakota State Historical Society.

Residents in Custer, Montana, were more fortunate than most citizens within the state. Civil defense director Glen Gibson reported that the old Northern Pacific Railway tunnel near the town would provide shelter for about 565 people in case of emergency. This number approximated the population within a 25-mile radius of the community, encouraging the director to note that Custer was probably the only city in the northwest United States to provide shelter space for all of the local residents.[39]

Military bases across the region also responded to the emergency, dispersing their aircraft to a number of civilian airports. The air force moved fighter aircraft from Malmstrom AFB in Montana to a small civilian airfield in Billings, Montana. Officials declined to comment on the number of aircraft involved but did say that "the dispersal is in accordance with a predetermined dispersal plan. The idea is to get all of our eggs out of one basket and provide a much better combat capability."[40] Billings mayor Harold Gerke told reporters that the city stood ready to assist the military during the crisis. The military took over the airfield, though the move did not affect civilian passenger planes or their flights. Airfield manager Kenneth Rolle played down the situation, pointing out that military aircraft routinely landed at the airport and that airfields in Helena and Missoula would receive military aircraft for the duration of the crisis.[41]

Transfer activities continued around the Great Plains and the nation as the air force ordered planes dispersed. But the air force denied that the international situation played any role in transferring aircraft back to their home station in Sioux Falls, South Dakota. The Air National Guard unit in Sioux Falls had transferred its F-102 fighters to Ellsworth AFB in Rapid City while crews made repairs to the runway at their home station. With the repairs completed, the aircraft returned to Sioux Falls as a matter of routine. Apparently only the northern bases exercised the dispersal tactic, as authorities sent aircraft from both Minot and Grand Forks AFBs in North Dakota to Hector Field in Fargo. Veterans recalled that officials had crammed aircraft onto Hector Field wherever they could find room, and each of the active duty F-101 and F-106 fighters had nuclear-tipped missiles for use against the anticipated Soviet bomber attack. Air National Guard units also played an important role during the Cuban Missile Crisis. They put as many fighters on alert as possible as tension increased.[42]

To illustrate the tension that pilots must have felt throughout the crisis, the North American Air Defense Command (NORAD) detected what it thought was a massive air invasion by the Soviet Union shortly after the Cuban Missile Crisis began. NORAD alerted the North Dakota Air National Guard, and crews loaded as many aircraft as possible with MB-1 nuclear air-to-air missiles. According to retired lieutenant colonel Ivan Lang, two aircraft with full armament flew out to inspect the threat. He described the faces of the pilots as "white as a sheet" upon receiving their orders. NORAD later determined that what appeared to be incoming Soviet aircraft was actually a highly reflective meteor shower.[43]

Newspapers across the nation proclaimed an end to the standoff on the morning of October 29, 1962, when Premier Khrushchev agreed to dismantle the nuclear missiles in Cuba and transport them back to the Soviet Union. Americans throughout the nation drew a collective sigh of relief at the news. The Kennedy administration had averted disaster but laid bare the problems at all levels of government, though many state officials vowed to continue to improve their civil defense measures. But the Cuban Missile Crisis points out a number of important lessons. It illustrated that no coherent civil defense plan existed on the northern Great Plains at the time, though political leaders did their best to reassure citizens and reacted courageously to meet the demands thrust upon them. These states were not alone, as few states across the nation were prepared for a real emergency.

The Cuban Missile Crisis also illustrates that most citizens had not adequately prepared for the possibility of a nuclear war. The majority disregarded civil defense measures until 1962 and did not take the proper precautions to ensure their survivability. Once the crisis loomed over the region, people scrambled to prepare for war. While civil demonstrations occurred in many larger communities throughout the country, the northern plains experienced no such phenomenon. Citizens almost universally supported President Kennedy. Many even suggested that the confrontation was overdue. The federal government continued to encourage states to incorporate civil defense designs into new buildings after the Cuban Missile Crisis in 1962. The National Fallout Shelter Program was intended to provide shelter space for every American and promised to offer funding and building designs to meet that end.

The federal government published a booklet in 1965 entitled *New Buildings with Fallout Protection*, intended to encourage public school officials to incorporate shelter designs into new buildings. The pamphlet included design specifications and drawings of a new school built in Rogers, North Dakota, that placed its cafeteria underground, for use as a shelter. The Federal Civil Defense Administration even sponsored design competitions for shopping centers to incorporate shelter designs, but the main impetus was federal and state government buildings, which displayed the yellow and black shelter placard. The program was probably underfunded, however. Steve Matosich requested federal funding to incorporate a fallout shelter into the new junior high school in Whitefish, Montana, only to find out that no funding was available. "Lack of federal participation," he wrote, "is bound to eliminate shelter construction. If the government doesn't feel it necessary . . . then the people at large feel apathetic about such a program."[44]

The *New York Times* reported that civil defense agencies across the nation took steps to speed up lagging programs in the wake of the Cuban standoff. The Defense Department had developed plans to provide and stock some 60 million shelter spaces since the Berlin Crisis, but space for only a few hundred thousand people was ready for immediate use nationally. Throughout the states, civil defense officials reported that people who had been indifferent to civil defense programs were asking for information during the crisis. Another official remarked that citizens were "gobbling up" civil defense bulletins, which officials could not give away with a set of dishes only the week before.[45]

The Cuban Missile Crisis caused a sensation across the nation. But after Kennedy and Khrushchev solved the issue at hand, people went about their daily business and largely dismissed the possibility of nuclear war. A meeting of civil defense officials in North Dakota in 1963 again cited public apathy as the major obstacle to establishing an effective civil defense program, even though most people knew about the civil defense initiative.[46] At the end of November 1963, a year after the missile crisis, Montana civil defense had only marginally increased the amount of shelter space available for residents. The state had 488 buildings that could shield only 21 percent of the population: 104,000 citizens. The year before, the state had been able to protect only some 58,000 citizens.[47] This represented a marked improvement but was still far short of the goal of 50 percent protection for the population that President Kennedy had called for. Constance L. Fisher of Missoula wrote to Montana senator Lee Metcalf only three months after the missile crisis, asking him to oppose a huge civil defense appropriation that President Kennedy was asking from Congress: "I deeply believe that fallout shelter buildings serve to condition people to expect war and to feel unwarranted security, an unrealistic optimism about the results of a thermonuclear war."[48]

Montana officials began experimenting with a number of fallout shelter designs to help shore up shelter deficiencies. In addition, the Walla Walla District Corps of Engineers, which included Montana, began evaluating the possibility of using mines within the state for fallout shelter purposes and published a report in June 1966. The report explained that the National Fallout Shelter Survey had identified approximately 338,000 shelter spaces for a population of 675,000, leaving a 50 percent deficiency. The Corps of Engineers surveyed over 10,000 mines, finding

650 suitable for civil defense purposes. Little was actually done with the mines except to file the information for use at a later time if necessary.[49]

Government officials and journalists have commented that citizens on the northern Great Plains were apathetic about civil defense before the Cuban Missile Crisis, but they certainly took an immediate interest in protection measures during the event. They quickly forgot their enthusiasm when the crisis ended, however. This phenomenon followed the national pattern, as new issues such as civil rights and the Vietnam War distracted Americans from civil defense concerns. After President Kennedy's death in 1963, the momentum for fallout shelters disappeared, and few states accomplished much beyond Kennedy's initial instructions.[50] As this chapter demonstrates, many people on the northern plains had no idea how to survive a nuclear attack and made no plans to ensure their survival. Moreover, officials had not identified adequate shelter space for the population and had not stocked most of the existing shelters with basic food and medical supplies prior to the Cuban Missile Crisis in 1962, let alone during the height of the Cold War in the 1950s. This episode further illustrates that the civil defense program developed at the national level and pushed to the state level for implementation was never successful.

The Cuban Missile Crisis had a number of other consequences. Secretary of defense Robert McNamara reevaluated America's nuclear strategy and decided that the U.S. nuclear policy was incomplete. Heretofore, civilian and military leaders had sought to reduce civilian casualties in the event of war by aiming only for military targets. The missile crisis pointed out the futility of this strategy, as civilian areas were the most vulnerable. In order to make nuclear war unthinkable, civilian targets must be the primary objective for both sides. MAD (Mutually Assured Destruction) became the dominant blueprint for a peaceful world.[51]

To this end, air force bases and the Minuteman missile silos under construction would take on a new role: deterrence. The missile silos dotted the landscape in all three northern plains states, and air bases became a major force there as well. To the citizens of the northern plains, strategy was not as important as the federal dollars that these facilities promised. Air bases, missile silos, and an Anti–Ballistic Missile (ABM) complex designed to knock incoming missiles out of the skies are the subjects of the next three chapters.

Chapter 7

Airpower and Air Bases

The weakened cattle heard the rumble as it echoed across the frozen ground. The sound was faint at first but gained momentum as the aircraft approached. The withered animals struggled to their feet, showing interest after lying despondently in the same spot for days, perhaps weeks. The small calves had the hardest time. They had not eaten in a month, the temperature had not risen above zero during that time, and the wind whipped incessantly, adding to their misery. The pilot knew his business after weeks of practice dropping food to the starving animals in the fields below, bringing life to a range where no truck could penetrate the driving snow. He gave the signal to the crew: hay bales fell out of the back of the plane and to the ground at precisely the right moment. In a flash and a roar the plane was gone, leaving behind it the smell of newly arrived grass. The cattle had tried to scramble away from the penetrating howl when the plane flew over, but they were too weak and the snow was too deep for them to get very far. They stumbled toward the aromatic pile of sweet hay, their ambling turning into a stampede as the realization struck them that nourishment was at hand. Some of the cattle plowed through the barbed wire fence to get the hay as others floundered through the deep snow. On the perimeter of the herd, cattle too weak from lack of food struggled to rise. Eventually all of the cattle in that particular herd somehow made it to the hay bale.[1]

Blizzards devastated the West and stranded millions of cattle, sheep, other livestock, and thousands of people during the winter of 1948–49. The only relief came from aircraft that dropped supplies to stranded citizens or dropped bales of hay to stranded livestock. The creatures starving on the plains were not unlike the humans struggling to survive at exactly the same time in the besieged city of Berlin. Half a world away, the Communists had closed all of the roads, train tracks, and waterways into Berlin, necessitating a similar airlift that brought thousands of tons of supplies per day. At the beginning of the Cold War, during the height of the Berlin Airlift, two very similar dramas played out at exactly the same moment.

Residents of that German city suffered from starvation nearly as much as the cattle on the Great Plains did. Citizens lined up at butcher shops at 4 A.M. to get a bowl of broth made from boiled bones or waited in other lines for the minimal rations of food coming into the city from the airlift. Anywhere the Americans had been, Germans scoured their garbage for whatever food was left behind. When a plane crashed coming into Gatow Airport, Germans combed the wreckage for the tiniest morsel, gathering up coffee beans one at a time or cooking topsoil in small pans to collect the lard that had seeped into it. When bags of dehydrated potato flakes burst open during unloading operations at Tempelhof Airport, German workers stuffed as much as they could into their mouths, resulting in horrible cramps as the flakes absorbed moisture and expanded in their stomachs. Ambulances took away three of the workers.[2]

The Berlin Blockade and the effort on the northern plains demonstrated yet again the importance of airpower and its unparalleled ability to bring destruction or salvation. World War II had shown that air forces could rain death from above to millions on the ground. The Berlin Airlift would show that the same forces could bring redemption to an entire city on a daily basis. While the national government directed military aircraft to provide food and supplies to Berlin, state and local officials used similar methods to provide essential provisions to stranded families throughout the northern plains. Flight crews for both situations came from different countries with different types of aircraft but with the same mission—to relieve the suffering of those under siege. This chapter demonstrates the importance of military bases and aircraft to the Cold War strategy and analyzes the effort to bring air bases into the region for economic benefits.

The Berlin Crisis was one of the first confrontations between the United States and Soviet Union after World War II. The British, Americans, Soviets, and later the French divided Berlin at the end of the war, as they divided all of Germany, into zones of occupation controlled by one of the wartime allies. Soviet premier Joseph Stalin wanted to oust the allied armies from Berlin and to prevent the incorporation of western Germany into the camp of the British and Americans. He surprised the world when he cut off all access to the city in June 1948, initiating the Berlin Blockade. The Americans and their allies had two choices: abandon the city to the Communists or supply the city through the air. The choice was obvious. American military leaders and their allies assembled a massive air armada to carry out one of the most audacious schemes in the Cold War era, the Berlin Airlift. The Soviets blockaded surface entrances into the city but left the air avenues unmolested. The airlift lasted 324 days, with the allies orchestrating an average daily delivery of over thirteen thousand tons of material.[3]

The Berlin Blockade was a prolonged period of worry for Americans, lasting from June 1948 to May 1949. It was all the more dramatic because it was so unexpected. On the northern plains another unexpected and dramatic event played itself out at the height of the Berlin Blockade in January and February 1949. The region's weather had been unseasonably warm at the beginning of the new year, with the mercury rising to almost fifty degrees. Los Angeles, ironically, was suffering through a freak cold spell that dropped six inches of snow on Southern California. When weather forecasters predicted increased snow and accumulation, nobody anticipated the disaster that loomed for the western states. Storms paralyzed businesses and industries, closed schools, and stranded thousands as the snow fell and drifted across roads. Hundreds of people died as well as hundreds of thousands of livestock. Millions of dollars in damage to property and crops took its toll from Arizona to the northern plains. Eight thousand motorists were stranded in cars and buses on the highways crossing the west, and a few thousand more were trapped in train stations or trains stopped on the rails. One family's home was buried under thirty-six feet of drifting snow. The occupants were freed by the assistance of neighbors. The effort to dig out of the mountains of snow turned into a massive rescue operation involving everyone from volunteers running snowplows and tiny airplanes to the United States Army operating bulldozers and the National Guard flying aircraft. For a country embroiled in the confrontation with the Soviets and a Cold War growing hotter at that time in Berlin, people on the northern plains confronted the disaster in the only terms they understood at the time: this was war.[4]

The snow started at the beginning of 1949 and continued to fall for days. As snow removal turned to rescue operations, journalists began to employ a litany of combat-related metaphors to describe the scene. Highway crews had begun to carry out the "campaign" against the blocked highways and to "battle" the miles of "blockaded" or snow-covered highways in the early stages of the storm. Plows and trucks "broke the siege" in order to deliver food and medical supplies to towns that had been isolated for weeks. Later plows "broke through" to Rapid City, where residents were trapped for ten days. When towns ran low on supplies and plows could not reach them, airplanes were the only answer.[5]

Already an "airlift" of volunteer civilian aircraft had begun dropping supplies to stranded towns throughout the West and northern plains or parachuting more delicate supplies such as units of blood plasma where needed. Volunteers and National Guard airplanes were required because active-duty units from the region were assisting with the situation in Berlin. Sixty B-29 bombers from Rapid City Air Force Base (AFB) were in England acting as a deterrent to Soviet aggression, while the C-54 cargo planes from Great Falls, Montana, participated in the airlift, bringing food and supplies to the desperate residents of Berlin.[6] Each volunteer pilot on the northern plains could identify with the pilots providing the lifeline to the residents of Berlin. Twenty small airplanes outfitted with skis enabled pilots to land and "evacuate" ill citizens. Others dropped supplies to South Dakotans stranded by the storm, such as the ton of flour dropped to faculty and students trapped at the Potato Creek Day School or the five hundred pounds of flour dropped to those at the Slim Butte School. Elsewhere in South Dakota pilots dropped a ton of flour, yeast, coffee, milk, lard, and sugar to those stranded at the Red Shirt Table day school. Other pilots flew "reconnaissance missions," to find livestock or to drop supplies to needy ranchers. Several pilots crashed and died for a variety of reasons, generally due to poor visibility. Major Donald C. Jones, the commanding officer of the North Dakota Air National Guard, died when his F-51 fighter crashed while seeking out those in distress.[7]

Though the civilian volunteers were essential, they needed more help. Two weeks into the unrelenting storms livestock owners throughout the

Dropping hay from a C-82 flying boxcar plane in support of Operation Haylift in 1949. Note the arrow pointing out the cowboy on horseback. Courtesy Special Collections Department, University of Nevada, Reno Library.

plains and the Rocky Mountain states requested government assistance in feeding their animals. Each plea from the stock owners in the affected state was more desperate than the last, with estimates of livestock losses rising above 50 percent and millions of dollars lost in states from Utah to North Dakota.[8] On January 24 air force officials announced that Operation Haylift would begin the following day. The objective was to use all available transport planes to drop hay to starving livestock herds all over the West and on the plains. Air force and National Guard planes greatly contributed to the relief measures, though the small-scale efforts continued unabated. The Royal Canadian Air Force began backing the relief effort by responding to Red Cross requests for emergency assistance. In fact the Canadians first coined the term "Haylift" to bring much-needed supplies through the air to starving livestock.[9]

One of the units involved in the Haylift was the Air National Guard unit from Fargo, North Dakota, formed in 1948. A pilot from that unit, Marshall Johnson, told reporters that his crew acted as if they were operating in a combat environment, as they tried to drop hay bales with the accuracy of a bombing mission. Johnson and other members of the crew looked for the "target" farm and then dropped to a couple of hundred feet above ground level as he made his pass. At exactly the right moment Johnson slowed the plane and rang a bell, which told the operator in the rear of the plane to discharge a load of bombs, paratroopers, or bales of hay. On one particular day the receiving end of the drop was John Slobajan's ranch, where over five hundred head of cattle looked skyward, waiting for the hay to arrive. Elsewhere photographs of hay "bombs" reaching their targets were adorning the front pages of many regional newspapers. The *Independent-Record* in Montana reported that cattle grew accustomed to "Hay Bombs" and did not seem to mind the roar of the planes. Within a week planes had dropped so much hay in the northern plains that stockpiles began to run low. The state legislature in Montana responded by issuing a hay embargo after listening to testimony from livestock associations, which emphasized the need for food supplies in Montana. The legislature made it illegal to sell hay to anyone outside the state.[10]

Throughout the early stages of the storms, city and county road crews provided the bulk of the personnel and machinery to clear the roads. By January 28, 1949, the situation was becoming desperate throughout the northern plains. The governors of the various states sent messages to President Truman, asking him to declare a state of emergency, thus allowing the regular army to "enter the fray" without having to wait for special funds. The governor of South Dakota, George T. Mickelson, sent word to Fifth Army Headquarters in Chicago that the situation was critical and that the state government could not handle it alone. That afternoon the president confirmed the state of emergency and got the army involved. He ordered the Corps of Engineers to start rolling immediately.[11] Once the regular army engaged, the metaphors emerged in the local papers. The *Billings Gazette* reported that "crews worked long hours in the 'battle' to open roads" while the *Huronite and Daily Plainsman* reported the 4,866 persons were "freed" by the greatest bulldozer operation ever organized.[12] Fifth Army commander Major General Lewis Pick "directed the war on drifts" as he coordinated the effort of almost four thousand soldiers involved in the struggle. Pick said of the relief efforts: "This is as near a wartime operation as we can expect in peacetime."[13] The *Bismarck Tribune* noted that the state had purchased three more snowplows to "battle the blockade." The paper noted the similarities between the international situation and the regional one when it announced "ND Winning Cold War" on February 5.[14]

By the beginning of February 1949 the blizzard had slowed to flurries and then stopped. Pick's Fifth Army reported its biggest "advance" in South Dakota, as army crews opened 4,915 miles of road, rescued 3,304 families, and "liberated" about 137,500 cattle, 37,600 sheep, and 3,800 other livestock such as horses and hogs. The *Bismarck Tribune* announced that the "battle" against McLean County's snow "blockade" had turned as plows opened several main roads in North Dakota by February 7. In isolated spots the battle continued. Wyoming officials sent two medium tanks into an area so packed with snow that even bulldozers could not make their way through the narrow mountain passes. No one had heard from several isolated families for three weeks, and the National Guard went to check on them. In Utah several sheepdogs were lost during the storm, requiring that replacements be parachuted into the isolated flocks to stand guard. Much work remained to be done, and it would take weeks until the West and the plains returned to some semblance of normalcy. In the middle of February Pick finally announced the cessation of operations in some areas of South Dakota and the beginning of the "demobilization" phase of the operation, though work would continue in North Dakota and Montana. On February 22 the area commander in North Dakota said that operations would begin to slow down the next day throughout the state, as roads remained open and families were out of danger. Not until the beginning of March was all of Montana "liberated" from "blockaded" snow, but both North Dakota and Montana had the Fifth Army to thank for opening thousands of miles of roads, saving thousands of families, and helping hundreds of thousands of animals get food to eat. The "war" on the northern plains ended in March 1949, and the Berlin Blockade ended in May of the same year in an allied victory of sorts when the Soviets opened the city to road, rail, and barge traffic. The residents of Berlin and the northern plains probably felt like combat veterans by the time their ordeals ended. Airpower had once again proved invaluable in desperate circumstances, leading to the development of numerous air bases in the region and around the nation.[15]

The Berlin Airlift and the Cold War itself were contests of will constructed as an example of good versus evil, but the international tension was also an economic opportunity for the states on the northern plains. Montana senator Mike Mansfield stood before a crowd of his constituents in October 1962 and announced with satisfaction: "Montana received $2.10 in federal funds for every $1.00 it paid to the federal government in fiscal year 1962." He noted that government agencies dispensed $346,321,832 in goods and services, while the Internal Revenue Service collected only $162,892,000 in taxes. "Military spending accounted for the greatest part of the increase," he continued. "The Defense Department expended a record $135.5 million, an increase of nearly $60 million over the previous year."[16] Expanding facilities at Great Falls and Glasgow air bases, along with construction of Minuteman missile sites, accounted for the growth.

The Cold War presented an excellent opportunity for western states and the northern Great Plains in particular. Intangible attributes such as patriotism guaranteed the region's support for the federal government's defensive initiatives, but tangible economic benefits simplified the decision to support these projects. A Soviet attack on the United States would follow a predictable path over the North Pole and Canada, commencing in the northern latitudes. A defensive ring in the northern reaches of the nation was the most prudent approach, putting the northern plains states in a unique position to leverage their geographic location into the construction of military bases and reverse the traditional colonial relationship between the states and eastern concerns. Instead of taking money out of the states, as was traditionally the case, the Cold War transferred money into the region, a trend begun during the Depression. Between

1933 and 1939 the government poured more than seven and a half billion dollars into the West in an effort to prop up the regional economy.[17] For citizens in North and South Dakota, this was a last resort. Dakotans did not want charity; they wanted assistance getting back on their feet. As the New Deal caught on and helped more people, they learned to live with it.[18] Residents realized that the federal government was a valuable source of funds.

Some of the military bases active on the northern plains during the Cold War actually dated from World War II. When the Japanese attacked Pearl Harbor and thrust the United States into war in December 1941, the U.S. military needed a number of new bases. Almost immediately military officials expedited the construction of airfields located within the United States, and hundreds of communities across the nation hoped to lure military bases to their locales. The Army Air Corps decision in June 1942 to locate a base in Rapid City, South Dakota, however, was the result of over a year of planning and negotiations.

South Dakota senator Francis Case knew that the air corps had authorized the construction of twenty-five bases across the nation in June 1941 and advised Rapid City, South Dakota, officials to get ready. While Case spoke to Army Air Corps officers about visiting western South Dakota to look over the land, the city needed to assemble pertinent information to attract the air corps and to begin negotiations about a base. The nation was at war, and South Dakotans would gladly assist in the defeat of the nation's enemies. But having a military base would also bring federal dollars into the state. To that end Case organized a committee of officials in Rapid City. They pooled their information regarding housing, water, public utilities, and the availability of tremendous tracts of land. Though differences of opinion arose among the representatives, they soon learned to put their disagreements aside for the good of the community.[19]

The U.S. military was initiating a massive buildup of forces and bases as the war progressed through its early stages. Army and navy officials had acquired over 12 million acres of land by November 1942 and had plans to acquire an additional 18 million the following year. These 30 million acres dwarfed the 3 million acres that they owned when the war commenced. Federal officials worked out a system in which they sent out questionnaires to communities where a new base seemed likely, and

Rapid City received one as a matter of routine. City leaders quickly responded and then waited for months. Many local residents doubted that they would ever hear from the military again. Much to their delight, city leaders learned that the air corps intended to look over the site in October 1941. The community spirit was the prime reason why the air corps eventually selected the site, according to Senator Case years later, but the military had other interests.[20]

Unknown to the South Dakotans, high-ranking military officials had more than a passing interest in the remote region. Senator Case had developed a close relationship with the head of the Army Air Corps, General Henry "Hap" Arnold, who had developed a love for the region when he flew airmail to President Calvin Coolidge and his wife while they vacationed in the Black Hills in 1927. General Arnold was also a close friend of the late Gutzon Borglum, the creator of the Mount Rushmore National Memorial. Arnold was an airpower visionary who predicted that the growing air corps would need a considerable amount of land to locate aerial gunnery ranges, a luxury not readily available in other regions of the country. More than anything, the availability of land for a gunnery range kept military officials interested in the site.[21]

Members of the air corps delegation examined the location, liked what they saw, and then kept the Rapid City commission in a state of suspense when no one heard from them for several months. A committee from Rapid City flew to Washington to meet with military officials and carry personal assurances of cooperation from the local government and local community. Soon after the committee left Washington, top military officials met to discuss the offer. The availability of land, water, and adequate housing within Rapid City made the site more enticing, but the promise of cooperation from city officials and residents also influenced their decision. The final factor, however, was the gunnery range necessary to teach pilots how to shoot. Federal representatives continued to request information from the Rapid City delegation; the city administrators duly answered. Military officials finally announced on January 2, 1942, that Rapid City would get its air base.[22]

In September 1942 the runways opened at Rapid City Army Airfield, providing a site for training thousands of B-17 bomber crews until the end of the war in 1945; instructors trained fighter pilots until the base shut down in 1946. The base closed for several months until the air corps reopened the base in 1947 as a home to B-29 Superfortress bombers and later the new B-36 Peacemaker bombers in 1949. The base was home to the B-52 Stratofortress throughout the Cold War and remains open today as the home of the 28th Bomb Wing, flying B-1B Lancer strategic bombers.[23]

While South Dakota officials worked to attract an army air base at the outset of World War II, Montana officials had similar hopes. By mid-1941 President Roosevelt could see that the United States was going to get involved in the conflict that was quickly spreading over the globe and ordered a massive increase in the number of heavy bombers available. He asked the secretary of war to "take whatever action is needed" for five hundred bombers to roll off production lines each month and to carry out this task "with all possible speed." Many community leaders knew that these planes needed homes.[24]

Once Roosevelt's request for more bombers became public in early 1941, rumors spread throughout Montana that army officers were making an inspection tour of civil airports within the state with an eye toward converting one or more of them to military use. A number of communities contacted their congressional leaders in Washington, asking that these officials intercede in their effort to lure a military base to their locale. James Murray contacted the air corps, which informed the senator that no such inspection tour was taking place. Perhaps, an air corps officer noted, pilots were simply touring the state, hoping to familiarize themselves with local facilities. More likely, community leaders had confused a military inspection tour with a survey of the airport facilities in Helena. The R. E. Morrison Flying Service was compiling a proposal to train aircraft mechanics and pilots for the war department.[25]

The rumors in May 1941 may have been false, but inspection teams did evaluate eleven cities within the state for possible bomber bases in November of that year, selecting sites at Great Falls, Cut Bank, Glasgow, and Lewistown, Montana. Great Falls was the main air base, with the others serving as satellite bases. The air corps completed construction on the four bases by late 1942. It needed a number of small northern bases to facilitate the Lend-Lease Program that supplied the Soviet Union with aircraft, spare parts, and supplies, flying from the continental United States to Fairbanks, Alaska. The bases continued this mission throughout the war, ending operations in September 1945. Additionally, four bombardment groups formed at the four air bases and conducted training over the Montana countryside, practicing assembling into group formations for simulated bombing missions. The bombardment groups trained from November 1942 until October 1943, when they left for Europe and participated in the bombing campaign against Germany.[26]

The war was an important turning point in the history of the West, marking a transition from resistance to opportunism. Citizens in the West, and their senators, worked to bring defense industries and military bases into the region. Rather than protest exploitation, westerners used the political system to bring federal dollars into the region. The open landscape and growing population formed a perfect marriage with the requirements of a nation at war. The country was not prepared for conflict but held enormous manufacturing potential, particularly in western states. The government invested some $70 billion into the West during the war years, much of it allocated through the Defense Plant Corporation, a subsidiary of the Reconstruction Finance Corporation. These government entities supplied the funding for numerous plants and factories throughout the region.[27] Western industries built ships, airplanes, and all manner of materiel. Additionally, the region saw the construction of numerous training facilities—army posts and naval bases—to fill the military pipeline with fighting men and women. In the 1930s fewer than one hundred thousand service members were stationed in the West; by 1945 more than 10 million members of the military were stationed there during the war. These initiatives transformed the economies of the various western states.[28]

Military bases also aided the South Dakota and Montana economies during the war. The air bases constructed in Mitchell, Pierre, Rapid City, Sioux Falls, and Watertown boosted the local economies, as did the Igloo Ordnance Depot in the Black Hills. Montana also had a series of air bases located at Cut Bank, Glasgow, Great Falls, and Lewistown, where women served indispensable roles as mechanics, drivers, and warehouse workers. The army established a War Dog Training Center near Helena to train sled teams to help downed pilots in the arctic and created a combined U.S.-Canadian special force that trained at Helena's Fort Harrison. North Dakota had no military bases during the war. The bases in Rapid City, South Dakota, and Great Falls, Montana, continued operation when the war ended, in a limited role.[29]

Citizens and officials on the northern plains had hoped that the war would bring defense industries and stimulate economic development. Influential leaders such as North Dakota governor John Moses and organizations such as the North Dakota War Resources Committee and the Greater North Dakota Association worked tirelessly to bring war industries into the state. North Dakota received only $9 million in war contracts, while Montana earned only $25 million of the $225 billion awarded by military contractors.[30] South Dakota fared better than its neighbors, earning over $50 million in defense contracts during the war, but still far below the $1.78 billion that Oregon garnered through construction contracts or the $4.5 billion for the state of Washington.[31] The manufacturing boom that the war generated bypassed the northern plains.

Historian Gerald D. Nash argues that western states benefited in at least four ways through Cold War spending: military installations, defense contracts and manufacturing, major science laboratories, and university research.[32] All of these possibilities with the exception of military installations eluded the northern plains during the Cold War. Manufacturing facilities that were growing in other parts of the West bypassed the plains, which had no industrial base to build upon. Corporations and universities on the northern plains could not compete with major science laboratories and research universities that other western cities already had at the start of the Cold War, saddling the region with additional handicaps. A critical weakness of the region was that it was still colonial in crucial respects.

When Congress funneled more than $100 billion into western military installations between 1945 and 1973, the political representatives and citizens of the northern plains states were determined to get a share.[33] Bases held the most promise for economic profit, given the geographic location of the northern plains states. Federal projects, and military bases in particular, played an important role in the economies of the states and local areas. The geographic location of the northern plains gave the region strategic importance to military planners, who intended to defend the nation along its northern border with new or reactivated air bases. Community leaders viewed new bases as a potential stimulus for struggling local economies, prompting an intense struggle to attract new bases away from other communities. While most Cold War historians have written at length about the fear that Americans felt throughout this period, the Cold War represented an economic opportunity to local communities in North Dakota, South Dakota, and Montana.

Local authorities in Glasgow, Montana, knew that the air corps might deactivate the air base at the end of the war and began working with political leaders to keep the facility open. Josef Sklower of the Glasgow Chamber of Commerce wrote to Senator Murray, asking that the air base continue flying operations or consider converting the unused buildings into a vocational school. The many buildings, barracks, and shops were not necessary for the continued operation of a civilian airport, and the facilities "can very advantageously be put to use for educational purposes. It is certain that many of our boys will wish to continue their interrupted education." Military officials had no plans to activate a vocational school at the facility and scheduled the site for deactivation. The air base gained a short reprieve at the end of the war, when the government decided to house prisoners of war at the site to assist in the cultivation and harvesting of beets, but the site shut down months later.[34]

Great Falls Army Air Base continued operations after the war, although the military closed down the satellite bases at Cut Bank, Glasgow, and Lewistown. The air corps needed only one facility to continue support operations to Alaska. The main base in Great Falls gained a new lease on life in 1948 upon the initiation of the Berlin Airlift. The military began supplying everything a city could need until Stalin lifted the blockade the following year. Great Falls Army Air Base was the only training facility for replacement C-54 aircrews and served as a training area for civilian pilots recalled to active duty. The Korean War kept the base open into the next decade, and the intensity of the Cold War necessitated stationing fighter aircraft at the base in the early 1950s.[35]

The Army Air Corps became the United States Air Force in 1948, leading to a number of transformations for the new military branch. Most noticeably, all facilities changed their names to reflect the designation. The name of the Montana base changed from Great Falls Army Air Base to Great Falls Air Force Base (AFB) after the transition. The air base in South Dakota changed name to Rapid City Air Force Base, but only temporarily. The name would change again in 1953 when the base experienced one of its worst disasters: a B-36 bomber crashed in Newfoundland, killing the twenty-three crew members, including Brigadier

(*Left to right*) Paul Ellsworth, Senator Karl E. Mundt, and Mrs. Mary Anne Ellsworth inspecting the plaque uncovered by President Dwight D. Eisenhower during a dedication ceremony renaming a base Ellsworth Air Force Base, June 13, 1953. Courtesy South Dakota Air and Space Museum.

General Richard E. Ellsworth. In recognition of the fallen general, President Eisenhower renamed the South Dakota center Ellsworth Air Force Base during his personal visit to the airfield on June 13, 1953.[36]

The air base in Montana received a new name in 1955, when air traffic controllers complained that Great Falls AFB and Great Falls Municipal

Airport sounded too similar, which presented a number of safety concerns. The air force hoped to name the base after one of its fallen heroes, but the community rejected the proposed names. The air force acquiesced to appease local residents. When Colonel Einar Malmstrom died in an airplane crash at the base, military and civic leaders reached a consensus. The community in Great Falls had great respect for Malmstrom, who served as the deputy commander for the Strategic Air Command (SAC) at the base. Malmstrom was a war hero, having downed six and a half enemy aircraft during World War II. He even donated a number of rare Scandinavian books to the local library. The chamber of commerce, Rotary Club, and city administration enthusiastically supported the name "Malmstrom Air Force Base."[37]

While Ellsworth and Malmstrom AFBs continued to grow and contribute financially to their local communities, a number of other cities hoped to attract an air force base to their area. The growing tension of the Cold War led to speculation across the northern plains that the air force needed to establish new fighter and bomber bases to meet the growing Soviet threat. The *Bismarck Capital* revealed in 1951 that North Dakota senator Milton Young had orchestrated a survey of existing airport facilities, passing the information to the air force in hopes of bringing a base to North Dakota. When officials responded with interest, it sparked a controversy within the state. Communities maneuvered to locate a base in their vicinity. Several cities, including Jamestown, Bismarck, Minot, Williston, and Wahpeton, contacted their political officials to seek information, while Fargo's mayor traveled to Washington, D.C., to discuss plans with military leaders.[38]

Air force officials were not interested in building new bases in 1951, but the same rumor mill that predicted new bases in North Dakota also fed speculation in Montana. H. O. Morgan, the secretary of the Glasgow Chamber of Commerce, wrote to the commander of the Strategic Air Command in Omaha, Nebraska, citing "persistent rumors that a jet fighter base will be established in western North Dakota or eastern Montana."[39] Morgan asked if there was any truth to the rumors: if so, he wanted to recommend Glasgow as an ideal community to host a base. It only needed to reactivate the abandoned facility just outside of town. The military forwarded the letter to Senator Murray, who had conducted inquiries "about the many rumors circulating in the cities of Glasgow and Lewistown, about such a proposed air base."[40] The military had no plans to build or refurbish air bases on the northern plains, the senator informed Morgan.[41]

Talk of the new base spread through the plains in eastern Montana and caught the attention of a particularly resilient lawyer named F. P. Holbrook, who wrote to his political representatives and the secretary of the air force endorsing Sidney, Montana, as a viable location for the new base. Joining Holbrook in petitioning the political establishment in Washington was E. E. Krebsbach, a business owner in Sidney. "We are very desirous of having the Air Force give this location a thorough consideration," he wrote. "We have a very attractive site for such a base in this area and a great acreage of perfectly level land in this section."[42] The air force saw it differently, telling both men: "The Department of the Air Force is not cognizant of any plan concerning the construction of a fighter base in the state of Montana at this time."[43]

Rumors also persisted that government officials were looking for a location for the new Air Force Academy, a financial windfall for any city. A number of cities in North Dakota, including Mandan, Minot, Grand Forks, Jamestown, and Devils Lake, all sent letters to North Dakota political leaders and to the Department of the Air Force, expressing their desire to host the academy and listing the numerous attributes of their locations. South Dakota officials in Sioux Falls also worked to bring the academy to their community, sending photos and information to air force authorities. Senator Case, however, seemed to prefer the city of Lakeport, South Dakota, sending the secretary of the air force an informative note, extolling the virtues of the site for the new academy and urging the secretary to endorse the idea.[44]

Civic leaders in Montana were also busy trying to attract the Air Force Academy to their state. The mayor of Ismay, Montana, sent a telegram to the secretary of the air force, requesting due consideration of his community, while the cities of Great Falls and Helena mounted an intensive effort to attract the school to their locations. The mayor of Great Falls, J. B. Austin, wrote to Senator Metcalf, asking for help in attracting the academy. Great Falls, Austin said, "has the greatest flying weather in North America, out of the heat, smog, and smaze, with two of the finest airports in the entire country."[45] The manager of the Great Falls Chamber of Commerce, R. F. Kitchingman, wrote to the air force chief of staff, asking him to intervene with the secretary on behalf of Great Falls. He cited the excellent weather, including harsh winter conditions that would undoubtedly aid in realistic training. Officials in Helena urged their political leaders to attract the academy first to Montana and then to their community, if possible. P. W. Singer of the Helena Chamber of Commerce also contacted the air force secretary, requesting his support.[46]

Only three states in the nation had not made some sort of effort to attract the Air Force Academy to their state. The secretary of the air force, Harold Talbott, formed a committee of five members that included Charles Lindbergh to sort through the long list of recommendations and to propose a site. Colorado proved tough competition in the drive to acquire the academy. The Colorado House of Representatives approved the expenditure of $1 million to purchase land in Colorado Springs, while residents pledged their support to raise additional funds. L. T. Skiffington, who represented Colorado Springs in the Colorado House of Representatives, said that the academy would have 2,600 cadets, an annual payroll of $18 million, and more than 1,200 employees. "It will be a $100,000,000 business a year for Colorado," Skiffington said. The attractive offer influenced the air force committee to select Colorado Springs to host the academy.[47]

While most residents of the northern plains enthusiastically desired an air base in their region, some communities in the Northeast did not share the excitement of having a military base located near them. A city official from Newington, New Hampshire, sent a telegram to Senator Young, who served as the chair of the Senate Military Appropriations Committee, urging him to reconsider the selection of the Newington community for the construction of the Portsmouth-Newington AFB in February 1952. The New Hampshire official, Kingsland Dunwoody, outlined several reasons why the citizens and local government were not interested in a base near their city. First, they knew that the base would lead the Soviets to target the area with nuclear weapons and were not interested in "bringing death and destruction to a heavily populated area."[48] Second, the air force simply announced that it was building the base in the vicinity and did not consult the local residents or respond to their protests. Finally, the air force should be satisfied with the number of air bases already located in the northeast, Dunwoody argued. Senator

Young wrote that New Hampshire state officials had approved the base and that he was reluctant to intervene, although "we in North Dakota would be very happy to have this installation. Anything that you can do to persuade them to move it out there would be appreciated."[49]

Dunwoody had more immediate concerns in his letter to Young than the probability of a Soviet attack. Construction of the base would require the air force to take most of the land of the communities of Newington, Portsmouth, and Greenland, New Hampshire. The cities were distressed with the decision and formed the Regional Citizens Committee, composed of various air base opponents. The effort was small but energetic. Opposition to the base began in earnest in 1951, and the effort delayed construction until 1956. Numerous newspaper articles of the day outlined the frustration of air force officials, who noted that construction was well behind schedule. When the Regional Citizens Committee organized a vote of affected communities, the residents of six towns voted against construction of the base. The enthusiasm of proponents soon obliterated the voices of the opposition. Political figures at the state and national level wanted the base, and some local officials rejoiced at the financial rewards that a base promised. Government officials estimated that for every job created on the base for civilian workers the local communities could expect the creation of one and a half additional jobs. The jobs created by the construction of a base, as well as the economic impact of 6,000 military personnel and their families on the local economy, left little doubt that the base would go through.[50]

Another city with a small but fervent opposition to a new air base was Plattsburgh, New York. Major resistance came from the student body of Champlain College, which had only opened its doors in 1946 in response to the massive number of veterans returning home to pursue a degree. Facilities for the new college consisted of the former Plattsburgh Barracks, a military base deactivated in 1944 and considered surplus government property. The New York legislature had created Champlain College on the former military grounds. As the Cold War intensified, military officials wanted the property back to form the foundation of a new base. Although college officials and students objected to the demolition of the college, many in the local community and the state favored the air base. Even college officials favored construction of the base, but only if federal officials spared the college. The objections delayed construction for one year, but the financial rewards were just too enticing. All but the most passionate objections soon disappeared. The final commencement ceremony took place in June 1953, after which the college transferred all its students and resources to colleges around the state.[51]

Financial reward enticed communities nationwide to support the federal government's military strategies. Senator Young got the help he needed to bring an air base to North Dakota from the new president. President Eisenhower was determined to balance national defense requirements with a sound fiscal policy. He and his staff worked throughout 1953 to formulate a new defense strategy and to reduce the military budget, which had ballooned to uncontrollable levels under the Truman administration. He outlined his plan for the military, called the "New Look," in his State of the Union Address on January 7, 1954: "Since our hope is peace, we owe ourselves and the world a candid explanation of the military measures we are taking to make that peace secure."[52] His military policy emphasized a powerful air force and a large stockpile of nuclear weapons in lieu of an expensive conventional military force. This approach necessitated the expansion of many bases, including Ellsworth and Malmstrom AFBs in South Dakota and Montana, and the construction of new bases such as those at Minot and Grand Forks in North Dakota and Glasgow AFB in Montana.

Officials in North Dakota, who worked toward acquiring new air bases in 1951, heard nothing from the air force until November 1953, when officials determined that its new military requirements included an increase in the number of air force units and sent inspectors throughout the state to evaluate existing airports. Air force officials notified North Dakota political leaders on February 25, 1954, that they intended to establish two air force bases in the state. Military engineers initially identified sites in Fargo and Bismarck as the most likely locations for the future bases because of the existing facilities there, contingent upon satisfactory agreements with the local communities.[53]

When news spread that the air force intended to locate two bases within the state, political leaders in Bismarck, Devils Lake, Fargo, Grand Forks, Jamestown, Minot, Valley City, and Washburn all asked their congressional representatives to petition the air force and secure a base near their community. Most of these cities even sent delegations to Washington to press their cases, with Senator Young making the necessary introductions. When officials in Minot wrote to Young seeking his assistance in securing an air base for their city, he wrote back that the air force was not considering Minot as a possible location and reiterated his stance of strict neutrality in the site selection.[54]

The competition to attract bases continued among the different communities, even though air force officials said that Fargo and Bismarck appeared to have the best chance of securing the bases by expanding their existing facilities. Competition increased when Fargo and Bismarck announced that they were having difficulty donating the required land to strengthen their cases. Donating land was not required to secure an air base but certainly made the community more attractive to the military. Other communities, specifically Grand Forks and Minot, had no such problems and let officials know their position. Grand Forks and Minot each raised approximately $65,000 and purchased almost one thousand acres for each base. Each community would donate the land free of charge should the air force decide to build bases there. Adjacent to these parcels of land were thousands of acres that the air force could purchase at an attractive price.[55]

Air force officials announced on June 11, 1954, that they had an obligation to taxpayers to construct the bases at the lowest possible cost. "When two or more locations existed within the area of requirement," they said, "other factors become important, such as the availability of land at little or no cost."[56] Five days later air force officials said that the new bases would be located in Minot and Grand Forks, not Fargo and Bismarck as initially announced. In the disappointment and confusion that followed, citizens demanded clarification. Military authorities acknowledged that they had originally considered the existing facilities at Fargo and Bismarck but admitted that these sites were only marginally acceptable, presenting little opportunity for expansion. Additionally, Brigadier General Joe Kelly argued that these locations were too far south to engage enemy aircraft effectively. This was an illogical contention: the air force had bases far to the south of those proposed for Bismarck and Fargo, in South Dakota and even Texas, for example. Kelly maintained that while donating land had helped their case, it was not the overriding factor in selecting Minot and Grand Forks.[57]

The rejected communities experienced a tremendous amount of frustration. Early in the competition for bases several local officials had charged Senator Young with favoring Fargo over the other cities, an allegation that he vehemently denied. Accusations of favoritism by both winning and losing communities arose again after the Minot and Grand Forks announcement. Young noted his frustration in response to a blistering telegram that he received from an official in Minot who believed that his community got the base in spite of Young working against them. "The many mean telegrams such as yours that I have received from both sides, including Fargo, Bismarck, Devils Lake, Grand Forks, and Minot, present a difficult situation," Young wrote. "I am sure when all the facts are known you will want to apologize for your telegram."[58] Young wrote to one constituent: "I certainly have been right in the middle of a bad situation which was misunderstood by practically everyone. I have received some mean letters from almost every city in North Dakota."[59] One of those mean letters came from Guy Larson in Bismarck, prompting Young to respond: "I do not blame you one bit for being disturbed about the Air Force handling of the jet air base deal. It was the worst job of public relations that has ever come to my attention and I have so advised the Air Force officials here."[60]

The press release announcing that the air force would construct bases at Minot and Grand Forks, North Dakota, included a statement that it would also build a base near Glasgow, Montana. Unlike North Dakotans, most people in Montana knew that the air force would probably reactivate one of the older air bases used during the war if it needed another air base within the state. It was cheaper to reactivate and expand an existing facility than to start from scratch. But other communities could still try to divert an air base to their location.[61]

Cut Bank, Lewistown, and Glasgow clearly had an edge in attracting the air base that the military had announced it needed in Montana. Glasgow had an advantage over the other bases in that the military officials had inspected the base there and recommended that the air force use those facilities. Members of the Miles City Trades and Labor Council wrote to Senator Murray, however, urging him to intervene on behalf of their town. Miles City, the union members asserted, had a more pressing need economically than Glasgow did. Industrial layoffs in railroad shops and the drop in construction activity had left many skilled workers unemployed. Union members claimed that these workers could better serve the state and the nation by building a new air base in Miles City than

The pilot (*left*) and radar operator (*right*) of a jet fighter preparing to take off on an intercept mission at Glasgow Air Force Base. Crews practice "shooting down" bombers and targeting jet planes by radar. No date given. Courtesy Montana Historical Society Research Center Photograph Archives, Helena, Montana.

by sitting by idly, waiting for work. Murray forwarded the request to the secretary of the air force, without any enthusiasm for the proposal.[62]

Senators Murray and Mansfield knew that attracting an air base was good for Montana, regardless of where it went in the state. They also knew that the existing facilities at the former bomber bases represented the best possible chance of attracting an air base, so they publicly and privately endorsed them. Once they were certain that the air force intended to select Glasgow as a definite air base site, they began pushing to reactivate the bases at Cut Bank and Lewistown. The air force needed "back stop strength" in the state, residents argued. The air force was not interested in additional bases but promised to consider the idea should the need arise.[63]

While the senators were endorsing Glasgow and the other sites for the new air base, the cities of Glendive and Sidney were asking their congressional leaders for help in acquiring the base. Murray and Mansfield were Democrats, and Republican representative Wesley A. D'Ewart sensed political dividends if he could undercut the Democrats and please constituents elsewhere. D'Ewart endorsed Miles City as the best site within the state, and to a lesser degree Sidney and Glendive. The air force had all but officially selected Glasgow as the site of the next air base in Montana, but many communities held out hope that they could somehow manage to lure it away.[64]

Glasgow was not sitting by idly, waiting for the air force to change its mind or allow another city to acquire the base. Political leaders and members of the Glasgow Chamber of Commerce immediately set aside $8,000 and hired a full-time manager to work on the housing situation. The city needed a massive amount of housing to meet the demands of the service members and their families and began construction projects before the air force officially announced that Glasgow was the site of the new air base. The Glasgow community soon turned the $8,000 into $32,000 through public subscription and promised the air force that the community would purchase all of the required land and donate it for the base. Glasgow's work paid off. The secretary of the air force officially notified the congressional delegation from Montana on June 17, 1954, that Glasgow was the site of the next air base within the state. When engineers finished construction in 1960, the base hosted long-range bombers, a fighter-intercept squadron, and refueling capabilities.[65]

Air force officials announced in early 1955 that it would expand the facilities at Ellsworth AFB because of Eisenhower's new military strategy. Improvements included new hangars, runways, and utilities with contracts exceeding $20 million, to make way for the new B-52 bombers beginning to roll off assembly lines in large numbers. The last B-36 left Ellsworth on May 29, 1957, with the first B-52 arriving sixteen days later. Malmstrom continued its role as a fighter base, ready to defend the continental United States from attack or escort long-range bombers to their targets.[66]

South Dakota political leaders continued to court the air force, hoping to bring another military base to their state. Senator Case was particularly resilient in this regard, working to bring a satellite base to the airfield in Mitchell, South Dakota, used as a bomber base during World War II. The federal budget precluded a complete air base, but a satellite base (used to disperse aircraft away from the major base at Ellsworth) was another matter. Case announced on June 26, 1956, that the Senate Armed Services Committee had allocated over $6 million for the construction of Mitchell AFB in the southeastern portion of the state, which would contain approximately fifteen of the new B-52 bombers, their flight crews, and support personnel. Military officials planned to begin construction in 1958.[67]

The months between Senate approval and the anticipated beginning of the construction project were intense. Air force administrators visited the location numerous times, and local officials did everything they could to allay any fears or problems. Citizens and government representatives knew that something could go wrong until bombers were landing at the airfield and service members were purchasing their goods locally, but there seemed little reason for concern. Senate committees and air force officials were satisfied with the location, and the money seemed readily available to build it.[68]

While state and local officials attempted to finalize plans to bring the bomber base to Mitchell, a number of other communities worked to steal the base and bring it to their own community, including Aberdeen, Bowdle, Britton, Huron, Lemmon, Pierre, Plankinton, Platte, Provo, Roslyn, and Yankton, South Dakota. Each of these cities wrote to Senator Case, requesting information and assistance to redirect the location of the base destined for Mitchell, claiming to have better facilities than Mitchell did or better reasons for having the base. Perhaps the most interesting attempt to acquire the base came from the mayor of Bismarck, North Dakota, Evan Lips.

Lips wrote to Senator Young in North Dakota, suggesting that the Mitchell community really did not want the air base, referring to a small number of local farmers who expressed their opposition to the base, and suggested that the air force could acquire land far more inexpensively around Bismarck than in Mitchell. Lips argued that the air force had pulled a dirty trick by not giving Bismarck the air base that it had promised several years before. Hence the community deserved the facility. Young responded quite diplomatically, pointing out that Senator Case had worked for years to bring an air base to Mitchell and that crossing the two South Dakota senators and two representatives might not be a wise move. "I would be very reluctant to incur their ill will," Young remarked, "by attempting to take a base away from them which had already been located in their state."[69]

Even so, the base at Mitchell proved more elusive than originally thought. The community, the air force, and the Senate all agreed that the

An air policeman (*left*) guarding SAC aircraft and maintenance support (*right*) at Glasgow Air Force Base. No date given. Courtesy Montana Historical Society Research Center Photograph Archives, Helena, Montana.

base was a good idea, but the federal budget simply could not support the proposal. Congress cut the air force budget for 1958, reducing the $23 billion budget to only $17 billion. Under such a dramatic reduction, the air force anticipated closing six bases throughout the United States and halting or canceling construction on other bases. Many local and federal authorities held out hope that Washington had merely postponed and not canceled the project, but authorities never seriously considered the base again.[70]

The situation with the federal budget did not improve in the 1960s; it got worse, especially as the nation's commitment in Vietnam increased. The air force announced the closure of Glasgow Air Force Base, Montana, on November 19, 1964, due to budget considerations. Officials planned to transfer all aircraft and personnel to other bases and cease all operations by June 30, 1968. The air force could transfer the planes to bases where it had like-model aircraft, saving the cost of running another base. The air force also cited the weather in Montana as a consideration. Snowstorms hampered operations and added expenses, and heated hangars were not available. Probably the most important reason that the air force cited for the closure was the Glasgow site's remoteness, far from any cities of significant size and without sufficient housing for military families.[71]

The announcement stunned the local population. The base had only been operational for four years when the air force made the announcement, and the government had invested almost $89 million in buildings, runways, and infrastructure improvements. Glasgow resident Ruben Sinclair doubted the reasons that the air force cited for closing the base and wrote to air force officials to protest the decision. The weather, he argued, was not a factor, for "it is an official fact that Glasgow Air Force Base has the best flying record of any SAC base." He also noted that it was not wise to train military personnel under the most favorable weather conditions because modern militaries did not always fight wars in favorable situations. He also challenged the claim that housing was a problem, noting that the city of Glasgow had over four hundred vacant houses or apartments at the time he wrote his letter.[72]

James Campbell of Glasgow wrote directly to secretary of defense Robert McNamara to protest the decision as well. "The Mountain States Telephone Company, the Great Northern Railroad, the Montana-Dakota Utilities, and the Montana Power Company all had to invest a lot of money to serve the base," he argued. An oil refinery had borrowed money to enlarge operations on the strength of a ten-year contract to serve the base, and housing, schools, and businesses had expanded to serve the military needs. "This is one of our newest bases, one of the most modern, and I think we should keep it in operation," he concluded.[73]

Even Paul Harvey, in his syndicated newspaper column, questioned the wisdom of closing down the base. "You and I sowed a hundred million dollars on the prairies of Montana," he wrote. "Now, before the crop has matured, Uncle Sam wants to plow it under." He continued: "if we are now plowing under, vacating, abandoning, our nation's newest and most modern SAC base, either the war [Vietnam War] is over or somebody goofed!" The citizens of Glasgow did not intend to let the base close without a fight and organized their meager forces to do battle with the government.[74]

The Glasgow United Community Committee asked the Montana Department of the American Legion to lead the way in urging Congress to launch an investigation of the Defense Department's decision to close the base, while Montana's congressional body urged McNamara to reconsider his decision. The data that he used to reach his decision, they argued, were outdated. Glasgow did not have a housing problem and had good flying weather 94.7 percent of the time. But the effort was futile. The escalating effort in Vietnam was draining the Defense Department budget to the point that McNamara identified ninety-five bases in the United States and overseas to scale back or close due to budgetary restrictions.[75]

While the base at Glasgow, Montana, closed on schedule, the other bases on the northern plains remain open and functioning. Citizens and politicians recognized the benefits that a military base had brought to their state. Though they were quick to denounce most federal intrusion upon their states, federal spending and largesse was another matter. Early political leaders such as Young, Case, Murray, Mansfield, and Metcalf understood this and worked diligently to bring and keep military bases in the region for economic reasons.

States on the northern plains have long depended upon the federal government for financial support and still do. Every time the Base Realignment and Closure (BRAC) committee meets, communities on the northern plains collectively cringe, hoping that the committee has not targeted their base for closure. The addition of a military base near a remote community is often a financial windfall for these areas, and people are reluctant to give up those federal dollars once obtained. During the Cold War even the possibility of a military base near a community often encouraged civic leaders to pull every political string available to divert a military base from one region to another. People wanted desperately to attract an air base to their proximity. They demonstrated that financial rewards far outweighed any civil defense considerations during the Cold War. This approach allowed citizens and state representatives to offer patriotic support in the federal government's battle against communism while enjoying significant financial benefits as a means to prop up the state economies. Other military opportunities with financial incentives soon presented themselves to the northern plains, as outlined in the next two chapters.

Chapter 8

Missiles on the Plains

"The Minuteman missile program is the darndest thing to hit Montana since they found copper in Butte Hill. Or maybe even in the history of the Treasure State," said Murray M. Moler in a 1960 issue of the *Great Falls Tribune*. "The impact, figuratively, of the program on the state will be tremendous, economically, socially, and physically." Moler acknowledged that the Minuteman missile project would bring approximately 4,600 jobs and a total expenditure within the state of $79 million, plus millions more in salaries. The farmers selling pieces of their land could count on considerable dislocation, but the project included improved roads and electrical service in rural areas. Air force officials planned more missile projects in South Dakota and North Dakota as well.[1]

Residents on the northern plains knew that the financial rewards associated with the missile project were based on having state residents find employment constructing the missile silos. Moler's hyperbole notwithstanding, prosperity would only last as long as the thousands of construction workers had jobs. The missile crews were small and lived on or close to the main air force base, negating any significant benefit to the state economy once the project was over. Farmers and ranchers could only hope to make a fair profit from the sale of a few acres of land that the military might need for the silos or launch facilities. Residents on the northern Great Plains looked forward to the benefits that the Minuteman project provided and embraced this project conceived at the federal level and implemented throughout the several states.[2]

Nuclear-tipped missiles were a fantasy when Dr. Robert Goddard began his work. Goddard, an American physicist at Clark University in Wooster, Massachusetts, was the inventor of the modern rocket. He began experimenting with liquid and solid fuels. By 1914 his work had progressed to the point that the American government awarded him patents for his many technological innovations. Goddard continued to refine his experiments and launched the first successful liquid-fueled rocket in 1926. He established a research facility near Roswell, New Mexico, in 1930, though the American government was not interested in rockets until after World War II.[3]

Goddard was not the only scientist experimenting with rockets. Germany had a highly successful program as well. Germans first built the "flying bomb" or V-1 rocket in 1935, a rocket with wings that catapulted from a platform. Its guidance system was wildly inaccurate: only 31 percent of all attempts landed within fifteen miles of a target. The Germans followed up this first attempt with the V-2 rocket, a supersonic missile completely redesigned. The V-2 reached an altitude of sixty miles above the earth's surface, and the guidance system disengaged at the apogee of its flight. This rocket was only slightly more accurate than its predecessor, as glide and gravity simply carried the rocket the rest of the way to its target. The real genius of the V-2 was not its guidance system but its engines.[4]

German scientists helped boost American missile research and development after the war. By 1950 both the army and the air force had active missile programs. The army concentrated on air defense, while the air force was more interested in strategic bomber fleets than in missiles. NSC-68 changed that. This review of American capabilities and Communist intentions by the National Security Council sparked President Truman's interest in improved military capability. The massive defense spending that such a vision evoked meant that the air force could have both bombers and missiles. In July 1951 improved guidance and propulsion systems made inter-continental ballistic missiles (ICBMs) feasible. Additionally, the advent of thermonuclear weapons, at once both lighter and more powerful than the original atomic bombs dropped on Hiroshima and Nagasaki, solved major problems with payload. The new weapons were light enough and powerful enough to enable workable designs. Many air force officers viewed the developments with disdain, feeling that air force officers flew fighters and bombers but did not launch missiles. President Eisenhower put intense pressure on the generals to accelerate ICBM development.[5]

While missile advocates continued to discuss the strategic importance of ICBMs, a new study in 1955 outlined what many thought the Soviets were doing: building intermediate-range ballistic missiles (IRBMs). The IRBMs only had a range of five hundred miles, but many scientists believed that they were easier to build. If the Soviets had them, they could intimidate American allies. When the Soviets launched *Sputnik*, the world's first artificial satellite, uncertainty swept the United States. Most Americans had assumed that the United States was the richest and most powerful nation in the world, blessed with the best-educated and advanced scientists. In an instant *Sputnik* swept away this illusion and brought a new dimension to the Cold War, terrifying American government and military officials. A missile that could launch a satellite into space could surely carry a nuclear warhead to the United States. Khrushchev's claim that the Soviet Union turned out nuclear weapons "like sausages" did little to alleviate these fears. What American planners did not know was that the Soviet Union had only six long-range nuclear missiles even as late as 1964 and only fifty intermediate range missiles as late as 1962. As Khrushchev's son Sergei observed, "We threatened with missiles we didn't have."[6]

The "missile gap" was front-page news all over the country. Politicians, the air force, and the aircraft industry all used the news for their own ends, giving rise to what Eisenhower termed the "Military Industrial Complex." The rhetoric did not fool Eisenhower, for he knew from classified U-2 photographs that there was no missile gap. He could not use the pictures to bolster his position because the U-2 project was highly classified. Neither the United States nor the Soviet Union wished to publicize that the United States was violating international law with the overflights. Khrushchev's bluster and political expediency led John F. Kennedy to rally against the "missile gap" that he believed had developed under the Eisenhower administration. Only after taking office did Kennedy learn the truth; the United States was far ahead of the Soviets on long-range missile construction.[7]

The military had many versions of the ICBM, which all had an inherent problem: the older, liquid-fueled weapons tended to explode prior to launch. The air force eventually solved the problems associated with older-generation missiles, designing a new and smaller missile that used solid fuel and carried a thermonuclear warhead, called the Minuteman.

The air force selected Boeing Airplane Company of Seattle, Washington, as the Minuteman assembly and test contractor in 1959, and construction proceeded rapidly. The Minuteman was a clear improvement over previous missiles. It required only a crew of two to work in launch control facilities for every ten unmanned silos, the hardened structures could withstand a close nuclear blast, and the missiles required a minimum of maintenance and support equipment.[8]

The first full test was a complete success in 1961, though in 1962 officials had to destroy a missile in flight that veered off course and headed for the Florida mainland. Most of these malfunctions were presumably fixed by 1966, when the Strategic Air Command's arsenal stood at eight hundred Minuteman I missiles. The Minuteman eventually came in three operational configurations. The earliest model, Minuteman I, was the first-generation missile; the Minuteman II had an improved engine; and the Minuteman III carried more than one warhead (Multiple Independent Reentry Vehicle [MIRV]). Ten missiles made up a flight, controlled by one launch facility; five flights made up a missile squadron; and three squadrons composed a wing. Each air base had a total of 150 missiles and fifteen launch facilities. Robert McNamara fixed the ICBM numbers at a thousand Minuteman missiles in 1966, plus 54 Titan IIs under construction, a level that remained unchanged for twenty-five years.[9]

The effective range of the missiles determined the first deployment, as a flaw in the first stage of the missile's propulsion system reduced the flight from 6,300 miles to 4,300 miles. Originally supposed to deploy to Vandenburg Air Force Base (AFB) in California, this flight limitation dictated that the first missiles would go to Malmstrom AFB in Montana. It might take six months to a year for engineers to fix the engine problem. Deploying the missiles in Montana also had some advantages. Montana was closer to Soviet targets, and its elevation gave the missiles added range. Other factors also influenced the decision to deploy the missiles to Montana: Montana was out of range of Soviet submarine-launched missiles and missile sites should utilize existing air force facilities, preferably close to communities with populations of fifty thousand or more.[10]

The required space to locate the missiles also indicated that the northern plains were well suited for sites. Each missile required a number of

Deployment of Minuteman missiles on the Great Plains. At the height of the Cold War bases were located in Montana, South Dakota, North Dakota, Wyoming, Nebraska, Colorado, and Missouri. Inland locations in sparsely populated areas were ideal for very large bases that would be targets for enemy missiles. Map by Bill Nelson. Courtesy National Museum of the Air Force, Wright-Patterson Air Force Base, Ohio.

miles of separation to ensure that one Soviet blast could not destroy more than one missile. The hundreds of proposed silos required thousands of square miles to meet such a directive. Additionally, the plains were sparsely populated, making it easier to find available land for the project and reducing the likely number of casualties in the event that the Soviets tried to destroy the American missiles. If the Soviets did try to take out the missile fields, they would have to launch a missile at each silo. As the authors of the anti–nuclear weapon journal *Nuclear Heartland* pointed out, the Great Plains would serve as a "sponge" to "soak up" enemy warheads.[11]

Once officials selected Malmstrom as the first Minuteman missile site in December 1959, the newly formed Corps of Engineers Ballistic Missile Construction Office began designing the fifteen control sites and 150 Minuteman I silos intended to dot the northern plains in Montana. Simultaneously, the Seattle District of the Corps of Engineers began site feasibility studies, surveys, soil and foundation investigations, electrical surveys, and land acquisition. The most difficult task was obtaining land, 5,200 tracts scattered across central Montana, totaling 20,000 square miles. This was the single largest project that the Corps of Engineers had ever attempted. At its peak the corps employed up to eighty people at its real estate office, negotiating contracts with approximately 1,400 landowners. Design modifications and other changes required the corps to renegotiate easements with the landowners on twelve different occasions over the four-year project.[12]

In most cases the Corps of Engineers simply negotiated contracts to purchase tracts of land from the owners, but in less than 3 percent of the cases it acquired land by condemnation. Landowners wanted a fair price for their parcels of land, but the government offers were often exceedingly low and did not compensate owners for their inconvenience. This scenario upset many of the landowners as the project started, but other situations tested the patience of landowners. Construction crews cut fences, left trenches open in cattle pastures, destroyed crops, and interrupted water and power supplies. Despite the array of problems, patriotic sentiment ran deep in the region, so the local population generally cooperated with the government officials.[13]

The Corps of Engineers began construction of the first Minuteman launch facility around Malmstrom AFB in March 1961, but early complications surfaced, threatening the economic benefits to the state. Montana workers and construction firms accused the primary silo build-ing contractor, Fuller-Webb, of hiring too many workers from outside the state and awarding too many subcontracts to outside firms. Repre-sentative James Battin suggested that a congressional investigation might examine contract-awarding practices. The company replied that it was not the least bit worried.[14] The wound was even deeper because the lieu-tenant governor, Tim Babcock, had predicted just weeks before the con-troversy that he anticipated "a tremendous boost for Montana's economy if Montana firms and labor are used." Furthermore, "it was essential that employment, equipment, and supplies went to Montana workers in every possible instance."[15] A construction firm from outside the state, handing out subcontracts to other out-of-state firms, was exactly what Montana officials did not want.

The controversy prompted Montana governor Donald Nutter to meet privately with military and contracting officials to find out more about the employment and contracting practices for the Minuteman project. He was dissatisfied with the answers that he received and arranged a public hearing. At the public session Nutter and Battin questioned rep-resentatives of Fuller-Webb about their practices, while the military and state labor unions defended their procedures. Some of the specific com-plaints suggested that Fuller-Webb was simply a broker for construc-tion and did not perform any of the work itself. Other complaints came from nonunion workers, who claimed that the company hired them in order to meet quotas then quickly fired them and brought in out-of-state unionized workers. The governor also remarked that he was interested in this project if it brought a big payroll to Montana, as the contractors said it would. "But what I want to guard against," he added, "is that at the end of this project, we might find that Montanans have not benefited appreciably and that we will be left with many additional people on our relief rolls."[16]

The meeting with Fuller-Webb reassured Nutter that the company's performance was above reproach. He was satisfied with the answers he received in the public forum. "I have been assured by representatives of the contractors that they are making full use of Montana labor," he said. "I also have been assured that full use of the Montana Employment Service is being made for those jobs not coming under the jurisdiction of labor unions. If they are doing those things, I am satisfied."[17] A review in 1962 indicated that some 41 percent of workers throughout the project were from Montana, but the implications were clear. Montana was interested in the project primarily for the economic benefit that the Minuteman missiles brought to the state.[18]

The first Minuteman ICBM arrived by rail on July 23, 1962, and the first silo was operational four days later. As silos became operational throughout the fall, they played a significant role in the Cuban Missile Crisis. A number of silos went on strategic alert, one at a time, until all ten functional missiles of the first flight awaited launch orders as tension increased. According to the official website of Malmstrom AFB, the operational status of those few missiles in Montana may have played a decisive role in the crisis: President Kennedy knew he had an "ace in the hole" (or silo). The Minuteman could launch within seconds of notification, while the older generation of nuclear missiles required hours of preparation and maintenance preceding launch. Contractors continued building the missile silos after the missile crisis. By July 1963, after twenty-eight months of construction, contractors had completed all 150 silos and launch control centers at a cost of $70.7 million. Six men had been killed in construction accidents.[19]

Only thirteen months after completing the first Minuteman project, air force officials decided to deploy 50 more missiles to the Malmstrom area, this time emplacing the Minuteman II. Contractors began work in 1965, continued through the following year, and finished in May 1967, when the air force declared the final missiles operational. Two years later the air force replaced the original 150 missiles with the Minuteman II type. Throughout the rest of the Cold War, Montana silos contained 200 nuclear missiles centered on Malmstrom AFB in a missile field covering 12 percent of the state.[20]

Montana's missile program served as the blueprint for other system deployments. South Dakota's Ellsworth Air Force Base also received a number of ICBMs, although initially they were the earlier generation Atlas and Titan missiles that used liquid fuel. Fully aware that the Titan and Atlas missiles were obsolete, the air force began building Minuteman I silos throughout South Dakota in August 1961. Again the project called for building 150 silos and fifteen launch control facilities around Ellsworth AFB. When operational Minuteman missiles became available,

A launch control facility under construction near Malmstrom Air Force Base, Montana. Cold War requirements to build up U.S. nuclear defenses hastened Minuteman site construction. Builders often labored year-round in three shifts, seven days a week. The Army Corps of Engineers Ballistic Missile Construction Office and its contractors built 1,000 silos between 1961 and 1966. Courtesy National Museum of the Air Force, Wright-Patterson Air Force Base, Ohio.

air force contractors replaced the Titan and Atlas missiles with the Minuteman. In April 1963 technicians put the first Minuteman missile into a silo. Two months later the first flight of missiles became operational. The entire complement of 150 became operational by 1965, at a cost of $75.7 million and two fatalities.[21]

It is unclear if this price was reasonable. The Preparedness Investigating Subcommittee, a congressional body responsible for documenting military readiness and defense spending, revealed in June 1962 that cost overruns of $225 million occurred over the last year at Titan and Atlas missile sites in South Dakota. While the government investigated reasons behind the expense, investigative reporter Bob Lee of the *Sturgis Tribune* had the answer, which included an unprecedented waste of taxpayer money. Lee's report, released in September 1962, detailed a number of issues, including the labor union practice of refusing work to anyone that did not apply for union membership. Once they were in the union, lax supervision of work practices was the norm. A supervisor told one worker, George Levin, to "look busy" whenever a stranger came around the site, while a night shift worker was told to sleep if he wanted: the supervisor would call him if necessary. Workers on the Minuteman sites were all paid additional money for travel expenses, whether the worker participated in a car pool or drove separately. Most contracts, Lee learned, were operated on a cost-plus basis, meaning that labor was an added expense that the contractor could pass on to the government, with little incentive to control those costs.[22]

Although few South Dakotans actually saw the crews at work, their earliest memories of the missiles involved the construction companies. Ted Hustead, the owner of Wall Drug in Wall, South Dakota, recalled that his father used to open the business at 4:30 A.M. to pack lunches and fix breakfast for the construction crews. Later, when their shifts were over, the crews used to come back to drink beer in the bar. This was a good business for Wall Drug, although the overall economic impact was small outside of Rapid City. For the most part, Hustead recalls, the crews and the local communities did not interact much. The workers came for a short time (eighteen months from the start of the construction project until it was complete) and then moved on. Hustead remembered children of the workers that moved into the area and admitted that he had a crush on one or two of the girls.[23]

Other South Dakotans' first impression of the missile project was not overly positive. The Corps of Engineers came to negotiate for the land necessary to emplace the missiles and contributed to the negative connotations associated with the missile construction. While most South Dakotans outside Rapid City did not anticipate an economic boost, landowners hoped that officials would offer them reasonable prices for their land. This was not always the case. The engineers consulted a map, noted the precise locations that they wanted to buy, and then contacted the farmers or ranchers. According to Gene S. Williams, a farmer in western South Dakota, there was quite a discrepancy among prices offered to various landowners, with the government negotiators trying to get the land for the cheapest price possible. The real controversy started when the contractors insisted that a missile silo had to go in the middle of a farmer's field, as happened to the Williams family. Williams's father even offered to donate land closer to the road if they would move the proposed location, only to find that air force officials insisted on the location and took the land by eminent domain. An obstacle like this severely impeded farming operations in the area, but such arguments met with little sympathy from the government.[24]

Historian Gretchen Heefner addresses the intractable air force position of siting missiles wherever it wanted and the paltry sums offered to farmers and ranchers in her book *The Missile Next Door*. She points out that the ranchers were patriotic and often would have donated land for the missile silos if only they had a say in their placement. Air force officials invariably were inflexible as to their emplacement. In frustration the ranchers in South Dakota created the Missile Area Landowners Association (MALA) in 1961, whose purpose was to band together in hopes of forcing the government to negotiate on the issues. Hundreds of farmers, ranchers, and other concerned citizens began meeting to discuss the situation. Dozens refused to sign over the ground, forcing the government to sue in court, where a fair price was determined by a judge, not the Corps of Engineers.[25]

The problem, as the air force engineers saw it, was that missile silos had to be located a certain distance from each other, often restricting where certain silos could go. In such instances the government paid nothing extra for the owner's inconvenience. In the case of roughly 15 of the 150 silos, the landowner went to court and often won an increased sum. According to Williams, that sum was $1,500 in 1961. One member of the MALA even suggested that ranchers would settle their cases for the cost of a trial. That seemed the most reasonable alternative, though the government did not pursue this compromise. The group was loosely organized, and court decisions often had little influence in changing negotiation practices.[26]

The silos had other problems as well. A tremendous amount of cable ran from each silo to a Launch Control Facility, and the government simply informed landowners that they intended to lay cable through their fields and did not compensate owners for this. But the most aggravating issue was that crews ran the cable and then left gates open so that cows got out or did not properly fill in holes, so that cattle fell into them, injuring themselves. At other times helicopter crews flew over farms, scaring the newly weaned calves. As Williams recalls, "they are basically about as scared as kitties, and if you have a helicopter fly over a couple hundred freshly weaned calves, you'll find out just how many fences you can fix in short order."[27]

Aside from these issues, most people recall that the silos brought a number of benefits. For example, the electrical lines that supplied the silos also offered increased power to local farms. The government paid to maintain the roads to the silos that local inhabitants also used, which was a great asset in areas that did not have gravel readily available. Perhaps most importantly, South Dakotans recalled the amiable relationships between missile crew members and themselves. One South Dakotan recalled that his mother brought iced tea to air force personnel when it got extremely warm outside. Others recalled that motorists would stop to check on air force crews on the side of the road, to ensure that their vehicle had not broken down. Some service members recalled helping a rancher fix a fence: the rancher invited them out to go hunting on his property. Lieutenant Colonel Andy Knight formed a more lasting relationship with western South Dakota when he met his wife in Rapid City. "My wife is a fourth generation Rapid Citian," he recalls, "so when it came time to retire, there was no question where we were coming back to."[28]

North Dakota, often jokingly referred to as the third most powerful nuclear state in the world, became home to some 300 missile silos located throughout the state: Grand Forks and Minot Air Force Bases controlled 150 silos each. The government began the project in 1961 at Minot AFB, completed it in 1966 at Grand Forks AFB, and experienced many of the same problems as in Montana and South Dakota, but to a lesser extent. Senator Milton Young also cited the great economic boost to the state as the project's greatest benefit. North Dakota had two separate missile fields going into the state and expected to reap the financial rewards. The difference between North Dakota and the other states was that political leaders never got as territorial regarding the number of North Dakotans that the project employed or experienced the amount of dissatisfaction with the Corps of Engineers' purchase of land from the farmers and ranchers.[29]

The project was not without its disgruntled local population, however. Gilbert F. Petersen, one of the owners of North Central Engineering

Consultants, wrote to Senator Young, asking his assistance to bid on some of the subcontracting work on the missile silos. Out-of-state businesses received the bulk of the contracts, he argued, and "it is hard for us to believe that the engineers and architects from North Dakota are not as capable and qualified as engineers and architects from other states." Young wrote back that he had discussed the possibility of using North Dakota firms with the primary contractor, who agreed that it was a good idea. Young did not wish to stir up controversy over the employment issue but would help where he could.[30] Perhaps politicians in Montana were more cognizant of the benefits associated with the construction process or less concerned with the laborers.

Clayton Cudmore wrote to Senator Young, expressing concern over the number of out-of-state truck drivers hauling gravel for the missile project. Additionally, Cudmore charged, "local truckers are denied jobs or laid off after a few days."[31] Young made some inquiries with the air force and the contractors and discovered that most of the trucking firms hauling gravel were from North Dakota, as were most of the drivers. The out-of-state drivers were from Minnesota but were covered under the local union and therefore considered local. George Chaput applied for work several times through the local union, which told him that no work was available. Out of desperation and frustration, he wrote to Senator Young, complaining about the number of out-of-state laborers. Young wrote back, encouraging Chaput to continue to work through the union. As for the number of out-of-state laborers, Young could do nothing about it: "there is no way to keep people from outside of North Dakota from moving into the state and applying for this work."[32]

Young did try to assist farmers with issues arising from the missile project. Melvin Petersen of Devils Lake had a problem with the cable installation through his farm. He claimed that the cable installation cut his hay field in half, making it impossible to bale and necessitating the sale of cattle he could not feed. The Corps of Engineers offered $480 to compensate Petersen for the losses he incurred, which he called "peanuts." The Corps of Engineers countered that Petersen had simply abandoned his field, not turning the hay or baling it and allowing it to spoil, and charged that it was impossible to negotiate with him. The corps recommended condemnation and paid Petersen $400.[33] Another farmer who ran into problems negotiating the sale of his land to the air force was

Ernest Johnson of Dazey, North Dakota, who informed Senator Young that engineers had conducted soil samples on his farm and seemed satisfied with the results. For some unexplained reason, Johnson complained, the air force decided to use the land of "a very influential neighbor" located nearby, insinuating favoritism in the site selection.[34]

Simply acquiring land for the missile sites was a tremendous undertaking, but the Corps of Engineers had learned from its experience in Montana and South Dakota. Officials from the Corps of Engineers and the Department of the Air Force published advertisements in regional newspapers announcing their intent to buy land for the missile sites and held public meetings to answer questions throughout the state. Hundreds of people attended these meetings, and the Corps of Engineers handed out 28-page booklets, explaining the reasoning behind the missile construction and site selection, rules for acquiring land, and the rights of individual landowners. North Dakota experienced few cases of condemnation as a result. Once the officials acquired all of the necessary sites, they began construction.[35]

Out-of-state workers and land prices never caused the level of frustration in North Dakota as in other states. North Dakota, however, experienced a liquor store crisis that other states never did. While construction continued on the missile silos, air force representatives announced that Grand Forks AFB was entitled to a liquor store on the base because it was a remote location. The announcement sparked hundreds of letters and telegrams to Senator Young, protesting the decision and imploring him to stop the action. Minot had a government-owned liquor store on the base, they argued, and it severely cut business in town. "Businessmen of this community put up $60,000 to help purchase land for base. Didn't do that to have government go into competition against us," wrote one local businessperson.[36]

Grand Forks got the liquor store despite the outraged citizens, but other concerns aroused little protest. The missile silos were undoubtedly a high-priority target for the Soviets, likely to attract an enormous number of nuclear missiles in the event of war, but few citizens in the region seemed to mind. Kate Stephenson has lived among the nuclear missiles since the air force engineers built them and confirms this assumption. She recalls that she did not have time to worry about the missiles. Her farming family had a lot of work to do, and she was too busy raising

A typical two-man Minuteman I-A launch crew. These crewmen served with the 10th Strategic Missile Squadron, 341st Strategic Missile Wing, Malmstrom Air Force Base, Montana. The 341st was one of six Minuteman wings. Courtesy National Museum of the Air Force, Wright-Patterson Air Force Base, Ohio.

kids and working to worry about nuclear war.[37] Kathy Davison, who grew up in the northeastern portion of the state, puts the issue in simple terms. "Living among the missiles was like living [with the possibility of earthquakes] in California," she recalls. "You always knew that the big one could hit at any time, but you didn't think about moving away."[38]

Tony Ziden, a farmer in Pisek, North Dakota, was more nonchalant: "After you've walked around a barrel of dynamite for twenty years, and it doesn't hurt you, you sort of don't think about it."[39]

Once the construction was complete, the people on the plains largely forgot about the missiles. Nukewatch was an activist organization that led protests against the stationing of missiles on the northern plains. Most people that the activists talked to had no idea that so many missiles dotted the landscape.[40] Missile crews drove or flew from the main base out to the launch sites and had little interaction with the people. For citizens on the northern Great Plains, the missiles meant little but presented two financial opportunities: the possibility of selling land to the government at reasonable prices and working with the construction crews. Either of these possibilities meant the influx of federal dollars into the local economy, and the people living close to the missile project protected these objectives jealously.

International events determined that a number of citizens on the northern plains do not have to worry about missiles anymore. These issues did not affect Montana, but South Dakota, once home to 150 missiles adjacent to the Black Hills, now contains no missiles: the government deactivated them in accordance with the START (Strategic Arms Reduction Talks) Treaty in 1991. The treaty was an agreement between the United States and the Soviet Union to reduce the number of nuclear weapon systems that each country held. President George Herbert Walker Bush ordered hundreds of Minuteman missiles taken off alert status on September 28, 1991. Air force engineers began removing missiles from their silos immediately and continued through 1994. North Dakota once held 300 missiles, but the treaty dictated the removal of 150 missiles near Grand Forks, leaving the 150 missiles near Minot. Government engineers imploded all of the empty silos in North Dakota and South Dakota and graded the rubble, allowing Soviet spy satellites to verify that the United States could not use the silos to launch nuclear missiles. The treaty effectively reduced each nation's nuclear arsenal over a ten-year period by 30 to 40 percent. The National Park Service saved one of the launch control facilities and one missile silo in South Dakota, operating them as a national park and offering guided tours to the public. North Dakota also set aside a missile silo in Cooperstown and turned it into a historic site.[41]

While many people were thrilled with the progress that the treaty made toward eliminating nuclear weapons, the effort did not go far enough for others. Almost from the beginning of the missile age a number of individuals and organizations protested against their construction and deployment, holding rallies and demonstrations to get their message heard. One group in particular, Nukewatch, sponsored a number of antinuclear programs and events, including the publication of several books pointing out the location of the nuclear missile silos and their destructive potential. Most importantly, the leadership of Nukewatch wanted to inform citizens residing on the plains that the silos existed right in their own backyards. Other actions included demonstrations at nuclear missile silos. In some cases activists attempted to destroy sections of the silos. These demonstrations were small and often quickly forgotten.[42]

Even if the citizens on the northern Great Plains did not demonstrate against the construction of missile sites, their presence often called for reflection. Bob Lusk, the publisher of the Huron, South Dakota, newspaper *Daily Plainsman*, described a day in 1962 when he was standing near the town of Hermosa and noticed that to the west stood a huge Titan missile. The missile was not too far away, but in the distance he saw clearly the white, granite faces on Mount Rushmore. Lusk thought that the missile was probably aimed at Moscow, which he equated with the center of tyranny and enslavement. The faces chiseled in rock were memorials to the men who had created a great nation of free people. Lusk pondered the sight and thought that perhaps the answers to the problems that faced the nation were not so difficult. Humankind needed less faith in missiles and more faith in the principles of human freedom and dignity for which the leaders on the side of the mountain strove. Missiles might be necessary to preserve a free world but would never set the world free. Only the ideals put forth by leaders such as George Washington, Thomas Jefferson, Abraham Lincoln, and Theodore Roosevelt could have done that after a determined America had resolved to set humankind free. "Only when we have determined on a great crusade for freedom," Lusk concluded, "will the slow retreat before tyranny end, a retreat that leads inevitably to the triggering in desperation of the Titan Missile."[43]

The northern plains, with few exceptions, have largely shrugged off the existence of the hundreds of missile silos located throughout the region. For decades the majority of plains residents drove by silos and launch facilities without thinking much about them. Now that half of them are gone, no one really misses them. One fact remains clear: the missiles on the plains represented an economic opportunity for the states during the construction phase. The economic benefits were modest and temporary. Still, the federal government pushed the construction of missile silos in the states and localities that wanted them, despite making the region a strategic target. People wanted to benefit financially through employment in building the silos, by selling goods and services to the construction crews, or by selling land at reasonable prices to the government. The construction of missile silos throughout the northern plains was not a traumatic event but an economic opportunity for the region. Even modest financial interests were stronger than fears of nuclear disaster. Likewise, the construction of an Anti–Ballistic Missile Complex promised economic benefits to one of North Dakota's most remote locations, as explored in the next chapter.

Chapter 9

The Safeguard Complex

"**D**on't ever mention ABM in my presence again," read the sign worn around the neck of Conrad, Montana, mayor Robert Arnot, on May 28, 1972.[1] He had experienced more headaches associated with the military project than most people in town and could not help expressing his disgust. That morning the government announced the cancellation of the nation's second Safeguard Anti–Ballistic Missile (ABM) site located in the small Montana town, where many residents experienced something akin to shock as they realized that construction workers in the area would soon leave and the anticipated military families would never arrive. Residents weighed the impact. As school superintendent Robert Singleton noted, "we'll have an incredible teacher-student ratio for one year, that's for sure." The district had just hired ten new teachers to meet the demands of new families in the area. Not everyone was disappointed at the collapse of Safeguard, however, as rancher Robert Krupp noted: "There was built-in resentment to ABM. Inflation hit. Farmers weren't properly paid for their land."[2]

The project had split the community from the beginning. Many residents, anticipating the influx of federal workers and military families, expanded their businesses, while others looked upon the scenario as a complete nuisance. Hordes of construction workers, called "boomers," had crowded into Conrad and the surrounding towns, snatching up any available housing and stretching the limits of the local infrastructure. Their paychecks had boosted the local economy, but now the boomers and their spending money would leave town quickly. Communities on the northern plains had long recognized that federal government projects provided injections of money into the local economies, leading residents to try to attract military bases. The Conrad situation was different, at least initially. The ABM system was less attractive: it was designed to destroy nuclear missiles before they could strike the United States, making the area a high-priority target for America's enemies. More importantly, however, the Vietnam War made people question their government's priorities. They no longer believed the hype of Cold War rhetoric. Many residents in the area demanded fiscal responsibility from their government and felt that the project was a waste of money. When the federal government announced plans to construct the Safeguard ABM complexes in Montana and North Dakota, aversion to the projects disappeared as citizens recognized the monetary potential of the new missile sites. Again the federal government designed a project at the national level and implemented it at the state level, where citizens embraced Cold War opportunities.[3]

Political leaders throughout the northern plains tried to attract the ABM for financial reasons, while the residents there were at best apathetic. Communities throughout the nation demonstrated against the ABM concept, which was controversial from the beginning. The scientific community debated whether the system would even work. It split the government and the nation as people argued the wisdom of governmental priorities. The $6 billion cost of each system multiplied over the proposed twelve sites caused many to question the motives of their national leaders. Senate majority leader Mike Mansfield of Montana noted that federal spending priorities were "still being determined by yesterday's fears and fallacies. We should be spending more on programs which are attuned to the needs of the day and less on programs which are carry-overs from the needs of yesterday."[4] In the end an international treaty nullified the entire project in 1975 after spending billions of dollars, leaving residents on the plains bitterly disappointed.

Since the invention of rockets, experimenters have tried to invent a countermeasure to them. The Germans first demonstrated a missile's destructive power with the invention of the V-2 rocket that rained terror on the inhabitants of London during World War II. Londoners could do little but seek shelter underground. Only occasionally, and then by a stroke of luck, could the new British jet fighters shoot down a V-2 rocket or nudge it off course. This was not a defense, however: it was an accident. The U.S. government asked several companies to evaluate ABM possibilities before the end of the war, but technology did not exist that could defeat the missiles. General Eisenhower, an early skeptic about ABM systems, compared the idea of shooting down a missile with "hitting a bullet with a bullet."[5]

German rocket scientists aided Americans with their missile technology after the war with an infusion of knowledge that allowed the United States to make advances in antiaircraft technology. The United States Army placed contracts with Bell Telephone Laboratories and the Western Electric Company late in 1945 to design and build antiaircraft missiles and controls under the label Project NIKE. The first product was the Nike-Ajax missile, a radar-directed antiaircraft missile for use against enemy bombers. The next generation missile was the Nike-Hercules, similar to the Ajax, but with a nuclear weapon instead of a conventional warhead. Army officials asked Bell Telephone Labs to revisit the issue of ABM technology in 1955.[6]

The United States Army and Bell Labs began working on the problem of ABM technology, proposing that they adapt their antiaircraft Nike missile to the task. They developed the radar-guided Nike-Zeus missile (named after the Greek god of victory and the chief god) to counter the missile threat. The Nike-Zeus missile would carry a nuclear warhead into space, guided by the radar, detonating the warhead near the approaching missiles and destroying the threat. As soon as the army proposed this countermeasure, critics pointed out a number of problems, such as overwhelming the system with multiple warheads. The system clearly had limitations, because it worked on one missile at a time. The army tested the system in July 1962, when a Nike-Zeus missile launched from Kwajalein Island in the Pacific intercepted an Atlas-D target missile launched from Vandenburg AFB in California, almost five thousand miles away. Notwithstanding Eisenhower's analogy, a bullet could hit a bullet.[7]

Despite the results, the critics continued to voice concerns, arguing that the result was not worth the estimated $10–14 billion necessary to deploy a single system. These arguments prevented the army from fully deploying the system. But it continued to develop the technology through the administrations of Presidents John Kennedy and Lyndon Johnson. One innovation was the Nike-X project, which was a greatly enhanced system that eliminated many of its predecessor's shortcomings.

It featured a short-range Sprint missile for close targets, Spartan missiles for use against missiles still in the atmosphere, and improved radar that used phased array technology. The phased array radar emitted numerous radar beams and shifted them quickly, enabling the system to scan the horizon in a matter of microseconds. The new radar also had a better range and could track more targets than the earlier Nike-Zeus system. The Joint Chiefs of Staff believed in the new system, but the $30 billion price tag kept the White House from requesting full funding for deployment. A concentrated Soviet attack of thousands of missiles could still overwhelm the American system with only a few dozen missiles firing in defense.[8]

When U.S. intelligence agencies detected the Soviets building an ABM site near Moscow in 1964, the Joint Chiefs reconsidered their own ABM capabilities and recommended to Robert McNamara that he consider funding the ABM project. McNamara and other planners moved away from the ABM concept, however, as they began to rethink nuclear strategy. McNamara had originally believed that obliterating Soviet nuclear forces was the best strategy. But by the middle of the 1960s he believed that no amount of force could guarantee that the Soviets could not respond with a devastating counterstrike. Neither side could deny a retaliatory secondary strike, thus making nuclear war too costly to consider. An ABM site had no place in McNamara's policy. It would spark an arms race to ensure that each side could overwhelm the other's defensive measures, upsetting the delicate nuclear balance.[9]

McNamara might have been against an ABM site, but President Johnson clearly supported it. Notwithstanding deterrence theory, Johnson faced staunch criticism by the military and members of Congress for not deploying a defensive measure against nuclear attack. He was also concerned that Republicans would use this issue against him in the 1968 presidential election, leading McNamara to offer a compromise in 1966. Continue to conduct research and development studies, he proposed, but limit construction until the United States could negotiate a compromise with the Soviets on ABM sites. The Soviets were not interested in any deal that reduced their defensive capabilities, however. When McNamara broached the subject with Soviet premier Alexsei Kosygin in June 1967, Kosygin responded: "When I have trouble sleeping at night, it's because of your offensive missiles, not your defensive missiles."[10] The

Americans held a three-to-one advantage in long-range nuclear missiles, leaving the Soviets with little incentive to negotiate away their defensive measures.[11]

While the Americans and Soviets were discussing ABM restrictions in 1967, the Chinese exploded their first hydrogen bomb. Chinese nuclear capabilities had expanded rapidly. They had detonated their first nuclear weapon only a year before. McNamara outlined the threat, suggesting that the Chinese might believe that the United States would destroy their missiles and small nuclear capability in a preemptive strike. The Chinese might believe that their only choice was to launch their missiles or lose them. In another scenario McNamara feared that the Chinese might threaten to attack the United States or an ally, using the threat of overwhelming casualties to blackmail these countries. McNamara and the Joint Chiefs hoped to eliminate this threat to the United States through a limited ABM system.[12]

With Soviet intransigence regarding ABM limitations and the looming Chinese threat, McNamara reluctantly agreed to proceed with a limited ABM capability called Sentinel. The proposed Sentinel system would protect a number of cities in the United States from Chinese attack, while protecting only nuclear missile silos from a Soviet attack. When asked about this confusing scenario, McNamara explained that any attempt to shield the United States from a Soviet attack was futile. The Soviets could quickly build enough missiles to overwhelm the system, while the Chinese could not. Thus McNamara endorsed the ABM system by 1967, arguing that it did not threaten the Soviets because it posed no change in the ability of each nation to annihilate the other.[13]

Once McNamara and Johnson decided to build the Sentinel system, they wanted to do so as quickly as possible. Contractors had only fifty-four months to complete the system design and obtain operational readiness. Government officials demanded that in only four and a half years contractors complete research and development on all system components, produce the system components, and complete construction of seventeen sites in locations that officials had not even selected or acquired. The decision to implement the Sentinel system depended upon the ability to pull components "off the shelf," but this was impractical—no shelf existed. Many components were still in the design phase. Regardless of acquisition problems, planners allocated only eighteen

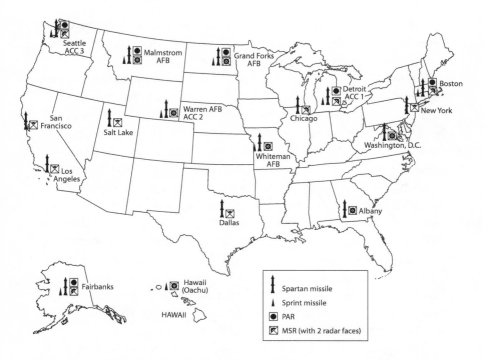

Proposed deployment sites for the Sentinel (later Safeguard) missiles. Widespread protests against the deployment led to construction of the first site in North Dakota. Crews began construction at a second site in Montana, but the SALT Treaty forced the abandonment of that project in 1972. Map by Bill Nelson. Courtesy of Mark Paine, creator of the image and owner of the website http://www.nuclearabms.info/HSentinel.html.

months to complete the design phase and begin construction on the first site, located near Boston, Massachusetts.[14]

Initially, the Boston Sentinel complex met with little interest by the local population, but dissent grew. The Corps of Engineers purchased a wooded site to locate the system then conducted a public relations meeting at North Andover High School in September 1968. A hundred people attended the meeting, which was generally amiable. The next meeting on January 29, 1969, was much different. Wide publicity had generated immense public interest, and estimates suggested that some five thousand people might attend the meeting held in the Reading High School auditorium. A winter blizzard reduced the size of the crowd but not its enthusiasm. Some thirteen hundred citizens and missile defense opponents filled the auditorium to hear the Corps of Engineers presentation and to offer boisterous criticism throughout the meeting.[15]

The most important consequence of the Reading meeting was that opponents in Boston contacted Edward Kennedy of Massachusetts, who soon joined the opposition. Senator Kennedy called on Secretary of Defense Melvin Laird on January 31, telling him that the system was "technically deficient, dangerously sited, unduly costly, and deleterious to domestic priorities as well as to prospects for an arms agreement with the Soviet Union."[16] Kennedy's concerns touched off a congressional debate, which led the House Armed Services Committee to threaten to cut off funding for portions of the Sentinel project unless the president reviewed the entire program. Other groups in Chicago, Detroit, and Seattle also had voiced their opposition to hosting a Sentinel site by this time, and a group from Chicago even sued the army to prevent construction of an ABM site near their community. Secretary Laird, in the midst of the flaring controversy, announced on February 6, 1969, that all Sentinel activities were suspended pending presidential review.[17]

During the review phase a number of constituents in South Dakota wrote to Senator Mundt, asking him to work against an ABM project. One was Byron Comstock of Sioux Falls, who suggested that the United States "stop wasting our national resources and energy on useless and dangerous military projects."[18] Officials of the Western South Dakota Development Company saw other possibilities, however. They wrote to Senator Mundt and U.S. representative E. Y. Berry, urging them to persuade Congress to move the ABM site to western South Dakota. Land was cheap in the state, they argued, and residents were used to living with nuclear weapons in the area, given the proximity of Ellsworth Air Force Base and the atomic bombs located there and the nuclear missile silos in close proximity. Both Berry and Mundt wrote to Laird and stressed the same points, urging the secretary to locate a system in South Dakota.[19] South Dakota was actively seeking the ABM complex, despite national distaste for the project.

Other Americans expressed their opposition to the ABM project during this period, and for the first time large numbers of citizens across the nation criticized the idea. Scientists, academics, and government officials argued that ABM systems were considerably more expensive and more complex than the missiles that they were supposed to destroy. The United States should simply invest in more missiles, they countered. Again critics raised the technical considerations of vulnerable radars and simply overwhelming the system with quantities of missiles.[20]

President Richard Nixon's advisors completed the review in early 1969, recommending that he deploy a limited system, which would defend the Minuteman ICBM fields instead of population centers. The term "Safeguard" probably came from Nixon's White House speech of March 14, in which he announced the modified plan. The new deployment, he said, "is a safeguard against any attack by the Chinese Communists that we can foresee over the next 10 years. It is a safeguard of our deterrent system, which is increasingly vulnerable due to the advances that have been made by the Soviet Union since the year 1967 when the Sentinel program was first laid out. It is a safeguard also against any irrational or accidental attack that might occur of less than massive magnitude which might be launched from the Soviet Union."[21]

The Pentagon formally adopted the name change on March 25 and reoriented the project to focus on the first Safeguard sites near Grand Forks AFB, North Dakota, and Malmstrom AFB, Montana. Government representatives had already planned to build Sentinel sites near the two bases, and building the first sites away from large population centers played heavily on the decision to begin construction on the northern plains. Later the complete system was to have twelve sites deployed around missile sites throughout the country. Simultaneously, the transition to Safeguard spelled the end of the Sentinel project near Boston. Local residents wanted to see the site restored to its natural beauty or a transition to a recreational area for residents. Ultimately the federal government transferred the site to the Massachusetts Department of Natural Resources, and it became a state park.[22] While the ABM project was also scorned nationally, citizens on the northern plains were not as critical. For the people there even a modest financial gain was a benefit. In this case, however, the citizens did not actively seek out the project, but their political leaders did.

Elsewhere, the change from Sentinel to Safeguard and the transition from protecting urban centers to missile fields did nothing to limit the acrimony within the country, as many American people began to organize against the project. Mrs. Richard Schwartz, the head of a grassroots organization called Citizens against the Tenafly Antiballistic Missile Site, was outspoken in her opposition to the site proposed outside New York City in Tenafly, New Jersey. "Although we are happy the ABM won't be located in communities such as Tenafly," Schwartz said, "we are distressed that there apparently will be deployment of the system at all." She went on to remark that citizens in her area opposed the ABM site because the scientific community argued that it would not work, because they believed that it would escalate the arms race, and because it was so expensive. It was a clear violation of our national priorities, she argued.[23]

Nationally, just over 50 percent of the nation supported the ABM concept. The argument split the scientific community as well, with some scientists arguing that such a system could never work and others arguing that it would. Some advocates of the system argued that a defensive system would render nuclear missiles obsolete, thus ending the arms race. Others argued that morality dictated that the government must save at least some percentage of the population. Perhaps the most ardent advocate of the system was Albert Wohlstetter, a researcher at RAND Corporation and Stanford Research Institute, who insisted that the United States needed the system to ensure the survivability of enough nuclear weapons for a second strike.[24]

The controversy split North Dakotans. An organization that called itself the North Dakota Citizens against the ABM promoted anti-ABM sentiment throughout the state, especially in the major cities during the late 1960s. Governor William Guy and North Dakota senator Quentin Burdick, both Democrats, were strongly opposed to the system, while Republican Milton Young strongly supported it. Pockets of opposition bloomed in some cities around the state, but most people were apathetic. Mayors in Fargo, Grand Forks, Dickinson, and Bismarck reported no major opposition or supporters. Closer to the construction site the project had a number of supporters. John Laqua, an attorney in Langdon, North Dakota, remarked: "I'm in favor of it, if those missiles are important for our defense. It's about time this country took a hard line on some of this stuff. We've had enough of the peaceniks. I wasn't opposed to the Minuteman missiles and I'm not opposed to the ABM."[25]

Even as construction began in Langdon, people were generally supportive of the project by 1970, with 58 percent of respondents expressing a favorable opinion in a local poll, though 16 percent disapproved. Sentiment clearly shifted by 1974, when a poll taken throughout the state indicated that four of five respondents believed that the project would benefit the state financially. Only one in ten thought that the project was detrimental to the state, while towns located near system components welcomed the influx of federal dollars. Everyone agreed on one point: the project would be a major economic boost to the state, though opponents argued that the state would benefit more from new schools and hospitals than from an ABM site.[26]

Notwithstanding public opposition, Congress finally passed the funding package for two of the twelve Safeguard sites by a one-vote margin in August 1969, as the vice president, Spiro Agnew, cast the deciding vote in a Senate tie. When Congress approved the fiscal year 1970 budget, it made funds available for the two sites, one in North Dakota and the other in Montana. Officials had already combed the area around the proposed North Dakota site under the Sentinel project and had completed much of the initial work, submitting a proposal to Congress in October 1969. In January 1970 the Corps of Engineers began acquiring land around Grand Forks AFB.[27]

The engineers had generally chosen the level farming area in the northeastern portion of the state close to the Canadian border. The Stanley R. Mickelsen Safeguard Complex (SRMSC), named for the commander of the army's Air Defense Command in the 1950s, consisted of four major elements. The Perimeter Acquisition Radar (PAR) located on 279 acres near Langdon, North Dakota, would use phased array radar to track potential targets and to guide long-range Spartan missiles for the farthest possible intercept. If enemy missiles made it through this measure, the Missile Site Radar (MSR) complex, located on 433 acres close to Nekoma, North Dakota, would track the targets for a closer intercept and launch the Sprint missiles located at any of the four Remote Sprint Launch (RSL) sites clustered within twenty miles of the MSR. For the Remote Launch Sites the corps purchased four tracts of land of thirty-six to forty-five acres each.[28]

The federal government had responsibilities other than acquiring land, such as completing environmental and community impact statements on the North Dakota communities. The first priority was to ensure that sufficient water supplies existed for the government facilities. The region had a precipitation rate of twenty-four inches per year, sufficient for community activities in the region but far short of the requirement for government facilities and their families. Local inhabitants generally drew their water from wells and were justifiably concerned upon learning that the government buildings might demand over one thousand gallons of water per minute. The problem demanded immediate attention.[29]

The public need not have worried, however, as officials had been working on this problem for years. Government engineers planned to tap into the Fordville aquifer approximately thirty-five miles from the PAR site and forty-six miles from the MSR site. Roger Schmidt of the North Dakota State Water Commission estimated that the aquifer could deliver over one thousand gallons of water per minute for a period of twenty-three years without incident. The corps planned to drill ten wells into the aquifer, build three booster stations, and lay over fifty-eight miles of pipe to deliver water into the government facilities. Local inhabitants, however, demanded a public review to assuage concerns before the state granted a permit. Quentin Burdick held these meetings in January 1970, when members of the Corps of Engineers, the U.S. Geological Survey, and the State Water Commission assured citizens that no adverse conditions would result from the army's needs. On March 9, 1970, the state awarded a water permit to the Corps of Engineers to use the aquifer. The corps awarded a $4 million contract to Zurn Engineers of Upland, California, to begin construction at the end of the month.[30]

While the Corps of Engineers worked through the water issues, government labor negotiators also needed to complete agreements with local construction unions that would actually build the ABM site. Labor relations issues were important to the Grand Forks unions, who viewed the contracts in North Dakota as a precedent for future construction sites around the country. Of particular concern were the issues of inflation, which would surely rise in the region with the influx of federal dollars, and the per diem rate that workers could expect, as many drove long distances to get to work. What few people envisioned in the early stages of contract negotiations was a clause found in the federal government hiring statutes and communicated to contractors and subcontractors: that construction companies make a "good faith" effort to hire between 6 and 10 percent minority workers. The companies viewed this requirement as excessive, as the population of North Dakota included only about 2 percent minorities, among them unskilled Indians living on reservations throughout the state. Cavalier County had no minorities in 1970, and the three adjoining counties had only 168. As difficult as it was, contractors ultimately met the goal of 6 percent minority representation on the construction sites, generally by recruiting minorities from outside the state.[31]

The government needed not only to solve environmental and labor problems but also to assess and solve infrastructure issues. The communities located near the military facilities were small. Many residents were concerned that the thousands of construction workers coming into the area, soon followed by hundreds of military personnel and their families, might stretch the resources of local schools, stores, and housing units. The Corps of Engineers organized a planning group to evaluate the problems and develop solutions and published a report entitled *Community Impact Report: Grand Forks Deployment Area*, which identified and addressed all of these issues. The report indicated that local resources would meet the anticipated population increase with proper planning—which proved to be a premature conclusion, as events unfolded.[32]

The planning group evaluated the communities and resources within fifty miles of Langdon, the largest community in the region, and all communities with a population over ten thousand people within one hundred miles of Langdon. The group estimated that the temporary population increase was just over eight thousand people in the fall of 1971, mingling with an established population of twenty-five thousand people. The permanent increase would be much less, about twenty-two hundred people at the end of the construction phase. In practical terms, this meant an increase of fifteen hundred students in 1970–71, to a peak of twenty-five hundred students in 1973–74 in the local school district. The planning group determined that the public sewer system in Langdon was inadequate for the increasing population, and the region needed three more police officers and four firefighters.[33]

Alleviating these problems depended upon the availability of federal funds, which Congress had allocated but the government process was slow in producing, aggravating local residents. Local housing was quite limited around the construction area. The main contractor purchased land around Langdon, placing over one hundred mobile homes in a trailer park in June 1970, for supervisory personnel and their families.

The Corps of Engineers had originally planned to build two separate mobile home parks for government workers, but the process soon bogged down after bids for the project far exceeded government estimates. The government canceled the housing project, but contractors soon reached an agreement with a local company to build Cavalier Estates, a mobile home park that eventually contained a few hundred homes. The park did not immediately solve the housing problem but mitigated it somewhat.[34]

Many workers needed decent housing, but area communities offered few rooms, apartments, or houses for the newcomers. This led to allegations of proprietors charging exorbitant rents; the small town did not offer many options. An unnamed Corps of Engineers spokesperson warned the Langdon property owners and business owners not to overcharge the workers, as government shopping facilities and housing would undercut their prices once they were constructed. "What many people in Langdon don't realize," said the corps representative, "is that the new people have a choice where they want to live. That could be Langdon, that could be someplace else."[35] Colonel Roy Beatty, the area Safeguard commander, sought to head off a confrontation and immediately indicated that he did not believe that the rates property owners or local businesses charged were excessive. "In trading up and down Main Street in Langdon," he proclaimed, "I have detected no escalation in price trends."[36]

Indeed, the businesspeople of Cavalier County reported significant increases in sales soon after the Corps of Engineers began construction, an unlikely phenomenon if the prices were exceedingly high. The local supermarket and jewelry stores both reported increased sales over several months, while the local shoe store owner reported a 50 percent increase in sales over two months. All of the local restaurants had more sales, while the local tavern also prospered. One tavern owner said that his quietest nights now resembled the busiest nights from only a year ago. "It varies from week to week," reported Darol Krueger, the manager of the local Ben Franklin. "On days when new families move into town, we go up sharply in sales. On other days, we dip," he reported, saying that he had seen "a number of new faces in town."[37] Even small towns located near Langdon noted an increase in business and that every available room and apartment had been rented. As the ABM project grew and construction workers moved into the area, local businesspeople were optimistic and believed that the demand for goods and services would only accelerate.[38]

Despite the appearance of amicable relationships, associations between the workers and local residents suffered at times. Deborah Levchak worked at the Safeguard Complex in 1974, during her summer away from college, and lived in the local community. She recalls that many local people wanted to work at the site, as federal service paid well and provided more financial stability for farm families. The government hired many local residents who learned trades and skills that became important later. While many local people worked with federal officials, a divide remained between the two groups. Local residents, she remembers, called the construction workers, soldiers, and Department of the Army civilians "missile people." They were often the object of scorn, as residents talked among themselves about the various threats that these groups posed to local girls and women. Some of the people in Nekoma also had "hard feelings" once the construction and missile workers arrived. They felt that businesses catered to outsiders, rather than to the local citizens. Many of the soldiers and civilians who worked at the site, however, recall the harsh winters and the difficulty building the site but more often mention the good friends that they met while stationed in North Dakota. Others recall the friends, and occasionally the spouses, that they met in the local community.[39]

Meanwhile, the infrastructure in Langdon continued to stretch under the weight of the incoming population. The federal money to alleviate these problems was slowly meandering through the bureaucracy, and the town began to show signs of the impact. By August 1970 the town of 2,100 people had grown to 3,300, with more on the way. Langdon mayor Harold Blanchard contacted federal agencies to let them know that the situation was critical. Langdon had plenty of water because of the reservoir, but the pumps were going around the clock to maintain water pressure, reduced to nearly nothing with all of the additional water lines going into the new trailer courts.[40]

While engineers dealt with the local issues, construction on the missile system got underway in earnest in North Dakota during the late spring of 1970, just as President Nixon was planning an expansion of the Vietnam War into Cambodia. This move sparked a nationwide movement, as college students across the country demonstrated against expanding the war. The protest spread to North Dakota, where students at the University of North Dakota organized a march designed to begin on the university campus and then move to Nekoma, one of the ABM construction sites. The students planned the demonstration long before the events at Kent State University, where Ohio National Guardsmen killed four students and wounded nine others during a protest over Nixon's expansion of the Vietnam War. Many within the state feared violence with the demonstration in Nekoma, prompting Governor Guy to call out the National Guard. In the end, however, the demonstration was uneventful. Students flew kites and planted "seeds of life" near a facility that they believed was designed for death.[41]

Construction continued in North Dakota, but the Montana project was well behind schedule, as congressional debate had hindered the site investigation there. Finally, the Corps of Engineers picked Conrad and Shelby Counties to locate the Montana site, but citizens received the news with a mixture of elation at the financial opportunities that the project would bring and concern over the limited infrastructure that the counties had to house, educate, and provide for families. Infrastructure problems in Montana closely resembled those in North Dakota. Corps officials eventually ran twenty-six miles of pipe from the Tiber Reservoir, capable of transporting a million gallons of water per day to the construction sites. Additionally, they built about sixteen miles of new road to the PAR construction sites, followed later by fifteen miles of new roads to other project areas.[42]

The human issues in Montana, particularly housing, also resembled the problems in North Dakota. Concerned citizens in the two counties contacted the governor, Forrest Anderson, and Senator Mansfield in an effort to ensure that federal dollars would arrive sooner in Montana than they had in North Dakota. Governor Anderson and North Dakota governor William Guy traveled to Washington in August 1970 to testify as to the adverse impact of Safeguard on their states, hoping to free federal dollars to alleviate these problems. As labor disputes limited the number of new workers and their families in the Montana communities, the urgency surrounding the issue dissipated.[43]

Construction in North Dakota had begun as scheduled in April 1970, though Montana labor unions, contractors, and representatives from the Corps of Engineers were just getting down to serious contract negotiations at that time. It soon became apparent that Montana unions made demands that could escalate construction costs by $5–10 million. The trouble began in 1968, when Montana labor unions set certain wage standards in anticipation of Sentinel construction: specifically double-time wage rates for any work over forty hours and a per diem rate of twelve dollars per day the first year, rising to fourteen dollars per day by the third year. There was little opposition to this measure in Montana, as few union members worked more than forty hours per week and few workers traveled great distances to a job site.[44]

During contract negotiations in April 1970 the Montana unions wished to incorporate existing wage agreements. The contractors declined at the time but promised to revisit the issue when the government awarded the final contracts. Eventually the winning contractors adopted the union requests, and construction began in May 1970. Workers completed the initial phase of construction by January 1971, but the spiraling labor costs forced the government to rethink its bid process, hoping to cut costs that appeared to keep increasing. The government, contractors, and local unions failed to negotiate a contract in January or February 1971 and stopped construction on the Montana site. In addition to previous wage negotiation of double-time pay for all overtime, the unions demanded an hourly increase of two dollars per hour, twenty dollars per day per diem, and ten cents per mile travel allowance for a round trip.[45]

These increased wages could mean an increased cost of $25–30 million over the rest of the Malmstrom project, and much more than that if multiplied over the construction of up to ten more sites. This was unacceptable to government contractors, who attempted to negotiate contracts with national unions and hoped the Montana unions would adopt the national contracts. National negotiations ended in October 1971, with more reasonable wage agreements; whether the Montana unions would accept them remained uncertain. By February 1972 the work scheduled at the Malmstrom site had slipped by fourteen months. Four local unions agreed to the new contracts, enough so that the government issued final contracts and planned to begin construction as soon as the weather permitted. Planners estimated that the Malmstrom ABM complex would be complete in 1974 and commence full operation in 1976.[46]

International events, however, would have a tremendous impact on the ABM site in Montana. The United States and Soviet Union signed the ABM Treaty in May 1972, as part of the Strategic Arms Limitation Talks (SALT), limiting each country to two defensive sites: one at the respective national capital and one at another location. Each site could have a maximum of one hundred missiles, two hundred missiles in total. The intent of the treaty was to prevent either side from establishing a nationwide ABM defense. When officials signed the ABM Treaty in 1972, the North Dakota site was 80 percent complete, while construction on the Montana site had barely begun. The treaty only allowed one ABM site away from the capital, so Secretary Laird ordered the army to stop construction on the Montana site at the end of May 1972.[47]

Reactions to the announcement varied in Montana, as the project had stretched the resources of several small communities, the patience of its residents, and the labor unions' sense of fair treatment. Mayor Robert Arnot from Conrad, Montana, responded to the news by saying: "[L]et us get back to the way we were."[48] Others, however, had looked forward to the financial opportunities that the project offered. Montana's chief planning officer, Perry F. Roys, remarked: "There are some people in the private sector who are going to be hurt. I mean hurt like going broke."[49] Roys was referring to the investments in homes and businesses to accommodate the expected influx of workers. The government dismantled as much of the complex as possible for reuse in other facilities, and local communities tried to entice businesses to the area by turning over the remaining facilities to them.[50]

The signatories refined the SALT treaty in 1974, limiting each country to just one ABM site and reducing the total number of missiles allowed from two hundred to one hundred. The Soviets kept their system near Moscow, and the United States kept the nearly completed Safeguard site in North Dakota. The SALT treaties prevented each nation from establishing a full ABM defense system and placed restrictions on the research and development of new system components or missiles. This treaty marked a turning point in nuclear negotiations between the superpowers, as each side acknowledged the attributes of Mutually Assured Destruction (MAD).[51]

Construction continued in North Dakota until the Safeguard complex received initial operational status on April 1, 1975, and reached full operational status on September 28, 1975. Army officials realized that the system was technologically obsolete almost as soon as it began operations, for the Soviets would overwhelm a single site in a large-scale attack, which it was never designed to counter. This led to the decision to maintain the site for a year and then shut it down. When the army's plan to cease operations reached Congress, it moved quickly to cut appropriations for the site, as it had recently voted to cut defense costs by $9 billion. Cutting the Safeguard project would save a significant amount of money rather quickly. The House voted on October 2, 1975, to deactivate the system due to the high operating costs and its limited effectiveness, barely a week after it achieved full operational status.[52]

Senator Milton Young worked hard to keep the complex running but noted that his greatest obstacle was the willingness of North Dakota representative Mark Andrews to close the facility. This gave critics such as Massachusetts senator Ted Kennedy and others an edge in their argument to stop funding and close the complex. Young managed to keep the PAR running (it is used even today to track space debris), but on February 10, 1976, the Joint Chiefs of Staff ordered the termination of the Safeguard mission. This decision ended the operation of the only ABM system in the free world after less than five months of full operation and a cost of nearly $6 billion.[53]

When the site shut down, many of the local residents were stunned. "It all looks like a big WPA project now. That's what it amounts to. What a waste. All it did was provide some jobs," proclaimed Dr. Harold Blanchard, now the former mayor of Langdon. "We're finally getting it where it should be and all of a sudden we are overbuilt."[54] Blanchard also realized that the shutdown meant that many workers would leave the area. He noted that the schools now had too many teachers, so the local housing market would suffer severely. Residents had borrowed money to refurbish stores and houses, and some businesses would close down. Other residents focused on the incredible waste of money. "I can't see how they can shut it down. Not with the billions they've spent there," declared Cavalier mayor Robert Olson.[55] The effect of the shutdown was a severe blow to the area's economy.[56]

The Safeguard Complexes in Montana and North Dakota had international, national, and local implications. From the beginning American political leaders had hoped to build the ABM systems and use them as a bargaining chip in negotiations with the Soviet Union, yet few communities in the nation were willing to assume this role. While several

The missile field and Missile Site Radar at the Stanley R. Mickelsen Safeguard Complex in Nekoma, North Dakota. People who have seen the Missile Site Radar often refer to it as the "Pyramid on the Plains." Courtesy United States Army.

cities around the nation protested against the possibility of hosting a Safeguard site, residents in North Dakota and Montana were generally apathetic toward the system but soon appreciated the financial opportunity that the project offered. When the sites in Montana and North Dakota shut down, many were shocked and disappointed. Most could not help remarking that the project was a colossal waste of money.

For the citizens of the northern plains the Safeguard Complex began as a proposition that excited few and was ignored by others. The facility cost too much money for those who insisted upon fiscal responsibility from their government. Others did not want a high-value target located near them. Still others argued that the system would not work. When the federal government insisted that the ABM system was viable and wanted to build it on the northern Great Plains, citizens slowly changed their stance. They recognized the financial possibilities that the project presented. For these citizens the ABM complex fit well within the framework that others had already recognized. The federal government and its projects benefited the area's residents. People cared little that the Soviets might target their region in the event of attack and worried less about whether the system would work. On the northern plains the Safeguard Complex represented an opportunity that could transform the agricultural economy of the local community. When the federal government shut down the centers in Montana and North Dakota, residents felt betrayed. They perceived the rules changing. The federal government was supposed to offer opportunities, not take them away. In the end there were limits to how far regional interests could work the system for federal dollars. The fate of the ABM system was sealed by larger diplomatic and strategic developments, irrespective of local interests.

Conclusion

This examination of the northern Great Plains shows that many Cold War events resulted from programs generated at the federal level and brought to the state and local level for implementation. Every citizen was a soldier on the front lines of the Cold War who needed constant reassurance that the American way of life was worth guarding and protecting. To meet these ends the federal government fostered programs designed to tap into patriotic or religious feelings on one hand and actively opposition to subversives on the other. The Cold War offered citizens the opportunity to engage in near-military operations in civil defense and the Ground Observer Corps and unprecedented financial opportunity in terms of military bases and weapons systems.

The history of the Cold War on the northern Great Plains does not fit neatly into Great Plains historiography. Most historians concentrate on the theme of dependency or colonialism. The research outlined here counters that interpretation, empowers citizens, and considers the choices that they made during a defined era. Economic issues associated with the Cold War allowed the northern Great Plains states to reverse the trend of colonialism. This was a phenomenon already underway by the Great Depression, when citizens and political leaders understood that the federal government could provide economic benefits. Citizens throughout the region attempted to attract federal dollars through manufacturing during World War II, but this effort fell short. Agricultural subsidies assisted greatly in bringing the northern Great Plains out of the Depression. Political leaders aggressively pursued federal projects to bring home to their states, including dams, highways, and military bases.

Contrary to earlier examinations of dependency by highly regarded regional authors that cast citizens of the area as victims, this book shows that people were not subject to overriding deterministic forces. They took advantage of opportunities, ameliorated damage, and in general responded assertively where it seemed appropriate or not at all when events indicated another path. Many citizens supported patriotic and religious endeavors advocated by the federal government but often ignored or rejected concerns with Communists even though national figures suggested that they were a threat. Many residents of the region doubted that a nuclear war was likely and did little to prepare for one, even though state and federal authorities recommended that they do so. But citizens did get excited about the prospect of military bases located near their communities because of their economic possibilities.

This examination of the Cold War does not fit into recent Cold War historiography either. While most studies concentrate on the terror that the confrontation with the Soviets generated, this trepidation never surfaced in the evidence. Anxiety over nuclear annihilation or Communist subversion was never a pervasive emotion in the daily lives of citizens. This study in a particular region demonstrates the importance of going to the sources to determine ways in which people responded to significant events. It also reveals the shortcomings of such documents, which are not all-encompassing and do not represent all aspects of public opinion. But making use of presidential and congressional records, newspaper accounts, magazine articles, and oral histories allows the thoughts and actions of particular citizens and politicians to come through and provides evidence for the historian. As this study shows, citizens on the northern Great Plains often did not see the Cold War as frightening or traumatic but as a source of opportunity and transformation.

As shown here, the citizens on the northern plains responded to calls for action. They welcomed the Freedom Train as well as the Friendship Train and participated in the Freedom Crusade initiative and the Ground Observer Corps. They were also quick to accept the increasing importance of the church as a means to battle Communists. As the first part of this study indicates citizens embraced patriotic and religious gestures but rejected anticommunist rhetoric. Though much smaller than many of the cities where the Freedom Train stopped, communities on the northern plains broke or approached attendance records at nearly every stop. Some residents had personal or regional connections with the sacred documents or their authors. Many of those who viewed the Freedom Train and its cargo also contributed to the Friendship Train as it gathered goods for those less fortunate or participated in Crusade for Freedom drives. The people of the region responded to the call for worship and religious observance. Despite the seemingly disparate religious and political affiliations of citizens in the Dakotas and Montana, they responded in a nearly uniform fashion, honoring patriotism and religion.

When the air force called on volunteers to staff Ground Observer Corps posts and report aircraft during all hours of the day and night, people volunteered. They disregarded their own safety out of altruism and agreed to help their neighbors. Across the nation the air force trained over 1 million people to watch the skies for enemy aircraft, lest some enemy bomber should cross the country's northern border and drop its deadly cargo on an American target. This mission was critical in the states of the sparsely populated northern plains, which might provide the first warning of attack for the rest of the nation. People banded together to form observation posts in homes, silos, or other structures. Though never called on to report actual enemy planes, the Ground Observer Corps was highly successful, allowing people to feel that they were contributing to the nation's defense.

Citizens in the region responded to the federal government's call to action in these areas out of patriotism, not emotion. The fear of Communists in the region was probably less than in other areas, as the lack of anticommunist legislation indicates. Senator Joseph McCarthy's colorful career indicates that many Americans believed his dire warnings. Even some citizens on the northern plains supported his claims, but their enthusiasm may have been directed at his investigations of the federal government in Washington, not locally. Relatively few members of the Communist Party lived in the area. The citizens did not react to the possibility of Communists in their midst and did not encourage the creation of investigative committees to expose them the way other states did. This is not to argue that the citizens had no opinion on communism. People in the region were ardently patriotic and opposed Marxist ideology. They simply did not believe that radicals were a menace in their communities. They saw the issue as more relevant to large urban areas, while patriotism, religion, and regional interests were more compelling to them.

As the rest of the nation looked for Communists in their neighbor-hoods or in local governments, the residents of the northern Great Plains generally dismissed the idea that Communists were a threat to them personally. Communists, if they existed in America, were in New York, Washington, or some other far-away city. Legislatures in the region rarely enacted loyalty oaths as the federal government did or investigated peo-ple for Communist sympathies with the same zeal as seen in other states. When accusations arose that Communists had infiltrated the Farmers Union, people responded with anger not against the suspected Com-munists but against outsiders who were making the accusations. The people generally hated Communism but refused to abandon their senses and embrace the hysteria. When South Dakota senator Karl Mundt pro-posed the Mundt-Nixon Bill that would greatly infringe upon the lib-erties of Americans suspected of Communist sympathies, many in the region rejected it, though others supported it. Nearly all the people in the area graciously welcomed the visiting Soviet farmers into their com-munities and their homes. The threat of Communist insurgency was not traumatic for most citizens of the northern plains.

The people had slight regard for radical insurgents, so few felt the need to prepare for a Soviet nuclear attack. Almost all of the funding for civil defense training and equipment came from state and local governments, which were often strapped for cash. Civil defense was at least initially a state responsibility, and government leaders generally ignored the threat. Montana had no civil defense plan during the 1950s, and North Dakota and South Dakota had only a semblance of a plan, vague and of little value. During the Cuban Missile Crisis the government hastily tried to concoct a coherent civil defense plan and to provide shelter space for its citizens. Few residents of the region put any thought into emergency procedures: they had no idea what to do in the event of an attack.

People on the northern Great Plains seem to have been largely apa-thetic about preparing for the possibility of nuclear war, especially dur-ing the 1950s. Civil defense officials constantly tried to frighten citizens out of their complacency, usually with little success. Some people were simply fatalistic and believed that they would die in any event. Others knew that any exchange of nuclear weapons would include slow and vulnerable Soviet bombers, providing six to eight hours of warning be-fore bombs reached their targets, and had faith that the air force could intercept and neutralize the planes. In addition, the government spent a considerable amount of time, effort, and money to convince people that they could survive a nuclear attack if they took a few precautions. The government did not want to spend vast sums of money to prepare fall-out shelters, so it convinced the population that elaborate shelters were unnecessary. By the end of the 1950s people were weary of hearing civil defense rhetoric and apathetic. This is not to suggest that some people never experienced fear. But dire warnings did not transform into action.

President John F. Kennedy aided in the development of a coherent civil defense plan when he authorized Congress to increase spending dramatically on fallout shelter construction in the wake of the Berlin Crisis in 1961. But events only a year later demonstrated that little had been accomplished. When the Cuban Missile Crisis occurred in 1962, the state and local governments and the civilian population were un-prepared to handle the situation. People on the northern plains did not know where to go in the event of emergency. Often they had no place to go, as shelters were incomplete or unidentified. Montana had no civil defense plan, and Governor Babcock called out the National Guard to help the state prepare for an emergency. North and South Dakota did not have enough shelters. Those that were available were not stocked with food or medical supplies. During the confusion government agen-cies reacted quickly and decisively, creating shelters and calming citizens. When the crisis subsided peacefully within a week, people went back to their apathetic ways. Any fear that the population had experienced had dissipated.

While residents ignored some aspects of the Cold War, they enthu-siastically embraced other features. The geographical location of the northern plains made it an ideal site for air force bases, which would dramatically affect the economies of those communities with a base. Cit-ies on the northern plains battled to host an air force base simply for the economic benefit. The construction of missile silos could also have a statewide effect on the economy, and each state jealously guarded the right to have its citizens help in their construction. Farmers also hoped for a generous price when the government offered to buy parcels of farm-land to locate the missile sites and went to court over what they consid-ered ridiculously low offers. The construction of (ABM) sites in North Dakota and Montana promised economic opportunity, but the closure of the sites for political reasons was a great disappointment to people in the region.

The projects were prime targets for Soviet bombers and then nuclear missiles as the Cold War progressed. Many communities throughout the nation rejected the construction of bases or weapons systems that would surely attract Soviet attention. Some areas even witnessed demonstrations designed to discourage government intervention. No such attitude prevailed on the northern plains, and no marches materialized. Financial opportunity through government investment was a constant objective. Fear was less ubiquitous.

William H. McNeill examines the concept of defining an individual or group working against an enemy in *Mythistory.* "Mythistory" describes the relationship between myth, a story commonly considered fiction, and history, which supposedly is nonfiction. A story or belief may be labeled myth by one group and history by another. History, McNeill says, is our mythology serving to define and excite us.[1]

History helps to define collective identities because a common past helps to define a collective group.[2] Members of the baby-boomer generation have written much of the Cold War history, often presenting the view that people were perpetually terrified during this era but managed to rise above the chaos and perpetuate the ideals of a God-fearing and liberty-loving nation. Michael Kammen, a historian who studies historical monuments, argues that anxiety defined the nation during the Cold War in the collective memory. The question remains as to whether or not these memories are real. Kammen notes that "we arouse and arrange our memories to suit our psychic needs. Historians . . . are surely correct in referring to the 'social production of memories.'"[3] He offers a warning that historians should be careful when considering the cohesion and clarity of popular or collective memory. Both warrant scrutiny and mistrust. With Kammen's warnings in mind, the proposition that the Cold War was as traumatic as many historians have argued is ripe for reconsideration.[4] Perhaps a more concrete definition of the term "fear" is appropriate going forward.

Whether or not the Cold War was a harrowing experience on the northern Great Plains, it was profitable. Many of the beneficial agricultural reforms remained in place. Farmers were finally making money, and the previously antagonistic colonial relationship with the East receded into the background. Government was now more salient and important to regional life than ever. The accumulation of air bases, missile silos, and other military facilities helped to bridge the gap between the era of colonial dependency and the more independent situation of the region since the 1990s.

Even as personal memory of the Cold War in the region fades, its material effect remains. A reduced number of missiles still stand at the ready, and historians will continue to contend their meaning.

Notes

Introduction

1. "S.D. Solons Back Proposals for President Truman to Administer Oath to Armed Forces Volunteers," *Huronite and Daily Plainsman*, February 12, 1948.

2. Ibid.

3. "Governor Urges President Truman to Visit State," *Huronite and Daily Plainsman*, February 17, 1948.

4. Stock, *Main Street in Crisis*, 206.

5. Lauck, *Prairie Republic*, 9, 42, 49.

6. Emmons, *The Butte Irish*, 95.

7. Ibid., 102.

8. Putnam, *Bowling Alone*, 19, 292.

9. Robbins, "The 'Plundered Province' Thesis," 577–78.

10. Robinson, *History of North Dakota*, vii; Kraenzel, *The Great Plains in Transition*, 228–29.

11. Danbom, "A Part of the Nation and Apart from the Nation," 174–80; Robinson, *History of North Dakota*, 358–60; Cooper, *Citizens as Soldiers*, 194; Hofer, *The History of the Hutterites*, 62; Gross, *The Hutterite Way*, 124.

12. Schell, *History of South Dakota*, 270–73; Frazier, *The Great Plains*, 194–95; Janzen, *The Prairie People*, 137. Note: Many Hutterites also experienced hostility for not supporting the war effort enthusiastically.

13. Malone and Roeder, *Montana*, 207, 215.

14. Kennedy, *Over Here*, 23; Spritzer, *Roadside History of Montana*, 294.

15. Rieselbach, "The Basis of Isolationist Behavior," 645; Billington, "The Origins of Middle Western Isolationism," 51, 60.

16. "Frazier, Lemke Hit 'War Fever,'" *Grand Forks Herald*, June 15, 1940; Griffith, "Old Progressives and the Cold War," 337; Robinson, *History of North Dakota*, 423; Cole, *Senator Gerald P. Nye and American Foreign Relations*, 72.

17. Heidepreim, *A Fair Chance for a Free People*, 41.

18. Robinson, *History of North Dakota*, 424.

19. Doenecke, *Not to the Swift*, 74; Heidepreim, *A Fair Chance for a Free People*, 49; Jerry Maguire to Karl Mundt, n.d., Box 234, Karl Mundt Papers (hereinafter Mundt Papers), Karl Mundt Library, Dakota State University, Madison, South Dakota; Heidepreim, *A Fair Chance for a Free People*, 41.

20. Chenoweth, "Francis Case," 75–77.

21. Ibid., 83.

22. Ibid., 88; "Memorandum of Telephone Conversation, Case to Holcomb," December 8, 1941, Box 33, Francis Case Papers (hereinafter Case Papers), McGovern Library, Dakota Wesleyan University, Mitchell, South Dakota.

23. "Radio Address By Hon. James E. Murray, United States Senator from Montana," March 2, 1941, Box 940, James E. Murray Papers (hereinafter Murray Papers), K. Ross Toole Archives, Mansfield Library, University of Montana, Missoula, Montana.

24. Ibid.

25. Spence, *Montana*, 160–61.

26. Wheeler, *Yankee from the West*, 36.

27. Smith, *Jeannette Rankin*, 157; Spence, *Montana*, 161.

28. Robinson, *History of North Dakota*, 430; Lillehaugen, "Survey of American Policy in the Cold War," x.

29. Schell, *History of South Dakota* (4th ed.), 319; Karolevitz, *Challenge*, 277.

30. Spence, *Montana*, 162; Bucklin, *From Cold War to Gulf War*, 7.

31. Harris et al., *The Homefront*, 64; "Rationing Reminders," *Bismarck Capital*, May 11, 1943.

32. Lauck, *American Agriculture and the Problem of Monopoly*, 65.

33. Nash, *The American West Transformed*, 6.

34. Gaddis, *The United States and the Origins of the Cold War*, 348–52; Davis, *The Cold War Begins*, 33.

35. Gaddis, *The United States and the Origins of the Cold War*, 348–52; Dallek, *Harry S. Truman*, 59–60.

36. Johnson, *The Age of Anxiety*, 132.

37. Whitfield, *The Culture of the Cold War*, 27–28.

38. Powers, *Not without Honor*, 236, 266.

39. Fite, *American Farmers*, 85–87; Hurt, *Great Plains during World War II*, 157–59.

40. Lauck, *American Agriculture and the Problem of Monopoly*, 140–44; Hurt, *Problems of Plenty*, 120–22.

41. Nash, *The Federal Landscape*, 81. Nash's argument demonstrates the stark contrast between the West, with its universities and large industries, and the northern plains states.

42. Lawson, *Dammed Indians*, 18–22; Schell, *History of South Dakota* (4th ed.), 324–26.

43. Nash, *The Federal Landscape*, 78.

44. Jerome Tweton, interview with Senator Milton Young, August 1977, Milton R. Young Papers (hereinafter Young Papers), Chester Fritz Library, University of North Dakota, Grand Forks, North Dakota; Lonnquest and Winkler, *To Defend and Deter*, 115.

Chapter 1. Anticommunism

1. Johnson, *The Age of Anxiety*, 11–14. Johnson is the latest of a number of scholars to trace McCarthy's beginning to the Wheeling speech.

2. Bailey, *Joe McCarthy and the Press*, 192; Fried, *Men against McCarthy*, 287.

3. "'Odds against U.S. in Communism Fight'—McCarthy," *Huronite and Daily Plainsman*, February 16, 1950.

4. Johnson, *The Age of Anxiety*, 146.

5. W. E. Bond to William Langer, August 10, 1954, Box 252, William Langer Papers (hereinafter Langer Papers), Chester Fritz Library, University of North Dakota, Grand Forks, North Dakota.

6. Sophie M. Roberts to James Murray, July 20, 1950, Box 432, James Murray Papers (hereinafter Murray Papers), K. Ross Toole Archives, Maureen and Mike Mansfield Library, University of Montana, Missoula, Montana.

7. A. E. Godfrey to Karl E. Mundt, April 1, 1950, Box 690, Mundt Papers.

8. Pauline de Sherbinin to Karl Mundt, April 21, 1950, Box 690, Mundt Papers.

9. Dan Grigg to Karl Mundt, March 30, 1950, Box 690, Mundt Papers.

10. Gaddis, *We Now Know*, 5, 14.

11. Heale, *McCarthy's Americans*, 4.

12. Dyson, *Red Harvest*, x–xi.

13. Ibid., 9, 26.

14. Ibid., 31; Goldstein, *Political Repression in Modern America*, 99.

15. McDonald, *The Red Corner*, 92.

16. Ibid., 161, 165.

17. Goldstein, *Political Repression in Modern America*, 87, 125, 128.

18. Hoyt, *The Palmer Raids*, 11.

19. Coben, *A. Mitchell Palmer*, 217.

20. Griffith, *The Politics of Fear*, 33–34.

21. Thompson, *The Frustration of Politics*, 18–20.

22. Filene, *American Views of Soviet Russia*, 162; Heale, *McCarthy's Americans*, 3–5.

23. Griffith, *The Politics of Fear*, 97–98; Thompson, *The Frustration of Politics*, 20–25.

24. Thompson, *The Frustration of Politics*, 24–28.

25. "Do These Laws Protect?" *Independent Record*, June 30, 1955; "Too Many Loyalty Oaths," *Independent Record*, October 12, 1952.

26. Heale, *McCarthy's Americans*, 28–30.

27. Ibid., 36–43.

28. Ibid.

29. Ibid., 48–49.

30. Lee, "McCarthyism at the University of South Dakota," 435–36.

31. "S.D. Senate Gets Loyalty Oath Bill," *Bismarck Tribune*, January 26, 1955.

32. Lee, "McCarthyism at the University of South Dakota," 436.

33. "Oppose Loyalty Oaths," *Bismarck Tribune*, February 4, 1955; "Teacher Terms New Loyalty Oath Law a 'Mistake,'" *Bismarck Tribune*, April 4, 1955.

34. "Blue Laws to Be Repealed on July 1," *Huronite and Daily Plainsman*, June 16, 1955.

35. "Loyalty Oath Rejected by City Commission," *Fargo Forum*, January 4, 1955.

36. Ibid.

37. "State Personnel Commission Plans Loyalty Oath for Most Employees of Montana's Governmental Setup," *Independent Record*, December 5, 1953.

38. "Attorney General Rules on Oath for State Employees," *Independent Record*, February 1, 1954; "Loyalty Oath Said Confusing," *Billings Gazette*, February 1, 1954.

39. Heale, *McCarthy's Americans*, 282.

40. Miller, "Montana and the Specter of McCarthyism," 68.

41. E. V. "Sonny" Omholt, interview by William D. Miller, in "Montana and the Specter of McCarthyism," 69–70.

42. Charles Cerovski, letter to William D. Miller, in "Montana and the Specter of McCarthyism," 70. Cerovski was a Montana state legislator during the McCarthy era.

43. "Communists Here Post Bills at Anti-Red Talk," *Montana Standard*, August 22, 1950; Miller, "Montana and the Specter of McCarthyism," 71; "One Rotten Apple," *Montana Standard*, August 11, 1950.

44. "1948 Communist Party Membership by State," n.d., Box 167, President's Secretary File, Harry S. Truman Papers (hereinafter Truman Papers), Harry S. Truman Library, Independence, Missouri.

45. Heale, *McCarthy's Americans*, 14–15.

46. Hoover, *Masters of Deceit*, 4.

47. "Communist Party, U. S. A. Organizational Apparatus," n.d., Box 145, President's Secretary File, Truman Papers; Karl Mundt, "Your Washington and You," June 6, 1951, Box 1267, Mundt Papers; Milton Young interview by Jerome Tweton, August 8, 1977, Box 796, Young Papers; "One Rotten Apple," *Montana Standard*, August 11, 1950; Pratt, "Farmers, Communists, and the FBI in the Upper Midwest," 69; Pratt, "The Montana Farmers Union and the Cold War," 68–69.

48. Hoover, *Masters of Deceit*, 75–76; Belknap, *Cold War Political Justice*, 6.

49. "Medina Took $15,000 Judgeship in 1947, Giving Up $100,000 Private Law Practice," *New York Times*, October 15, 1949; Russell Porter, "11 Communists Convicted of Plot; Medina to Sentence Them Friday; 6 of Counsel Jailed in Contempt," *New York Times*, October 15, 1949; "Medina Considers Changing Name," n.p., n.d., newspaper clipping found in William Langer Papers (hereinafter Langer Papers), Chester Fritz Library, University of North Dakota, Grand Forks, North Dakota.

50. Heidepreim, *A Fair Chance for a Free People*, 108.

51. Thompson, "Legislation from the Past Speaks to Us Today," 83; "Wallace in Talk before Senate, Raps Mundt Bill," *Daily Inter Lake*, May 28, 1948.

52. Lisle A. Rose, *The Cold War Comes to Main Street in 1950*, 221.

53. George C. Fullinweider to Francis Case, June 2, 1948, Box 34, Case Papers.

54. Harry L. Burns to James Murray, August 22, 1950, Box 178, Murray Papers.

55. L. A. Forkner to Francis Case, Box 683, February 10, 1948, Mundt Papers. This was a carbon copy of a letter sent to Case found in the Mundt Papers.

56. Jack Williams to William Langer, August 18, 1950, Box 252, Langer Papers.

57. L. S. Boe to James Murray, March 24, 1950, Box 178, Murray Papers.

58. Unsigned letter to James Murray, April 6, 1950, Box 178, Murray Papers.

59. J. Howard McGrath to Senator Scott W. Lucas, August 26, 1950, Box 275, Langer Papers; "Logical, But Not Practical."

60. Rose, *The Cold War Comes to Main Street*, 221; Thompson, "Legislation from the Past," 85.

61. Thompson, "Legislation from the Past," 85.

62. William Langer, Report 1358, to accompany S. 2311, March 8, 1950, Box 275, Langer Papers.

63. Gerson, *Either the Constitution or the Mundt Bill*, 4–5; Thompson, "Legislation from the Past."

64. Johnson, *The Age of Anxiety*, 169–70.

65. "House Has 79 Introductions, 50 Notices as Deadline Nears; Constitutional Measure Dies," *Independent Record*, February 3, 1951.

66. "No Subversives Listed in State," *Billings Gazette*, February 5, 1952.

67. "Butte Resident Is Arrested on Anti-Red Act," *Billings Gazette*, April 6, 1956.

68. Ibid.

69. "Montana Judge Attacks Tactics of FBI's Hoover," *Daily Inter Lake*, April 15, 1956.

70. "Hellman Handed 5-Year Term in Federal Case," *Montana Standard*, June 17, 1958.

71. G. H. Ryan to Karl Mundt, March 31, 1950, Box 690, Mundt Papers. No confirmation of this official losing his job was ever found through newspaper accounts.

72. Pratt, "Farmers, Communists, and the FBI," 78.

73. Lee, "McCarthyism at the University of South Dakota," 433.

74. Thompson, *The Frustration of Politics*, 54–56.

75. Ibid., 56–57.

76. *Communist Invasion of Agriculture: Speech of Hon. Styles Bridges of New Hampshire in the Senate of the United States, September 7, 1950* (Washington, D.C.: Government Printing Office, 1951), Box 36, Young Papers.

77. Field, *Harvest of Dissent*, 4.

78. "Discuss Red Efforts to Win Over Farmers," *Sheboygan Press*, September 15, 1950; Pratt, "Farmers, Communists, and the FBI," 69; Pratt, "The Montana Farmers Union and the Cold War," 65.

79. Field, *Harvest of Dissent*, 2.

80. *Congressional Record*, 81st Cong., 1st sess., 1950, p. 14317.

81. Milton Young to S. C. Best, September 29, 1950, Box 36, Young Papers.

82. Harry Miller to Milton Young, September 9, 1950, Box 36, Young Papers.

83. Field, *Harvest of Dissent*, 91.

84. Ron Rice to James Murray, November 7, 1952, Box 432, Murray Papers.

85. "FU Challenge 'Phony': Matusow," *Lewistown Daily News*, October 19, 1952; "FU Delegates Challenge Red Charges," *Great Falls Tribune*, October 18, 1952.

86. "Official Declared Legion Not Sponsoring Ex-Red," *Great Falls Tribune*, October 22, 1952.

87. Richard C. Shipman to Harvey Matusow, n.d., Box 432, Murray Papers; Ron Rice to James Murray, November 7, 1952, Box 432, Murray Papers; "Speaker Brought to Montana But Not by Legion," *Great Falls Tribune*, October 22, 1952.

88. Vic Overcash, "Documentation of Communist Infiltration Tactics and Strategy," n.d., Box 595, Lee Metcalf Papers (hereinafter Metcalf Papers), Montana Historical Society, Helena, Montana.

89. Ibid.

90. Johnson, *The Age of Anxiety*, 249; Griffith, *The Politics of Fear*, 195.

91. "GOP Senators Schedule Visit," *Billings Gazette*, October 2, 1952; "McCarthy Lauds Sen. Ecton, Hits Mansfield," *Daily Missoulian*, October 15, 1952; Oberdorfer, *Senator Mansfield*, 102.

92. Advertisement, "In Cut Bank Tonight! Harvey Matusow, Ex-Communist Spy for the FBI," *Great Falls Tribune*, October 15, 1952; Oberdorfer, *Senator Mansfield*, 102–103.

93. Oberdorfer, *Senator Mansfield*, 103.

94. "Open Letter to Mike Mansfield: From a Father Whose Son Was Killed in Korea," *Lewistown Daily News*, October 31, 1952.

95. Advertisement, "A True Story about a Montana Soldier and Father," *Miles City Daily Star*, October 28, 1952 (the advertisement in the newspaper listed the time and radio station to hear this story and endorsed Senator Ecton).

96. Oberdorfer, *Senator Mansfield*, 103.

97. Ibid., 102–103.

98. Gallup, *The Gallup Poll*, 911. Interview dates: May 1–6, 1950. When asked if they had heard of McCarthy's charges that there were Communists in the State Department, 84 percent said yes, 16 percent said no. When asked if Senator McCarthy was doing more good than harm, 29 percent responded that he was doing more harm than good, 39 percent responded that he was doing more good than harm, and 16 percent had no opinion.

99. Gallup, *The Gallup Poll*, 924. Interview dates: June 4–9, 1950. When asked if they had heard of McCarthy's charges that there were Communists in the State Department, 78 percent said yes, 22 percent said no. Those who replied in the affirmative were asked what their opinion of these charges was: 31 percent approved or believed the charges, 10 percent had qualified approval, 20 percent disapproved or disbelieved the charges, 6 percent said that McCarthy was sometimes right and sometimes wrong, and 11 percent had no opinion.

100. Elmer Thurow to Karl Mundt, March 25, 1954, Box 558, Mundt Papers.

101. Heidepreim, *A Fair Chance for a Free People*, 171–72; W. H. Lawrence, "Mundt Will Direct Senate Unit Study of McCarthy Fight," *New York Times*, March 17, 1954; Karl Mundt to Ray Twyeffort, March 22, 1954, Box 558, Mundt Papers.

102. Maude Ridenour to James Murray, March 25, 1953, Box 432, Murray Papers.

103. Emma Reppert to James Murray, May 3, 1954, Box 432, Murray Papers.

104. Fred Christopherson to Karl Mundt, May 4, 1954, Box 558, Mundt Papers.

105. C. S. Rothwell to Joe McCarthy, May 5, 1954, Box 390, Metcalf Papers.

106. Paul Noren to Joe McCarthy, May 4, 1954, Box 558, Mundt Papers.

107. John E. Griffin to Karl Mundt, May 5, 1954, Box 558, Mundt Papers.

108. Heidepreim, *A Fair Chance for a Free People*, 182; James Reston, "McCarthy Changes Plan, When Cameras Turn, He Makes Himself a Central—Not a Secondary—Figure," *New York Times*, April 23, 1954.

109. Fred Christopherson to Karl Mundt, June 15, 1954, Box 558, Mundt Papers.

110. "Time for Mundt to Use Iron Fist," *Daily Argus-Leader*, June 11, 1954, Box 558, Mundt Papers.

111. Richard Johnston, "M'Carthy Expects 2 Inquiry Reports, He Tells Sioux Falls Legion Parley There Will Be No 'Clear-Cut Decision,'" *New York Times*, June

14, 1954; Lloyd Noteboom, "SD Legion Hears McCarthy, Controversial Figure Praises Work of Mundt at Hearings," *Daily Argus Leader*, June 14, 1954.

112. Anthony Leviero, "6 Senators Named as a Panel in McCarthy Case," *New York Times*, August 6, 1954; Heidepreim, *A Fair Chance for a Free People*, 188.

113. C. P. Trussell, "Army-M'Carthy Verdicts Put Blame on Both Sides; Watkins Silences Senator, McCarthy Gaveled Down as He Persists in Plea to Discredit Johnson," *New York Times*, September 1, 1954; Johnson, *The Age of Anxiety*, 434–35.

114. Trussell, "Army-M'Carthy Verdicts Put Blame on Both Sides"; Fried, *Men against McCarthy*, 287.

115. Gallup, *The Gallup Poll*. Interview dates: July 2–7, 1954.

116. Chenoweth, "Francis Case," 163–64.

117. Anthony Leviero, "M'Carthy Ignores Plea for Apology to Avoid Censure," *New York Times*, November 12, 1954; Chenoweth, "Francis Case," 170.

118. H. R. Davidson to Karl Mundt, November 17, 1954, Box 557, Mundt Papers.

119. Rovere, *Senator Joe McCarthy*, 56.

120. Jesse M. Olson to Karl Mundt, November 15, 1954, Box 557, Mundt Papers.

121. Douglas Hancock to Karl Mundt, November 19, 1954, Box 557, Mundt Papers.

122. Mary Lear to James Murray, July 19, 1954, Box 432, Murray Papers.

123. Maude Gushart to James Murray, August 18, 1954, Box 432, Murray Papers.

124. "Case Denies Political Pressure on Changed McCarthy Stand," *Lincoln Star*, November 24, 1954; Chenoweth, "Francis Case," 172–73; "National Affairs," *Time*, November 29, 1954.

125. Anthony Leviero, "Final Vote Condemns M'Carthy, 67–22, for Abusing Senate and Committee; Zwicker Count Eliminated in Debate," *New York Times*, December 3, 1954; Herman, *Joseph McCarthy*, 293.

126. C. Maxwell Brown to Milton Young, December 10, 1954, Box 59, Young Papers.

127. Max E. Lang to Milton Young, December 12, 1954, Box 56, Young Papers; Milton Young to Max E. Lang, December 18, 1954, Box 59, Young Papers.

128. Willard E. Fraser to Anton Gerharz, November 30, 1954, Box 433, Murray Papers.

129. Vera Praast to James Murray, December 2, 1954, Box 433, Murray Papers.

130. Karl Mundt telegram to Dwight D. Eisenhower, September 27, 1954, Box 1121, Mundt Papers.

131. Ibid.

132. Karl Mundt to Richard Nixon, September 10, 1954, Box 1121, Mundt Papers.

133. Karl Mundt to Barry Goldwater, September 10, 1954, Box 1121, Mundt Papers.

134. Karl Mundt to Barry Goldwater, October 18, 1954, Box 1121, Mundt Papers.

135. Chenoweth, "Francis Case," 174–75.

136. William White, "M'Carthy Censure Wins, 67 to 20, In Tentative Vote on 2 Counts; Knowland Widens Split in G.O.P.," *New York Times*, December 2, 1954.

137. Broyles, *The John Birch Society*, 5–7.

138. Johnson, *The Age of Anxiety*, 463–64.

139. Broyles, *The John Birch Society*, 3; Karl Mundt to C. E. Baughman, January 27, 1962, Box 165, Mundt Papers.

140. Broyles, *The John Birch Society*, 4.

141. Harry Johansen, "The Demos and the Birchers," *San Francisco Examiner*, August 18, 1963.

142. Wallace Turner, "Birch Aide Cites Gain in Montana," *New York Times*, June 1, 1963.

143. Unsigned letter to Lee Metcalf, July 2, 1963, Box 116, Metcalf Papers.

144. Cora E. Van Deusen to Lee Metcalf, January 8, 1962, Box 116, Metcalf Papers.

145. Barbara Hauge to Lee Metcalf, April 9, 1961, Box 116, Metcalf Papers; unsigned letter, Flathead County Democratic Women's Club to Lee Metcalf, August 14, 1961, Box 116, Metcalf Papers.

146. Newman, "A Study of the Beliefs, Methods of and the Impact or Effect of the John Birch Society," 18–19; "Tactics of Birchers under Fire," *Fargo Forum*, May 7, 1961.

147. Newman, "A Study of the Beliefs," 19–20.

148. Ibid., 20.

149. "Landsberger Workshop," January 18, 1968, *Fargo Forum*; Newman, "A Study of the Beliefs," 23.

150. "Sees Peril in Hatred of Communism," *Fargo Forum*, September 16, 1950.

Chapter 2. One Nation, under God

1. "Christ for Greater Billings Crusade," *Billings Gazette*, December 15, 1951.

2. "Merv Rosell in Billings for Midland Empire Crusade," *Billing Gazette*, November 10, 1951.

3. Whitfield, *The Culture of the Cold War*, 83.

4. Herzog, *The Spiritual-Industrial Complex*, 36.

5. Ibid., 32, 35.

6. Whitfield, *The Culture of the Cold War*, 83.

7. Ellis, *To the Flag*, 130–37.

8. Whitfield, *The Culture of the Cold War*, 89.

9. "In 1951 as in 1776," *Bismarck Tribune*, February 22, 1951.

10. "Mayor Proclaims June 11 'Wake Up America' Day," *Bismarck Tribune*, June 8, 1950.

11. "Closure Ceremonies Climaxed," *Bismarck Tribune*, June 11, 1953.

12. "Ike Says Red Honor Doubtful," *Billings Gazette*, October 31, 1953.

13. "DAR Concludes Annual Session," *Huronite and Daily Plainsman*, March 23, 1958.

14. "More Spent on Dog Food Than Christian Education—Bishop," *Daily Republic*, May 9, 1960.

15. "Vets Day Marked by Lions Club," *Montana Standard*, November 13, 1956.

16. "Communist Threat Growing, Bishop Gilmore Declares," *Independent Record*, October 24, 1954.

17. Herzog, *The Spiritual-Industrial Complex*, 62–63.

18. Ibid., 63–64.

19. Powers, *Not without Honor*, 227.

20. Herzog, *The Spiritual-Industrial Complex*, 56, 62, 77.

21. Ibid., 65.

22. Ibid., 40–43.

23. Ibid., 62–64.

24. Malone and Roeder, *Montana*, 269.

25. Emmons, "Irish Miners," 50.

26. "Cardinal's Conviction Part of Soviet Plan, Bishop Gilmore Avers," *Independent Record*, February 8, 1949.

27. "Communist Threat Growing, Bishop Gilmore Declares"; Oblinger, *My Priests Can Do Anything*, 13–15, 24–25.

28. "Communist Threat Growing, Bishop Gilmore Declares"; Oblinger, *My Priests*, 101–106.

29. "Communist Threat Growing, Bishop Gilmore Declares."

30. "St. Patrick Day Is Marked at Butte Banquet," *Montana Standard*, March 18, 1947.

31. "Butte Friendly Sons of St. Patrick Hold Annual Banquet," *Montana Standard*, March 17, 1948.

32. "Irish and Their Friends Have Gala Time at St. Patrick's Day Banquet," *Montana Standard*, March 18, 1958.

33. "100th Anniversary of Founding of St. Ignatius Mission Is Celebrated by Catholic Diocese," *Independent Record*, September 24, 1954; "St. Ignatius Will Be Host to Throngs for Centennial," *Daily Inter Lake*, September 21, 1954.

34. McCumber, *Time in the Ditch*, 21.

35. Nichols, "Something Old, Something New," 295.

36. Fixico, "Dislocated," 295.

37. Herzog, *The Spiritual-Industrial Complex*, 65.

38. "Catholic Youth Stand as Bulwark against Communistic Inroads," *Montana Standard*, September 29, 1946.

39. "Bishop Proclaims Prayer Crusade," *Montana Standard*, September 13, 1959 (quotation); "May Day for Peace Rites Attended by More Than 1,200 Persons Despite Rain Sunday," *Independent Record*, May 17, 1953; "More Than Thousand Catholic Students to Participate in Pilgrimage Sunday Evening," *Independent Record*, May 22, 1952; "Ringing Tower Bells This Evening Will Herald Carroll Pilgrimage of Peace," *Independent Record*, May 25, 1952.

40. Lauck, *Prairie Republic*, 57, 62.

41. Allitt, *Religion in America since 1945*, 12–15.

42. Ibid., 14.

43. Whitfield, *The Culture of the Cold War*, 77–79.

44. "Over-Capacity Crowd of 5,000 Hears Dr. Schuler [*sic*]," *Daily Argus Leader*, October 16, 1950; "Sioux Falls Greatest Revival of Century Nears End," *Daily Argus Leader*, October 20, 1950.

45. "Annihilation Possible Says Californian," *Daily Argus Leader*, October 24, 1950.

46. "Will You Be Free to Observe Easter in the Future?" *Montana Standard*, March 9, 1958.

47. Allitt, *Religion in America*, 25.

48. "Speaker Tells of Red Tactics," *Billings Gazette*, February 28, 1959.

49. "Legion Speakers Hit at Apathy," *Billings Gazette*, July 20, 1958; "Red Fighter Will Have Large Audience Here," *Montana Standard*, February 8, 1959.

50. "Speaker Tells of Red Tactics," *Billings Gazette*, February 28, 1959.

51. "5,000 Jam 2 Buildings for Roberts' Revival," *Bismarck Tribune*, November 4, 1955; "Roberts to Be Here Four Days," *Bismarck Tribune*, November 2, 1955.

52. "Roberts Continues to Jam Buildings," *Bismarck Tribune*, November 1, 1955.

53. "Florida to Be Winter Home of Passion Play," *Daily Republic*, August 14, 1952; "Passion Play Site Like Boyhood Dream—Meier," *Daily Republic*, August 4, 1951; "Schools and Churches Endorse Play," *Independent Record*, November 20, 1955; "Veteran Passion Play Christus Will Turn Over Role to Nephew," *Billings Gazette*, July 31, 1951.

54. "7,500 Saw Passion Play in Bismarck," *Bismarck Tribune*, January 13, 1949.

55. "Passion Play Hits High Attendance," *Huronite and Daily Plainsman*, September 18, 1953.

56. "Black Hills and Badlands Draw More and More Tourists Yearly," *Daily Republic*, September 11, 1959.

57. "Passion Play Will Be a Powerful Sermon," *Billings Herald*, September 1, 1949.

58. "Passion Play Site Like Boyhood Dream—Meier."

59. "Church Official Addresses Club," *Billings Gazette*, November 24, 1953.

60. "Christianity Can Defeat Communism Minister Asserts," *Bismarck Tribune*, September 19, 1952.

61. "Church Bells to Ring Throughout State July 4th," *Daily Republic*, July 3, 1951.

62. "Touring Russians Plan Visit to Stock Farms, Picnic, Huron Ice Show," *Huronite and Daily Plainsman*, August 3, 1955.

63. "Huron in International Spotlight as Russian Farmers and Ice Show Stars Mingle in Evening of Conviviality," *Huronite and Daily Plainsman*, August 5, 1955; "Russia Was Never Like This: Ice Show Beauties Plant Kisses on Cheeks of Visiting Soviet Farmers," *Huronite and Daily Plainsmen*, August 5, 1955.

64. "Russian Tour By-Product," *Huronite and Daily Plainsman*, August 5, 1055.

65. Herzog, *The Spiritual-Industrial Complex*, 8.

Chapter 3. Freedom Crusades

1. "10,000 See Parade; Barkley Due Here," *Bismarck Tribune*, June 12, 1950; "ND Elks 1950 State Meet," *Bismarck Tribune*, June 12, 1950.

2. "Discovery of Oil Fueled Bismarck's Largest Growth Spurt in the '50s," *Great Plains Examiner*, October 27, 2011.

3. "Barkley Warns of Red Menace," *Bismarck Tribune*, June 13, 1950.

4. Cherny, *The Candy Bombers*, 127.

5. "Bakers Pledge Aid in Saving Grain," *Fargo Forum*, October 18, 1947; "Luckman Says Distillers to Close Down," *Montana Standard*, October 14, 1947; "Writer Lists Reasons for Sudden Change in Poultryless Thursday," *Billings Gazette*, November 9, 1947.

6. "Dahl Urges ND Horse Surplus Feed Europe," *Bismarck Capital*, May 7, 1946.

7. "Sen. Young Says Food Scarcities Europe Problem," *Bismarck Capital*, September 19, 1947; "U.S. Wheat Exports Setting New Records," *Bismarck Capital*,

December 12, 1947; "Young Urges More European Wheat Shipments," *Bismarck Capital*, September 26, 1947.

8. "Senator Young Announces Results of Poll in N.D.," *Bismarck Capital*, March 26, 1948.

9. "Campaign on Rats," *Fargo Forum*, November 9, 1947; "Grain-Eating Rats Invade State," *Montana Standard*, December 28, 1947; "Positive, Vigorous Program for Wiping Out Costly Rats Suggested," *Daily Republic*, November 22, 1947; "State Pheasant Season Reopening Refused; Give Farmers Shooting Rights," *Huronite and Daily Plainsman*, December 17, 1947.

10. "Local Restaurants to Serve Patrons Just What They Order," *Daily Inter Lake*, October 21, 1947; "Meatless Days Observed at S.F.," *Daily Plainsman*, October 15, 1947; "Poultryless Thursday Called Off," *Fargo Forum*, November 8, 1947; "Save Grain by Marketing Poultry and Livestock," *Daily Plainsman*, October 19, 1947.

11. "Trumans Keep Egg, Meat Bans," *New York Times*, January 8, 1948.

12. "'Friendship Train' to Get Relief Food," *New York Times*, October 27, 1947; "Hollywood Fanfare Sends Friendship Train East to Collect Contributions for Europe," *New York Times*, November 8, 1947.

13. "Christmas Ship for Europe," *Billings Herald*, December 18, 1947; "Ford Commends Montana Aid," *Billings Gazette*, February 17, 1948.

14. Cherny, *The Candy Bombers*, 127.

15. Ibid., 227.

16. "Ford Receives Berlin Letter," *Billings Gazette*, May 23, 1948.

17. "Food Arrives for Austrians," *Billings Gazette*, March 24, 1948; "Northwest Group Goes to Europe," *Billings Gazette*, March 2, 1948; "Plate from Mayor of Berlin in Historical Library," *Helena Independent Record*, August 4, 1948.

18. "Friendship Train Gets Thinnest Welcome in Milan," *Independent Record*, January 3, 1948; "Sicilians Storm Friendship Train," *Billings Gazette*, January 25, 1948; "Suspect Sabotage as Friendship Train Food Burns," *Daily Republic*, January 30, 1948.

19. "French Gifts to Be Auctioned," *Huronite and Daily Plainsman*, February 25, 1949; "Local 40 et 8 Sets Display of Merci Train Gifts Friday," *Bismarck Tribune*, February 12, 1949; "Six Million Frenchmen Can't Be Wrong," *Herald*, March 17, 1949.

20. Fried, *The Russians Are Coming!* 29–30.

21. Ibid., 31.

22. Ibid., 31–35.

23. "Freedom Train Is Christened," *Billings Gazette*, September 18, 1947.

24. "Priceless Documents of Nation's Freedom Will Be Displayed Aboard Freedom Train," *Billings Gazette*, April 4, 1948.

25. Ibid.

26. "Gov. Sam C. Ford Calls Attention of Montanans to Visit of Freedom Train to Helena," *Independent-Record*, September 16, 1947.

27. "Many Planning to Go to Missoula, See Freedom Train," *Daily Inter Lake*, April 14, 1948; "School Group Announces Plans," *Billings Gazette*, April 9, 1948; "Thousands Expected to View Freedom Train Exhibit Today," *Billings Gazette*, April 20, 1948.

28. "Historic Freedom Train Here Today," *Daily Missoulian*, April 15, 1948.

29. "10,146 Southwestern Montanans Visit Freedom Train in Butte," *Montana Standard*, April 17, 1948.

30. "Thousands Greet Freedom Train," *Great Falls Tribune*, April 19, 1948.

31. "City's Churches to Note Freedom of Religion," *Billings Gazette*, April 18, 1948.

32. "Freedom Train Committee Named, Program-Planning Sessions Set," *Billing Gazette*, March 7, 1948; "200 Too Late to View Train," *Billings Gazette*, April 22, 1948.

33. "City Jammed for Freedom Train: Every West River Town Represented in Crowd Here to See Documents," *Rapid City Journal*, April 21, 1948.

34. Ibid.; "Record Crowd in City for Freedom Train Exhibition," *Rapid City Journal*, April 23, 1948.

35. "Thousand View Freedom Train," *Aberdeen American News*, April 24, 1948.

36. "Aberdeen Is Freedom Train's Next Stop after Capital City," *Daily Argus Leader*, April 24, 1948; "Record Crowds See Train at Pierre, Rapid," *Daily Argus Leader*, April 23, 1948.

37. "Officials Aid Canadian Who Flew to See Train," *Bismarck Tribune*, April 27, 1948.

38. "Freedom Train Viewed in Minot by 10,907 for Western Record," *Minot Daily News*, April 28, 1948.

39. "Thousands Gather to View Train," *Jamestown Sun*, April 28, 1948.

40. "8,785 People Here Pass through Freedom Train," *Jamestown Sun*, April 29, 1948.

41. "Record 10,925 Tour Freedom Train," *Fargo Forum*, April 30, 1948.

42. "Signature of Fargo Woman's Relative on Freedom Train," *Fargo Forum*, April 28, 1948.

43. "Crowds See Freedom Train," *Grand Forks Herald*, April 30, 1948.

44. "County's First White Woman Sees Train," *Watertown Public Opinion*, May 11, 1948;

45. "Early-Rising Youths Flock to Train Site," *Daily Argus Leader*, May 12, 1948; "Plane Armada Roars over S.F.," *Huronite and Daily Plainsman*, April 18, 1948.

46. Cummings, *Radio Free Europe's "Crusade for Freedom,"* 6–12.

47. Ibid., 23–25; "To Listen May Mean Imprisonment, Death or Torture, But Thousands Listen Every Night to 'Radio Free Europe,'" *Independent Record*, November 16, 1952; "'Truth Dollars' Feature Crusade," *Daily Inter Lake*, February 13, 1956.

48. Cummings, *Radio Free Europe "Crusade for Freedom,"* 12–17.

49. Ibid., 36; "Names of 13,186 Montana Men, Women, and Children Leave on Plane Today for Berlin," *Independent Record*, October 19, 1950.

50. "Freedom Crusade Sets Up Quarters in A of C Office," *Bismarck Tribune*, September 25, 1950.

51. "Freedom Crusade Gains Momentum," *Bismarck Tribune*, September 26, 1950.

52. "South Dakota Joins Group for Freedom," *Daily Argus Leader*, September 3, 1950.

53. "The Bell of Freedom," *Daily Inter Lake*, October 15, 1951; "United Nations Day Set for October 24," *Daily Argus Leader*, October 19, 1950.

54. "Pierre Liberty Bell Facsimile Will Toll United Nations Day," *Daily Argus Leader*, October 23, 1950.

55. Cummings, *Radio Free Europe's "Crusade for Freedom,"* 59–61, 201; "Mitchell Lad, 11, Wins Britannica Set in Contest," *Daily Republic*, June 24, 1960.

56. "Freedom Drive Motorcade Due Here Tomorrow," *Daily Inter Lake*, September 19, 1951; "Special Events to Highlight 'Freedom Crusade Week' in City," *Billings Gazette*, September 9, 1951; "27 Communities See Motorcade," *Billings Gazette*, September 16, 1951.

57. Cummings, *Radio Free Europe's "Crusade for Freedom,"* 64.

58. "Local Girl's Idea Will Sell Freedom," *Bismarck Tribune*, February 5, 1955; "S.D. Gets Freedom Balloons," *Bismarck Tribune*, February 26, 1955.

59. "Balloon on Flight from Sioux Falls," *Huronite and Daily Plainsman*, March 8, 1959; "S.F. Balloon Down after Short Flight," *Huronite and Daily Plainsman*, March 9, 1959; "Sioux Falls Man to Make Balloon Hop," *Huronite and Daily Plainsman*, March 1, 1959.

60. "Public May Hear Gruenther at Capitol," *Bismarck Tribune*, February 18, 1959.

61. "Crusade for Freedom Float Wins First Prize in Big Fair Parade," *Daily Inter Lake*, September 14, 1951; "Crusade Leader Leaves on Radio Free Europe Tour," *Daily Republic*, October 1, 1959.

62. Cummings, *Radio Free Europe's "Crusade for Freedom,"* 171–74, 203–207.

63. Ellis, *To the Flag*, 130–37; "U.S. 'United Front' Will Combat Reds," *Bismarck Tribune*, January 30, 1956.

64. Putnam, *Bowling Alone*, 19, 292.

65. Fried, *The Russians Are Coming!* 17; Whitfield, *The Culture of the Cold War*, 45.

66. Fried, *The Russians Are Coming!* 54–58.

67. "Observe Loyalty Day," *Bismarck Tribune*, April 24, 1954.

68. "Foss Proclaims May 1 as Loyalty Day in the State," *Huronite and Daily Plainsman*, April 25, 1956.

69. "Montana VFW Posts Prepare to Celebrate 'Loyalty Day,'" *Daily Inter Lake*, April 28, 1955.

70. "40-Year Battle for Women's Vote Reviewed in USD Bulletin," *Daily Republic*, October 24, 1959.

71. "Three Out Of Four Rural Women in Demonstration Clubs in S.D.," *Huronite and Daily Plainsman*, April 18, 1949.

72. "Business and Professional Women Observe Special Week," *Independent Record*, October 11, 1953; "Governor J. Hugo Aronson Proclaims This Week as 'National Business Women's Week' in State," *Independent Record*, October 11, 1953.

73. George Sokolsky, "Aroused Women Form Grass-Roots Clubs," *Bismarck Tribune*, May 28, 1952.

74. "Dean Chaffin to Be Guest Speaker at First Meeting of Newly Organized Freedom Club of Helena," *Independent Record*, January 13, 1953.

75. "Oro Fino Chapter, DAR, Has Fine Education Program," *Independent Record*, February 6, 1955.

76. "North Dakota DAR Good Citizens," *Bismarck Tribune*, March 4, 1950.

77. "Freedom Shrine Program Arranged," *Bismarck Tribune*, February 23, 1956; "This Is Communism? It's Mayhem!" *Bismarck Capital*, November 12, 1954.

78. Fried, *The Russians Are Coming!* 139.

Chapter 4. Civil Defense

1. Daniel M. Burnham, "'Target Town' Great Falls, Montana, Flanked by Bombers and Missiles, Is Seemingly Undisturbed," *Wall Street Journal*, September 8, 1961.

2. Ibid.

3. Tanaka and Young, *Bombing Civilians*, 2–5.

4. Dwight D. Eisenhower, "Press Release, Speech before Congress," February 22, 1955, Highways and Thoroughfares, Box 728, Dwight D. Eisenhower Papers (hereinafter Eisenhower Papers), Dwight D. Eisenhower Library, Abilene, Kansas; Schwartz, "Excerpts from Atomic Audit"; Oakes, *The Imaginary War*, 53.

5. Garrison, *Bracing for Armageddon*, 13, 35; Oakes, *The Imaginary War*, 38–39.

6. Dwight D. Eisenhower, "Press Release, Speech before General Assembly of the United Nations," December 8, 1953, Speech Series, Box 6, Eisenhower Papers; Chernus, *Eisenhower's Atoms for Peace*, 4, 106–107; Ambrose, *Eisenhower*, 342–43.

7. Elton C. Fay, "President Gives Congress New Look at U.S. Weapons," *Evening Tribune*, January 8, 1954; Ambrose, *Eisenhower*, 343.

8. "Atomic Exhibit to Tour N.D.," *Bismarck Tribune*, July 30, 1958; Chernus, *Eisenhower's Atoms for Peace*, 99; "New Words to Be Defined at Bismarck Atomic Show," *Bismarck Capital*, March 4, 1952; Ambrose, *Eisenhower*, 343.

9. Dwight D. Eisenhower, "Annual Message to the Congress on the State of the Union," January 7, 1954, Eisenhower Papers, Speech Series, Box 6; Rose, *One Nation Underground*, 4.

10. Gaddis, *The Cold War*, 80–81.

11. Garrison, *Bracing for Armageddon*, 36; Rose, *One Nation Underground*, 18; Schwartz, "Excerpts from Atomic Audit."

12. Gallup, *The Gallup Poll*, 1162. The poll was conducted between July and September 1953: 32 percent thought that their communities stood a "Good Chance" of being hit; 24 percent thought that their communities stood a "Fair Chance"; 37 percent thought that their communities stood "Not Much Chance"; 7 percent had no opinion.

13. Ibid., 1434–35. Interview dates June 15–20, 1956: 63 percent thought that the hydrogen bomb would be used; 17 percent thought that it would not be used; 20 percent were either unsure or had no opinion.

14. Ibid., 1162. The poll was conducted between July and September 1953: 4 percent said that they were doing civil defense work; 3 percent said that they had done no work yet signed up to help; and 93 percent admitted that they had done no work in civil defense.

15. Ibid., 1741. Interview dates September 21–26, 1961. In an earlier poll conducted between July 27 and August 1, 1961, only 5 percent had made any changes to their home to protect against a nuclear attack. In the same poll 20 percent said that they had stored extra food with an enemy attack in mind.

16. Ibid., 1445. Interview dates August 3–8, 1956: 23 percent disapproved of the plan, and 13 percent had no opinion.

17. Ibid., 1671. Interview dates April 28 to May 3, 1960: 19 percent opposed such a law, and 10 percent had no opinion.

18. "Advisory Group Calls CDA a Flop," *Daily Inter Lake*, March 6, 1956.

19. "Civil and Defense Mobilization," *New York Times*, January 17, 1961; "Scientific Blueprint for Atomic Survival," *Life* 42 (March 18, 1957): 26.

20. "Right to Die," *Time* 72 (August 17, 1958): 52.

21. "Atomic Shelter Idea Losing Support," *Independent Record*, April 15, 1960.

22. Ibid.

23. "Protest against Shelters Is Effort to Evade Issue," *Independent Record*, November 20, 1961.

24. Ibid.

25. "We're All in Same Shelter," *Montana Standard-Post*, September 25, 1961.

26. "Civil Defense Setup Makes Little Headway against Public Apathy," *Billings Gazette*, June 28, 1959.

27. "CD Director Peterson Argues over Value of Shelters," *Inter Lake*, February 19, 1957.

28. Rose, *One Nation Underground*, 10–11.

29. Ibid.

30. "Civil and Defense Mobilization," *New York Times*, January 17, 1961; Rose, *One Nation Underground*, 18.

31. *Fallout Shelter Survey Data.*

32. "Transcript of Kennedy Address to Congress on U.S. Role in Struggle for Freedom," *New York Times*, May 26, 1961.

33. "More Funds Asked for Civil Defense," *New York Times*, July 25, 1961; "Shelters in Big Cities Sought by Kennedy," *New York Times*, July 27, 1961.

34. Burnham, "'Target Town.'"

35. "Unit Formed by Aandahl," *Fargo Forum*, August 9, 1950.

36. "Bismarck May Be Target in War," *Bismarck Capital*, December 15, 1950; Lloyd Omdahl, email to author, December 12, 2006.

37. "Edwards Warns ND May Become a Battleground," *Bismarck Capital*, February 20, 1950.

38. "Col. Tharalson Fighting Apathy in Building State Civil Defense," *Minot Daily News,* September 14, 1955.

39. "State Civil Defense Group to Meet Sept. 16," *Bismarck Capital,* September 6, 1955.

40. "South Dakotan Works to Avert Disaster in Air," *Bismarck Tribune*, June 2, 1955.

41. Ibid.

42. Lloyd Omdahl, "Did They Intend to Bomb Us?" *Fargo Forum*, December 11, 2006.

43. "Agriculture and Biosystems Engineering," http://www.ag.ndsu.nodak.edu/abeng/ cropsplans.htm; Don Bachmeier, email to author, October 29, 2006; Lloyd Omdahl, email to author, December 12, 2006.

44. Advertisement, "Have Your Home 'Atomasticated!'" *Bismarck Capital*, September 18, 1953.

45. "Sure Sign of Atomic Age," *Bismarck Capital*, September 1, 1950.

46. *State of South Dakota Civil Defense Plan.*

47. *Civil Defense Report to the Governor and Legislature*, 3, 6.

48. *Operational Survival Plan*, 3–4.

49. "We're All in Same Shelter," *Montana Post-Standard*, September 25, 1961.

50. "Fallout Shelter for Family of Six Completed in City," *Rapid City Daily Journal*, March 27, 1960.

51. "Governor Dedicates Fallout Shelter Here," *Rapid City Daily Journal*, March 30, 1960.

52. "There's No Logic to Shelter Collapse," *Daily Plainsman*, June 24, 1962.

53. "Shelters First Step in Aiding Medics in Case of Disaster," *Daily Republic*, October 1, 1961.

54. Rose, *One Nation Underground*, 8, 202.

55. Bob Lusk, "The Publisher's Notebook," *Huronite and Daily Plainsman*, October 2, 1955.

56. "Fallout Shelter No Longer Cause for a Horselaugh," *Daily Plainsman*, August 27, 1961.

57. "Huron Has Fallout Shelter Space for 6,500 Persons in 18 Spots," *Daily Plainsman*, July 21, 1964.

58. Hugh Potter to James Murray, July 17, 1953, Box 165, Murray Papers.

59. Cole Sullivan to James Murray, July 16, 1959, Box 165, Murray Papers.

60. Hugh Potter to James Murray, March 13, 1957, Box 165, Murray Papers.

61. "Atomic Shelter Apathy Scares Defense Chief," *Billings Gazette*, April 30, 1960.

62. "Director of Civil Defense Gives State Heads Facts," *Independent Record*, June 3, 1960.

63. "CD Recommends Sample Fallout Shelter in City," *Billings Gazette*, October 30, 1959.

64. "Civil Defense Chiefs Told 'Time to Fill Sandbags,'" *Independent Record*, September 13, 1961.

65. "'Be Prepared' Is CD Message," *Montana Standard and Butte Daily Post*, September 13, 1961.

66. Ibid.

67. Garrison, *Bracing for Armageddon*, 165.

Chapter 5. The Ground Observer Corps

1. "Billings Filter Center Project Spotlights Montana Air Defense," *Aircraft Flash* 3 (December 1954): 3. *Aircraft Flash* was an official Air Force magazine published monthly to illustrate the achievements of its volunteers at the observation posts and the filter centers.

2. "How Russia Can Strike: An Enemy Air Force Has the Power to Hit Us in Three Ways," *Life* 30 (January 22, 1951): 78.

3. Gallup, *The Gallup Poll*, 1445. Interview dates August 3–8, 1956: 64 percent of those surveyed approved of a plan that would require every man and woman to contribute an average of one hour per week in civil defense work; 23 percent disapproved of the plan; and 13 percent had no opinion; ibid., 1671. Interview dates April 28 to May 3, 1960: 71 percent favored a law that would require each community to

build public fallout shelters; 19 percent opposed such a law; and 10 percent had no opinion.

4. "How Russia Can Strike," 79–80.

5. "N.D. Important in U.S. Defense, Officer Stresses," *Bismarck Tribune*, March 11, 1954; "New 24-Hour Watch Effective July 14 Stresses Need for Ground Observer Corps Aides," *Independent Record*, June 27, 1952.

6. Zaloga, *The Kremlin's Nuclear Sword*, 12–16.

7. Ibid.

8. Wilson, "Interview with General Chidlaw," 30.

9. "Worth Quoting . . . ," *Aircraft Flash* 5 (March 1957): 2.

10. "Ground Observer Corps Expansion Will Blanket Entire United States," *Aircraft Flash* 3 (November 1954): 3; "Salute to GOC," *Aircraft Flash* 7 (January 1959): 4.

11. "Flashes," *Aircraft Flash* 2 (October 1953): 7. "Flashes" denotes that standard section of *Aircraft Flash,* which contains snippets of GOC information from around the nation. The cited pages have no other title.

12. "Flashes," *Aircraft Flash* 4 (May 1956): 10; "Stanton Sets GOC Training Meeting," *Bismarck Tribune*, April 15, 1954.

13. "New Hradec Sets Example," *Dickinson Press*, March 5, 1953.

14. "Flashes," *Aircraft Flash* 5 (August 1956): 10; "O'Callaghans Contribute to Country's Defense," *Bismarck Mandan Shopper*, October 10, 1956.

15. "Flashes," *Aircraft Flash* 4 (November 1955): 11.

16. "Flashes," *Aircraft Flash* 4 (October 1955): 11.

17. "Air Force Jets Called in Search of 'Fireball' over Kalispell," *Missoulian*, September 5, 1956; "Flashes," *Aircraft Flash* 2 (October 1953): 6.

18. "Flashes," *Aircraft Flash* 4 (June 1956): 10; "Pilot to Bomb Minot with Balloons Saturday," *Ward County Independent*, February 26 1953; "Publicity and Promotion Assist the GOC," *Aircraft Flash* 4 (January 1956): 7.

19. GOC advertisement, "Another Town Is Safer Tonight," *Newsweek* 46 (November 28, 1955): 28.

20. GOC advertisement, "Do the Russian Leaders Want Peace?" *Golden Valley News*, April 20, 1954; GOC advertisement, "WARNING: Russian War Planes in a Single Raid," *Minot Daily News*, April 23, 1955.

21. "Women of the GOC," *Aircraft Flash* 7 (August 1958): 3–5; "Stanton Sets GOC Training Meeting," *Bismarck Tribune*, April 15, 1954.

22. "Custer Monument GOC Post at Symbolic Place," *Missoulian*, n.d., newspaper clipping in file, Box 1, Margaret Owen Papers (hereinafter Owen Papers), Ross Toole Archives, Maureen and Mike Mansfield Library, University of Montana, Missoula, Montana; "These Soldiers Don't Fade—They're a Crack GOC Team," *Missoulian*, n.d., newspaper clipping in file, Box 1, Owen Papers.

23. "Beulah Boy Scouts to Complete GOC Tower," *Beulah Independent*, May 26, 1955; Bill Lardy, email to author, February 27, 2008; "Flashes," *Aircraft Flash* 2 (March 1954): 6; John Sullivan, email to author, March 1, 2008.

24. "Private Lumber Firms Join Air Defense Team," *Aircraft Flash* 2 (January 1954): 3–4; "Smoke Spotters—Plane Spotters," *Aircraft Flash* 2 (August 1953): 3–4; "Volunteers Man CD Look-out Post," *Daily Inter Lake*, November 27, 1953.

25. "Electric Co-Op Crews in North Dakota Become Mobile Observers for GOC," *Aircraft Flash* 2 (August 1953): 3; "Flashes," *Aircraft Flash* 5 (March 1957): 11; "Smoke Spotters—Plane Spotters," 4–5 (quotation); "Flashes," *Aircraft Flash* 3 (August 1954): 7.

26. "Air Defense Exercise Held in Western ND," *Bismarck Capital*, January 21, 1953; "GOC Emergency Assistance," *Aircraft Flash* 3 (April 1955): 6; "Flashes," *Aircraft Flash* 4 (November 1955): 10.

27. "Flashes," *Aircraft Flash* 4 (December 1955): 9.

28. "DP Works in Filter Center," *Aircraft Flash* 2 (October 1953): 3; "Flashes," *Aircraft Flash* 4 (May 1956): 11.

29. "Flashes," *Aircraft Flash* 4 (May 1956): 11.

30. "Chippewas Double as Guided Missile, Skywatch Guards," *Minot Daily News*, August 11, 1956; "Flashes," *Aircraft Flash* 2 (December 1955): 6.

31. "Flashes," *Aircraft Flash* 2 (December 1953): 7; "GOC Emergency Assistance," *Aircraft Flash* 3 (April 1955): 4; "Honor 2 Regent Men for Jet Crash Work," *Bismarck Tribune*, May 6, 1954.

32. "GOC Alert, Helpful in Severe Weather," *Aircraft Flash* 6 (September 1957): 11.

33. "Flashes," *Aircraft Flash* 3 (May 1955): 6; "Flashes," *Aircraft Flash* 5 (June 1957): 9.

34. "Flashes," *Aircraft Flash* 3 (May 1955): 6.

35. "2 from Here to See Tuesday Atomic Test," *Bismarck Tribune*, April 25, 1955; "Flashes," *Aircraft Flash* 4 (September 1955): 10.

36. "Sioux Falls Air Defense Plan," *Aircraft Flash* 3 (March 1955): 3.

37. "Operation Lifesaver Will Utilize ADC's Far-Seeing Radar Net," *Billings Gazette*, October 24, 1954; "Operation Lifesaver Ceremonies Attract Hundreds to Airport," *Billings Gazette*, November 1, 1954.

38. "Drake Chosen as GOC Post of the Month," *Drake Register*, April 22, 1954; "North Dakota OP Draws Rebekahs," *Aircraft Flash* 3 (August 1954): 6.

39. "GOC Members Receive Praise," *Montana Standard*, November 22, 1958; "GOC Phase Out," *Aircraft Flash* 7 (January 1959): 3–4; "Sioux Falls GOC Advisory Council Marks Fourth Year," *Aircraft Flash* 6 (April 1958): 2; "To Deactivate Filter Center at Sioux Falls," *Huronite and Daily Plainsman*, November 21, 1958.

40. "GOC Phase Out," *Aircraft Flash* 7 (January 1959): 3–4.

41. "Salute to GOC," *Aircraft Flash* 7 (January 1959): 4.

42. "General Neely Pays Tribute to GOC Workers at Banquet," *Bismarck Tribune*, January 23, 1959.

43. "They Also Serve," *Aircraft Flash* 3 (August 1954): 1.

Chapter 6. The Cuban Missile Crisis

1. "F-M Business Slows as President Speaks," *Fargo Forum*, October 23, 1962.

2. "America Didn't Lose Its Sense of Humor," *Fargo Forum*, October 28, 1962; "U Reaction to Kennedy Talk Solemn," *Grand Forks Herald*, October 23, 1962.

3. George, *Awaiting Armageddon*, 1.

4. Gaddis, *The Cold War*, 114–15; "Shelters in Big Cities Sought by Kennedy," *New York Times*, July 27, 1961.

5. Gaddis, *The Cold War*, 76.

6. Kennedy and Schlesinger, *Thirteen Days*, 33–34, "Word 'Quarantine' Used to Avoid Warlike Note," *New York Times*, October 24, 1962.

7. Anthony Lewis, "President Grave: Asserts Russians Lied and Put Hemisphere in Great Danger," *New York Times*, October 23, 1962; Kennedy and Schlesinger, *Thirteen Days*, 54–55; Seymour Toppling, "Moscow Says U.S. Holds 'Armed Fist' over Cuba," *New York Times*, October 23, 1962.

8. "Dr. Pauling Terms Speech 'Horrifying,'" *New York Times*, October 23, 1962; E. W. Kenworthy, "Action Is Based on '47 Rio Pact," *New York Times*, October 23, 1962; "U Reaction to Kennedy Talk Solemn," *Grand Forks Herald*, October 23, 1962.

9. Nan Robertson, "Anxiety Coupled with Support Here on U.S. Move," *New York Times*, October 24, 1962.

10. Austin Wehrwein, "Students to March in Blockade Protest," *New York Times*, October 26, 1962.

11. "Midtown Barred to Pickets Protesting Blockade," *New York Times*, October 25, 1962.

12. "Mayor Urges Participation in UN Program," *Minot Daily News*, October 24, 1962; "U.S. Day to Be Marked in Williston Today," *Williston Herald*, October 23, 1962.

13. David H. Smith and Rob Renshaw, "Sioux Falls Citizens Endorse President's Stance," *Daily Argus Leader*, October 23, 1962.

14. George Remington, "Montanans Back JFK," *Montana Standard Post*, October 28, 1962.

15. "Raid Sirens Not Too Good," *Grand Forks Herald*, October 24, 1962.

16. "Siren Causes Scare in Texas," *Daily Argus Leader*, October 24, 1962.

17. "Siren Creates Near Panic," *Grand Forks Herald*, October 27, 1962.

18. "Advice Given in Case of Enemy Attack Here," *Grand Forks Herald*, October 28, 1962; "No Orders for City Officials," *Daily Argus Leader*, October 24, 1962.

19. "Fire Alarm to Sound for Civil Defense," *Miles City Star*, November 1, 1962.

20. "Buzzer Alarm System Would Alert U.S. Homes: Kennedy Asks 10 Million to Start the Program," *New York Times*, July 27, 1961; "Shelters in Big Cities Sought by Kennedy," *New York Times*, July 27, 1961.

21. Catherine Coffin to Senator Karl E. Mundt, July 28, 1961, Box 65, Mundt Papers.

22. "Stepped-Up CD Program Is Outlined," *Rapid City Journal*, October 28, 1962.

23. William Guy, interview by author, Fargo, North Dakota, October 9, 2007.

24. "Guy Urges Civil Defense Efforts," *Grand Forks Herald*, October 30, 1962.

25. "Guy Orders CD Alert for Monday," *Fargo Forum*, October 23, 1962.

26. "Flurry of Activities at State Capital," *Dickinson Press*, October 30, 1962; "N.D. Civil Defense Head Cites Strength of Program," *Fargo Forum*, October 24, 1962; "State CD Alert Shows 'Improvement,'" *Williston Herald*, October 30, 1962.

27. "City Asks Civil Defense Planning for Williston," *Williston Herald*, October 24, 1962; "Civil Defense Director Reports on Organization," *Williston Herald*, October 31, 1962.

28. "Advice Given in Case of Enemy Attack Here," *Grand Forks Herald*, October 28, 1962; "Mark City Fallout Shelters," *Grand Forks Herald*, October 24, 1962;

"Whistle Blast to Open Fete," *Grand Forks Herald*, October 28, 1962; "Williston Public Shelters Could Hold 1,000 Persons," *Williston Herald*, October 25, 1962.

29. "Bismarck Lacks Fallout Shelters," *Rapid City Journal*, October 24, 1962; "Fallout Shelter Space Leased for 9,000 Persons in Bismarck," *Bismarck Tribune*, October 24, 1962.

30. "Fallout Shelters Would Be Hard to Find," *Bismarck Tribune*, May 5, 1969; "Mark City Fallout Shelters," *Grand Forks Herald*, October 24, 1962; "Shelters Marked," *Bismarck Tribune*, October 20, 1962.

31. "Questions on Local Defense Unanswered," *Rapid City Journal*, October 24, 1962.

32. "BHTC Conducts Defense Drill," *Rapid City Journal*, October 27, 1962; "Civil Defense Meeting Is Set at Sturgis," *Rapid City Journal*, October 26, 1962.

33. "Interest Perks Up in Civil Defense," *Rapid City Journal*, October 24, 1962.

34. "No Orders for City CD Office," *Daily Argus Leader*, October 24, 1962.

35. "Civil Defense Activities on Increase across State in Wake of Worst World Crisis since Pearl Harbor," *Daily Capital Journal*, October 24, 1962; "County CD Unit Placed on Alert," *Daily Capital Journal*, October 23, 1962.

36. "Guard to Assist in Civil Defense Work," *Dickinson Press*, October 28, 1962; "National Guard to Aid Civil Defense," *Montana Standard Post*, October 26, 1962.

37. "Guard to Assist in Civil Defense Work."

38. "Butte Fulfilling Its Role in Civil Defense," *Montana Standard Post*, October 25, 1962; "National Guard to Aid Civil Defense," *Montana Standard Post*, October 26, 1962.

39. "Rail Tunnel Fallout Shelter," *Billings Gazette*, November 2, 1962.

40. "Air Force Shifts Number of Jets to Billings," *Montana Standard Post*, October 24, 1962.

41. "Mayor Claims Air Force Takes over Billings Field," *Great Falls Leader*, October 23, 1962.

42. Colonel Tom Larson, email to author, December 19, 2006; "F102 Fighters at EAFB Back to Sioux Falls," *Rapid City Journal*, October 24, 1962; "Fighter Aircraft Dispersed," *Minot Daily News*, October 24, 1962.

43. Colonel Tom Larson, email to author, December 19, 2006.

44. *New Buildings with Fallout Protection*, 1; Steve Matosich to Lee Metcalf, February 23, 1965, Box 92, Metcalf Papers.

45. Charles Grutzner, "Crisis Spotlights Civil Defense Lag," *New York Times*, October 24, 1962; Saul Pett, "America Didn't Lose Its Sense of Humor," *Fargo Forum*, October 28, 1962.

46. *Survey of Opinion on Civil Defense in North Dakota*, 5.

47. "Civil Defense Summary," November 12, 1963, Box 105, Metcalf Papers; "Press Release," August 23, 1962, Box 105, Metcalf Papers.

48. Constance Fisher to Lee Metcalf, January 15, 1963, Box 105, Metcalf Papers.

49. Lindsay Thompson, "In the Shadow of Nuclear War," 77; *Potential Shelter Space in Montana Mines*, 1.

50. Garrison, *Bracing for Armageddon*, 15, 36.

51. Gaddis, *The Cold War*, 80–81.

Chapter 7. Airpower and Air Bases

1. "Stark Drama Takes Place as Hungry Cattle Get First Hay in Month," *Independent-Record*, February 1, 1949.

2. Cherny, *The Candy Bombers*, 469.

3. Gaddis, *The Cold War*, 33–34, 56; LaFeber, *America, Russia, and the Cold War*, 76–77.

4. "Heat Hits ND and LA Shivers," *Bismarck Tribune*, January 5, 1949; "New Storms Strand Travelers; 4,000 Are Snowbound in Wyoming; Relief Work Slowed," *Independent Record*, February 8, 1949; "Six-Inch Blanket of Snow Buries Los Angeles Area," *Bismarck Tribune*, January 11, 1949; "Thousands of Train Passengers Marooned by Midwest Blizzard," *Billings Gazette*, January 5, 1949.

5. "New But Less Severe Storm to Hit Midwest; S.D. Roads Being Opened," *Huronite and Daily Plainsman*, January 7, 1949; "Snowbound Town Receives Supplies," *Billings Gazette*, January 12, 1949.

6. Sutherland and Canwell, *The Berlin Airlift*, 35, 39.

7. "F-51 Crash Fatal to Airlift's Chief," *Bismarck Tribune*, February 21, 1949; "'Little Airlift' Aids Montanans," *Daily Inter Lake*, January 20, 1949; "Mercy Flights Planned to Storm Areas," *Huronite and Daily Plainsman*, January 13, 1949.

8. "Stockmen Make Appeal for Help in Feeding Their Starving Herds," *Billings Gazette*, January 23, 1949.

9. "Air Force to Begin 'Haylift' Today to Aid Western Livestock," *Billings Gazette*, January 24, 1949; "Navy Relievers for 'Vittles Run,'" *Daily Inter Lake*, January 20, 1949; "Stockmen Make Appeal for Help in Feeding Their Starving Herds."

10. "Cattle Accustomed to 'Hay Bombs,'" *Independent Record*, February 9, 1949; Duane Lund, "Haylift Air Crews Using War Tactics," *Minot Daily News*, February 12, 1949; "Mercy Flights Planned to Storm Areas," *Huronite and Daily Plainsman*, January 13, 1949; "State Hay Embargo Sought as Cold, Snow Continue," *Independent Record*, January 30, 1949.

11. "Governor Says Situation Out of Control," *Huronite and Daily Plainsman*, January 28, 1949.

12. "4,866 Persons Are Freed by Storm Crews," *Huronite and Daily Plainsman*, February 3, 1949; "Crews Battle to Open Rural Roads in Area," *Billings Gazette*, January 21, 1949;

13. "4,866 Persons Are Freed by Storm Crews."

14. "ND Winning Cold War," *Bismarck Tribune*, February 5, 1949; "State Buys Three New Snowplows to Battle Blockade," *Bismarck Tribune*, February 4, 1949.

15. "Army Reports Big Gain in Storm Battle," *Huronite and Daily Plainsman*, February 6, 1949; "Dog-Lift Being Planned in Utah," *Independent Record*, February 9, 1949; "Plows Open Road Between Garrison, Elbowood Sunday," *Bismarck Tribune*, February 7, 1949; "Snow Operations to Be Suspended in Seven Counties," *Huronite and Daily Plainsman*, February 15, 1949.

16. "Statement of Senator Mike Mansfield," October 26, 1962, Box 56, Metcalf Papers.

17. Nash, *The Federal Landscape*, 5.

18. Stock, *Main Street in Crisis*, 98–107.

19. Redford H. Dibble, "Location of Base Result of Hard Work by Many Persons," *Rapid City Daily Journal*, October 10, 1942.

20. Ibid.; "Vast Military Acreage," *Helena Independent*, November 30, 1942.

21. Dibble, "Location of Base."

22. Ibid.

23. "Ellsworth Air Force Base History."

24. "President Asks for Large Increase in Heavy Bombers," *Helena Independent Record*, May 6, 1941.

25. "Air Facilities Here to Be Surveyed in Defense Plan," *Helena Independent Record*, May 2, 1941; Carl Rankin to Senator James Murray, April 26, 1941, Box 452, Murray Papers; Major Edward Curtis to James E. Murray, May 9, 1941, Box 452, Murray Papers.

26. "Army Bombers in State to Begin Practice," *Helena Independent Record*, December 1, 1942; Curt Shannon, "Malmstrom Air Force Base," *Great Falls Rivers Edge Journal* 38 (February 2007): 18; "Three Million Dollar Air Force Project Authorized in State," *Helena Independent Record*, May 6, 1942.

27. White, *It's Your Misfortune and None of My Own*, 497.

28. Etulain, *Beyond the Missouri*, 365.

29. Malone and Roeder, *Montana*, 309; Schell, *History of South Dakota* (4th ed.), 317; Spritzer, *Roadside History of Montana*, 30, 251.

30. Robinson, *History of North Dakota*, 427; Spence, *Montana*, 163.

31. Schell, *History of South Dakota* (3rd ed.), 379.

32. Nash, *The Federal Landscape*, 81.

33. Ibid., 78.

34. James Murray to Josef Sklower, May 7, 1945, Box 566, Murray Papers; Josef Sklower to James Murray, February 8, 1944, Box 566, Murray Papers.

35. Gaddis, *The Cold War*, 33–34; Shannon, "Malmstrom Air Force Base."

36. "Ellsworth Air Force Base History."

37. Major General Joe Kelley to Lee Metcalf, June 21, 1955, Box 58, Metcalf Papers; R. F. Kitchingman to Lee Metcalf, June 3, 1955, Box 58, Metcalf Papers.

38. "ND Officials Present Survey of Facilities to Air Force," *Bismarck Capital*, February 20, 1951; Nolan, "The Air Force Comes to North Dakota," 36.

39. H. O. Morgan to Commanding Officer, Strategic Air Command, June 6, 1951, Box 452, Murray Papers.

40. Lieutenant Colonel Earl Miller to H. O. Morgan, June 20, 1951, Box 452, Murray Papers.

41. James Murray to H. O. Morgan, June 29, 1951, Box 452, Murray Papers.

42. E. E. Krebsbach to James Murray, January 22, 1951, Box 452, Murray Papers.

43. F. P. Holbrook to James Murray, December 29, 1950, Box 452, Murray Papers; F. P. Holbrook to James Murray, January 11, 1951, Box 452, Murray Papers; Robert Eaton to James Murray, January 17, 1951, Box 452, Murray Papers.

44. Francis Case to Harold E. Talbott, March 26, 1954, Box 137, Francis H. Case Papers (hereinafter Case Papers), McGovern Library, Dakota Wesleyan University, Mitchell, South Dakota; Milton Young to George Longmire, May 10, 1954, Box 84, Young Papers; "Seek Air Academy for S.F.," *Sioux Falls Daily Argus-Leader*, February 23, 1954.

45. J. B. Austin to Lee Metcalf, February 2, 1954, Box 53, Metcalf Papers.

46. General Joe Kelly to James Murray, April 17, 1954, Box 452, Murray Papers; R. F. Kitchingman to General Nathan F. Twining, February 5, 1954, Box 53, Metcalf Papers; P. W. Singer to Harold Talbott, January 27, 1954, Box 53, Metcalf Papers; P. W. Singer to Lee Metcalf, January 27, 1954, Box 53, Metcalf Papers.

47. Press release, "Academy Site Selection Group Named by Secretary Talbott," April 6, 1954, Box 53, Metcalf Papers; Tom Gavin, "Colorado House Approves Million for Air Academy," *Rocky Mountain News*, n.d., Box 452, newspaper clipping in Murray Papers.

48. Kingsland Dunwoody to Milton Young, February 12, 1952, Box 84, Young Papers.

49. Milton Young to Kingsland Dunwoody, February 13, 1952, Box 84, Young Papers.

50. "17 Communities Ask Help with Air Base Plans," *Portsmouth Herald*, December 7, 1951; "Six Area Towns Vote 'No' on Jet Base Construction," *Portsmouth Herald*, March 12, 1952; "Newington 'Sold Down the River' on Air Base, Cry Angry Citizens," *Portsmouth Herald*, June 25, 1951.

51. "Carlson Reveals Plans to Close Champlain College," *Post-Standard*, March 20, 1953; "Champlain 'Orphans' Find Haven," *Oneota Star*, November 26, 1952; "Seek Airport on Champlain College Site," *Syracuse Herald-Journal*, May 20, 1952.

52. Dwight D. Eisenhower, "Annual Message to the Congress on the State of the Union," January 7, 1954, Eisenhower Papers; Elton C. Fay, "President Gives Congress New Look at U.S. Weapons," *Minneapolis Tribune*, January 8, 1954.

53. Brigadier General Joe W. Kelly to Senator Milton Young, February 25, 1954, Box 84, Young Papers.

54. Milton R. Young to Byron J. Kluesing, March 22, 1954, Box 520, Langer Papers; Milton R. Young to M. M. Oppegard, June 19, 1954, Box 84, Young Papers.

55. Memorandum, "Grand Forks Air Force Base," n.d., Box 84, Young Papers; memorandum, "Minot Air Force Base," n.d., Box 84, Young Papers; Nolan, "The Air Force Comes to North Dakota," 41.

56. Brigadier General Joe W. Kelly to Senator Milton Young, June 11, 1954, Box 84, Young Papers.

57. Brigadier General Joe W. Kelly to Senator Milton Young, June 17, 1954, Box, 84, Young Papers; Colonel William C. Warren to Milton R. Young, June 22, 1954, Box, 84, Young Papers.

58. Milton R. Young to Dr. Archie D. McCannell, June 24, 1954, Box 84, Young Papers.

59. Milton Young to Dennis W. Kelly, June 29, 1954, Box 64, Young Papers.

60. Milton Young to Guy Larson, June 23, 1954, Box 64, Young Papers.

61. "Minot Base Will Have Supersonic Jet Planes," *Bismarck Tribune*, March 2, 1955.

62. Herbert F. Smith to James Murray, June 9, 1954, Box 451, Murray Papers; James Murray to Herbert F. Smith, June 10, 1954, Box 451, Murray Papers.

63. Brigadier General Joe Kelly to Senator Murray, February 25, 1954, Box 451, Murray Papers; Senator James E. Murray to George McCabe, February 18, 1954, Box 451, Murray Papers; Senator James E. Murray to Harold Talbott, February 18, 1954, Box 451, Murray Papers.

64. Memorandum, "Summary of Telephone Call from Judge Shea, of Glasgow, to Senator Murray," June 16, 1954, Box 451, Murray Papers.

65. James Murray telegram to Joseph T. Gorman, June 17, 1954, Box 451, Murray Papers; Joseph T. Gorman telegram to James Murray, June 16, 1954, Box 451, Murray Papers; Joseph T. Gorman to James Murray, May 24, 1954, Box 451, Murray Papers.

66. Shannon, "Malmstrom Air Force Base"; "Ellsworth Air Force Base History"; "20 Million Dollar Building Program Seen Here," *Rapid City Daily Journal*, February 9, 1955.

67. Bruce Stoner, "Satellite B52 Base Is a Possibility for Mitchell," *Mitchell Daily Republic*, June 26, 1956.

68. Art Raymond, "City Officials Meet to Lay Plans for Air Force Survey," *Mitchell Daily Republic*, June 30, 1956; "Senate Passes Bill Providing Cash for Mitchell Air Base," *Mitchell Daily Republic*, July 16, 1956.

69. Evan E. Lips to Milton Young, January 25, 1957, Box 84, Young Papers; Milton Young to Evan E. Lips, January 29, 1957, Box 84, Young Papers.

70. Art Raymond, "USAF Wants Air Base Here; Money Lacking," *Mitchell Daily Republic*, January 31, 1957; Francis Case to Carney Peterson, February 4, 1957, Box 137, Case Papers.

71. "Glasgow AFB Shutdown Disrupts Community," *Glasgow Courier*, November 24, 1964; Memorandum, "Glasgow Air Force Base, Glasgow, Montana," n.d., Box 56, Metcalf Papers.

72. Ruben Sinclair to Lewis E. Turner, June 24, 1965, Box 56, Metcalf Papers.

73. James Campbell to Robert McNamara, January 8, 1965, Box 56, Metcalf Papers.

74. Paul Harvey, "Maybe the War Is Over!" *Lima (Ohio) News*, October 24, 1965.

75. "Battle to Save Glasgow Base Begins," *Independent Record*, December 6, 1964; "Glasgow Fights to Keep Air Base," *Glasgow City Courier*, December 8, 1964.

Chapter 8. Missiles on the Plains

1. Murray M. Moler, "Minuteman Is Greatest Project in Magnitude Ever in Montana," *Great Falls Tribune*, September 22, 1960.

2. Gretchen Heefner, "Missiles and Memory: Dismantling South Dakota's Cold War," *Western Historical Quarterly* 38 (Summer 2007): 84.

3. Lonnquest and Winkler, *To Defend and Deter*, 11; *SAC Missile Chronology*, 3.

4. Nuefeld, *The Development of Ballistic Missiles in the United States Air Force*, 40; Lonnquest and Winkler, *To Defend and Deter*, 15.

5. Schwiebert, *A History of the U.S. Air Force Ballistic Missiles*, 100–101; Lonnquest and Winkler, *To Defend and Deter*, 31–34; Nuefeld, *The Development of Ballistic Missiles*, 148.

6. Gaddis, *The Cold War*, 69–71 (quotation); *SAC Missile Chronology*, 31–34; Zaloga, *The Kremlin's Nuclear Sword*, 55, 77.

7. Kennedy, *The Strategy of Peace*, 33–35; Lonnquest and Winkler, *To Defend and Deter*, 65–66.

8. Lonnquest and Winkler, *To Defend and Deter*, 72–77; "Minuteman Is Smaller Missile, But Has Advantage over Big Ones," *Great Falls Tribune*, December 12, 1962; "Solid-Fuel Minuteman Missiles to Be Based in State Can Blast Off in Seconds; Won't Clutter Up Scenery," *Great Falls Tribune*, March 27, 1960.

9. Day, *Nuclear Heartland*, 9 (Samuel H. Day is co-director of Nukewatch, an organization concerned with peace initiatives, and was editor of the *Bulletin of the Atomic Scientists* before joining Nukewatch in 1981); *From SNARK to Peacekeeper*, 26; Lonnquest and Winkler, *To Defend and Deter*, 72–77; "Runaway Minuteman Destroyed," *New York Times*, October 18, 1962.

10. "Montana Is Becoming an Atomic Age Fort," *Great Falls Tribune*, September 29, 1960; "Program Director Says Minuteman Exceeds Hopes, Denies Inability to Reach Targets in Soviet Union," *Great Falls Tribune*, May 2, 1963, "Strategic Missile Wing Is Pioneering First for Montana," *Great Falls Tribune*, August 8, 1961.

11. Lonnquest and Winkler, *To Defend and Deter*, 77–78; Day, *Nuclear Heartland*, 10–12, 17.

12. "Malmstrom AFB"; "State Said Right for ICBM Sites," *Great Falls Tribune*, March 16, 1962.

13. Spritzer, *Roadside History of Montana*, 188–89; "Malmstrom AFB."

14. "Montana Missile Contractors Reply to Battin," *Daily Inter Lake*, April 9, 1961.

15. "Babcock Predicts Tremendous Boost in State Economy," *Daily Inter Lake*, March 15, 1961.

16. "Nutter Investigates Missile Controversy," *Daily Inter Lake*, May 11, 1961.

17. "Key Minuteman Officials Assure Gov. Nutter That 'Full Use Is Being Made of State Labor,'" *Great Falls Tribune*, May 11, 1961.

18. "Boeing Minuteman Operations Boost Great Falls Economy," *Great Falls Tribune*, October 7, 1962.

19. Day, *Nuclear Heartland*, 14; "First Fifty Missile Silos Soon Ready," *Great Falls Tribune*, May 9, 1962; "Malmstrom AFB"; "Minuteman Project Starts Today with Dynamite Explosion," *Great Falls Tribune*, March 16, 1961.

20. "AF to Update Minuteman I," *Great Falls Tribune*, May 20, 1965; Shannon, "Malmstrom Air Force Base"; "Malmstrom AFB."

21. "Ellsworth AFB"; "Ellsworth Air Force Base History."

22. J. D. Davenport to Loren Carlson, September 25, 1962, Box 136, Case Papers (Lee report); John Stennis to Francis Case, June 13, 1962, Box 136, Case Papers; untitled document, n.d., Box 136, Case Papers.

23. Ted Hustead, interview by Erin Pogany, Wall, South Dakota, January 7, 2003, Minuteman Missile National Historic Site Files, Phillip, South Dakota (hereinafter MIMI-NPS).

24. "Federal Land-Buying Hindered," *New York Times*, May 19, 1962; Gene S. Williams, interview by Erin Pogany, Wall, South Dakota, January 7, 2003, MIMI-NPS; Gene Pellegrin to Francis Case, June 21, 1961, Box 136, Case Papers; "Land Owners Talk Missile Site Values," *Rapid City Daily Journal*, March 23, 1961.

25. Heefner, *The Missile Next Door*, 82, 106–107.

26. Dick Rebbeck, "Land Owners May Take Problems to Washington," *Rapid City Journal*, April 7, 1961; Leonel M. Jenson to Francis Case, June 23, 1961, Box 136, Case Papers; Williams interview, MIMI-NPS.

27. Gene Pellegrin to John L. Burgum, June 21, 1961, Box 136, Case Papers; Williams interview, MIMI-NPS.

28. Andy Knight, interview by Steven Bucklin, Rapid City, South Dakota, May 19, 1999, MIMI-NPS; David Blackhurst, interview by Steven Bucklin, Rapid City, South Dakota, May 19, 1999, MIMI-NPS; Tim Pavek, interview by Steven Bucklin, Rapid City, South Dakota, May 20, 1999, MIMI-NPS; Williams interview, MIMI-NPS.

29. Milton Young to Betty Dawkins, February 26, 1964, Box 174, Young Papers.

30. Gilbert F. Petersen to Milton Young, March 9, 1963, Box 174, Young Papers; Milton Young to Gilbert F. Petersen, March 19, 1963, Young Papers.

31. Clayton Cudmore to Milton Young, January 21, 1965, Box 214, Young Papers.

32. Colonel John Dacus to Milton Young, March 1, 1965, Box 214, Young Papers; George Chaput to Milton Young, May 21, 1965, Box 214, Young Papers; Milton Young to Clayton Cudmore, March 3, 1965, Box 214, Young Papers; Milton Young to Colonel John Dacus, February 10, 1965, Box 214, Young Papers; Milton Young to George Chaput, June 1, 1965; Box 214, Young Papers (quotation).

33. Colonel John Dacus to Milton Young, June 30, 1966, Box 214, Young Papers; Melvin Petersen to Milton Young, April 18, 1966, Box 214, Young Papers; Milton Young to John Gaking, July 8, 1966, Box 214, Young Papers.

34. Ernest Johnson to Senator Milton Young, 11 April 1962, Box 115, Young Papers.

35. Colonel John J. Haley, Corps of Engineers to Milton Young, September 1, 1961, Box 115, Young Papers; Lex E. O'Brient to Milton Young, August 16, 1961, Box 115, Young Papers; pamphlet entitled "Facts about Minuteman Land Acquisition—North Dakota," 1961, Box 115, Young Papers.

36. Dean Tsoumpas telegram to Milton Young, April 25, 1962, Box 174, Young Papers; Frank J. Kosanda to Milton Young, April 27, 1962, Box 174, Young Papers.

37. Tristam, "American Impression."

38. Kathy Davison, interview by author, Bismarck, North Dakota, January 7, 2007

39. Day, *Nuclear Heartland*, 9.

40. Ibid., 5.

41. Ibid., 9; "Ellsworth AFB"; Palyan, "Silent Sentinels: 44th Missile Wing" (April 2012); "START Treaty Final Reductions" (December 5, 2001), http://www.state.gov/t/ac/rls/fs/ 2001/9624.htm; Heefner, "Missiles and Memory," 181; "Minuteman Missile: National Historic Site, South Dakota"; "Ronald Reagan Minuteman Missile Site."

42. Day, *Nuclear Heartland*, 7; John LaForge (Nukewatch co-director), interview by Mary Ebeling, Madison, Wisconsin, January 3, 2003, MIMI-NPS.

43. "A Crusade to Check Retreat to Tyranny," *Daily Plainsman*, July 1, 1962.

Chapter 9. The Safeguard Complex

1. James Stokes, "ABM: Withdrawal More Painful Than Habit," *Great Falls Tribune*, May 29, 1972.

2. "Contractor Told to End ABM Work," *Great Falls Tribune*, May 29, 1972.

3. "Conrad Trying to Forget," *Great Falls Tribune*, May 28, 1972; "Contractor Told to End ABM Work"; Stokes, "ABM: Withdrawal."

4. "Mike Says Priorities Out of Tune," *Great Falls Tribune*, August 15, 1970.

5. Graham, *Hit To Kill*, 3 (quotation); Kitchens, *A History of the Huntsville Division*, viii. This history of the ABM complex is pivotal to this work. The Corps of Engineers gave Kitchens unlimited access to the files and plans and asked him to write the official history.

6. Walker et al., *Strategic Defense*, 23; Graham, *Hit to Kill*, 4; Schwiebert, *A History of the U.S. Air Force Ballistic Missiles*, 144–45.

7. Walker et al., *Strategic Defense*, 23; Graham, *Hit to Kill*, 4; Schwiebert, *A History of the U.S. Air Force Ballistic Missiles*, 146–48.

8. Graham, *Hit to Kill*, 5; Schaffel, *The Emerging Shield*, 259.

9. Baucom, *The Origins of SDI*, 23; Lonnquest and Winkler, *To Defend and Deter*, 111.

10. Baucom, *The Origins of SDI*, 33–34.

11. Graham, *Hit to Kill*, 7; Lonnquest and Winkler, *To Defend and Deter*, 112.

12. Richard B. Stolley, "Defense Fantasy Now Comes True: In an Exclusive Interview, Secretary McNamara Explains in Full the Logic behind the ABM System," *Life* 63 (September 29, 1967): 28.

13. Stolley, "Defense Fantasy," 28.

14. Baucom, *The Origins of SDI*, 34–37; Walker et al., *Strategic Defense*, 38.

15. Kitchens, *A History of the Huntsville Division*, 27, 31; "Senate Critics Ask Delay on Sentinel, Arms Race Feared," *New York Times*, February 5, 1969.

16. "Rivers Temporarily Blocks Sentinel Missile System in House," *New York Times*, February 6, 1969.

17. Baucom, *The Origins of SDI*, 38–39; Donald Johnson, "Chicago Group Sues to Block Missile Facility," *New York Times*, January 18, 1969.

18. Byron Comstock to Karl Mundt, January 31, 1969, Box 65, Mundt Papers.

19. E. Y. Berry to Melvin R. Laird, February 17, 1969, Box 65, Mundt Papers; Karl Mundt to Melvin Laird, February 18, 1969, Box, 65, Mundt Papers; Western South Dakota Development Co. to Karl Mundt, February 12, 1969, Box 65, Mundt Papers.

20. John W. Finney, "Foes of Antimissile Net Increase in Senate Attacks on Pentagon," *New York Times*, February 2, 1969.

21. Kitchens, *A History of the Huntsville Division*, 34; Robert J. Bresler and Robert C. Gray, "The Bargaining Chip and SALT," *Political Science Quarterly* 92 (1977): 66–67; Robert J. Semple, Jr., "Nixon for Limited Missile Plan to Protect U.S. Nuclear Bases; Fears Major Test in Congress," *New York Times*, March 15, 1969 (quotation).

22. Kitchens, *A History of the Huntsville Division*, 38; "Sentinel Is Renamed The Safeguard System," *New York Times*, March 21, 1969.

23. Murray Illson, "Disappointment and Delight Greet Missile Decision," *New York Times*, March 15, 1969.

24. "Safeguard: Local, Regional, and National Attitudes"; "Scientists Wage Battle on ABM," *Bismarck Tribune*, May 14, 1969.

25. Larry Feinstein, "Opposition to ABM Silent in State," *Bismarck Tribune*, May 8, 1969; Illson, "Disappointment and Delight"; Thomas W. Graham, "The

Polls: ABM and Star Wars: Attitudes toward Nuclear Defense, 1945–1985," *Public Opinion Quarterly* 50 (1986): 126; William Guy, interview by author, Fargo, North Dakota, October 9, 2007; Illson, "Disappointment and Delight" (quotation).

26. "American Legion Supports Deployment of Safeguard," *Grand Forks Herald*, June 18, 1969; Jack Haggerty, "Young Asks Missile Site Protection," *Bismarck Tribune*, March 22, 1967; "Langdon Community Generally Favors ABM," *Grand Forks Herald*, May 3, 1970.

27. Bresler and Grey, "The Bargaining Chip and SALT," 67; Warren Wever, "Nixon Missile Plan Wins in Senate by 51–50 Vote; House Approval Likely," *New York Times*, August 7, 1969.

28. "Safeguard System Components"; Kitchens, *A History of the Huntsville Division*, 43; "Site Land Negotiations to Begin February 2 in Area," *Cavalier County Republican*, January 29, 1970.

29. Kitchens, *A History of the Huntsville Division*, 43; "Pipe Line Rights to Be Sought," *Cavalier County Republican*, March 12, 1970.

30. "Bids Called on ABM Water Wells," *Cavalier County Republican*, June 22, 1970; Kitchens, *A History of the Huntsville Division*, 44; "Fordville Aquifer Water Approved for ABM Use," *Grand Forks Herald*, March 16, 1970; "Langdon Community Generally Favors ABM," *Grand Forks Herald*, May 3, 1970.

31. Kitchens, *A History of the Huntsville Division*, 48–49.

32. "ABM Area Impact Briefings Scheduled," *Grand Forks Herald*, May 21, 1970; *Community Impact Report*, 2.

33. "Date Set on Safeguard Contract Awards, Area Impact Under Study," *Cavalier County Republican*, February 21, 1970; "Uncertainty Clouds ABM Area Community Impact," *Grand Forks Herald*, May 26, 1970.

34. "Housing Will Be Built for Missile Employees," *Cavalier County Republican*, April 2, 1970; Kitchens, *A History of the Huntsville Division*, 46; Deborah Levchak, interview by author, Bismarck, North Dakota, February 19, 2006.

35. "ABM Impact Figures Released; Uncertainty Caused by Alleged 'High Costs, Jacked-Up Rent,'" *Cavalier County Republican*, May 28, 1970.

36. "ABM Area Commander Beatty Clarifies Corps Position on Langdon Costs and Rent," *Cavalier County Republican*, June 4, 1970; Levchak interview.

37. "ABM Impact Dollars Flowing into Langdon Retail Stores," *Cavalier County Republican*, July 1, 1970.

38. "Uncertainty Clouds ABM Area Community Impact," *Grand Forks Herald*, May 26, 1970; "Walhalla Shows Impact of ABM Construction," *Grand Forks Herald*, August 21, 1970.

39. Levchak interview; "Guestbook," http://srmsc.org/fdb2000.html#x0023.

40. "ABM Impact Hits Langdon," *Grand Forks Herald*, August 2, 1970.

41. "Campus Protests Flare," *Grand Forks Herald*, May 2, 1970; "Nekoma to Be Site for Anti-War Demonstration," *Grand Forks Herald*, May 3, 1970; "Peace March and Rally Here Small and Peaceful," *Grand Forks Herald*, May 12, 1970; "Rally at UND Planned as Part of Anti-ABM Events," *Grand Forks Herald*, May 10, 1970; Guy Interview.

42. "Army Starts Safeguard Land Buying," *Great Falls Tribune*, January 16, 1970; Kitchens, *A History of the Huntsville Division*, 60; *Preliminary Re-Use Plan for Malmstrom Safeguard Complex, Montana*, 20–25.

43. "ABM to Have Adverse Effect, Governor Says," *Great Falls Tribune*, August 6, 1972; "Aid for ABM Towns Requested," *Grand Forks Herald*, August 5, 1970; Kitchens, *A History of the Huntsville Division*, 61.

44. Kitchens, *A History of the Huntsville Division*, 61.

45. "Administration May Slow Down Safeguard Work," *Great Falls Tribune*, January 28, 1971; "2nd ABM Bid Opening Today," *Great Falls Tribune*, May 14, 1970; Kitchens, *A History of the Huntsville Division*, 75.

46. "ABM Contract Signed," *Great Falls Tribune*, February 25, 1972; Kitchens, *A History of the Huntsville Division*, 77; "Missile Site Costs Rise," *Great Falls Tribune*, February 25, 1972.

47. "Laird Orders Army to Halt ABM Project in Montana," *New York Times*, May 27, 1972; "Montanans Stunned by End to Conrad ABM," *Great Falls Tribune*, May 27, 1972; Morgan and Berhow, *Rings of Supersonic Steel*, 33.

48. "Mansfield Seeks ABM Area Relief," *Great Falls Tribune*, May 29, 1972.

49. "Arms Curb to End Boom Town's Boom: Montana Aide Says Some in Business Will Go Broke," *New York Times*, May 27, 1972.

50. "Preliminary Re-Use Plan," 25.

51. Lonnquest and Winkler, *To Defend and Deter*, 115; "Safeguard: Montana Complex (Malmstrom AFB)," http://srmsc.org/mnt0000.html; "U.S., Russia Sign Missile Freeze," *Great Falls Tribune*, May 27, 1972.

52. "House Cuts Defense By $9 Billion," *Grand Forks Herald*, October 3, 1975; Lonnquest and Winkler, *To Defend and Deter*, 115; "Mothballing of ABM Reflected in Defense Cut," *Grand Forks Herald*, October 3, 1975; "Panel Would Mothball ABM at Once," *Grand Forks Herald*, September 26, 1975.

53. Senator Milton Young interview with Jerome Tweton, August 1977, Young Papers; Lonnquest and Winkler, *To Defend and Deter*, 115.

54. Warren Strandell, "Officials React with Disbelief to ABM Deactivation," *Grand Forks Herald*, September 28, 1975.

55. Warren Strandell, "Mothball Idea Stuns Mayor at Walhalla," *Grand Forks Herald*, September 26, 1975.

56. Levchak interview.

Conclusion

1. McNeill, "Mythistory, or Truth, Myth, History, and Historians," in *Mythistory and Other Essays*, 3, 10–11.

2. Ibid., 12–13.

3. Kammen, *Mystic Chords of Memory*, 9.

4. Ibid., 10.

Bibliography

Archival Collections

Dwight D. Eisenhower Papers, Dwight D. Eisenhower Presidential Library, Abilene, Kansas.

Francis H. Case Papers, McGovern Library, Dakota Wesleyan University, Mitchell, South Dakota.

Harry S. Truman Papers, Harry S. Truman Library, Independence, Missouri.

James E. Murray Papers, Ross Toole Archives, University of Montana, Missoula, Montana.

Karl E. Mundt Papers, Karl E. Mundt Library, Dakota State University, Madison, South Dakota.

Lee Metcalf Papers, State Historical Society of Montana, Helena, Montana.

Milton R. Young Papers, Chester Fritz Library, University of North Dakota, Grand Forks, North Dakota.

M. Margaret Owen Papers, Mansfield Library, University of Montana, Missoula, Montana.

William L. Langer Papers, Chester Fritz Library, University of North Dakota, Grand Forks, North Dakota.

Government Documents

Aircraft Flash: Official G.O.C. Magazine. Colorado Springs: Air Defense Command, 1952–59.

Civil Defense Report to the Governor and Legislature. Pierre: Office of Civil Defense, 1952.

Community Impact Report: Grand Forks Deployment Area. Omaha: U.S. Army Engineer District, 1970.

Fallout Shelter Survey Data. Bismarck: North Dakota Disaster Emergency Services, 1960.

From SNARK to Peacekeeper: A Pictorial History of Strategic Air Command Missiles. Omaha: Strategic Air Command, 1990.

How You Will Survive. Bismarck: North Dakota Civil Defense, 1960.
New Buildings with Fallout Protection. Washington, D.C.: Office of Civil Defense, 1965.
Operational Survival Plan. Pierre: Office of Civil Defense, 1958.
Potential Shelter Space in Montana Mines. Walla Walla, Wash.: Civil Defense Support Section, 1966.
Preliminary Re-Use Plan for Malmstrom Safeguard Complex, Montana. Washington D.C.: Office of Economic Adjustment, 1974.
SAC Missile Chronology, 1939–1988. Omaha: Strategic Air Command, 1990.
State of South Dakota Civil Defense Plan. Pierre: Office of Civil Defense, 1950.
Survey of Opinion on Civil Defense in North Dakota: Influential Leaders, Summarization Report. Grand Forks: Bureau of Governmental Research, 1963.

Interviews

Bachmeier, Don (Bismarck civil defense worker). Letter to author. October 29, 2006.
Blackhurst, David (Missileer and facility manager, South Dakota). Interview by Steven Bucklin. Rapid City, South Dakota. From *Minuteman Missiles*, Minuteman Missile National Historic Site Files, Phillip, South Dakota. May 19, 1999.
Davison, Kathy (Safeguard worker). Interview by author. Bismarck, North Dakota. February 19, 2007.
Guy, William (Former North Dakota governor). Interview by author. Fargo, North Dakota. October 9, 2007.
Hustead, Ted (Wall Drug owner, South Dakota). Interview by Erin Pogany. Wall, South Dakota. From *Minuteman Missiles*, Minuteman Missile National Historic Site Files, Phillip, South Dakota. January 7, 2003.
Knight, Lt. Col. Andy (Missileer, South Dakota). Interview by Steven Bucklin. Rapid City, South Dakota. From *Minuteman Missiles*, Minuteman Missile National Historic Site Files, Phillip, South Dakota. May 19, 1999.
LaForge, John (Nukewatch co-director). Interview by Mary Ebeling. Madison, Wisconsin. January 3, 2003. From *Minuteman Missiles—Oral Histories*, http://www.nps.gov/mimi/historyculture/oral-histories.htm.
Larson, Col. Thomas (Retired vice commander, North Dakota Air National Guard). Letter to author. December 19, 2006.
Levechak, Deborah (Safeguard worker). Interview by author. Bismarck, North Dakota. February 19, 2007.
Omdahl, Lloyd (Former North Dakota lieutenant governor). Letter to author. December 12, 2006.
Pavak, Tim (Deactivation program manager, South Dakota). Interview by Steven Bucklin. Rapid City, South Dakota. From *Minuteman Missiles*, Minuteman Missile National Historic Site Files, Phillip, South Dakota. May 19, 1999.
Williams, Gene S. (Landowner, South Dakota). Interview by Erin Pogany. Wall, South Dakota. From *Minuteman Missiles*, Minuteman Missile National Historic Site Files, Phillip, South Dakota. January 7, 2003.

Young, Senator Milton (Former North Dakota senator). Interview by Jerome Tweton. Lamoure, North Dakota. August 7–11, 1977.

Books, Articles, and Theses

Allitt, Patrick. *Religion in America since 1945: A History.* New York: Columbia University Press, 2003.

Ambrose, Stephen E. *Eisenhower: Soldier and President.* New York: Simon and Schuster, 1990.

"Another Town Is Safer Tonight" [advertisement]. *Newsweek* 46 (November 28, 1955): 28.

Bailey, Edwin R. *Joe McCarthy and the Press.* Madison: University of Wisconsin Press, 1981.

Baucom, Donald R. *The Origins of SDI, 1944–1983.* Lawrence: University of Kansas Press, 1992.

Belknap, Michal R. *Cold War Political Justice: The Smith Act, the Communist Party, and American Civil Liberties.* Westport, Conn.: Greenwood Press, 1977.

Billington, Ray A. "The Origins of Middle Western Isolationism." *Political Science Quarterly* 60 (March 1945): 44–64.

Bresler, Robert J., and Robert C. Gray. "The Bargaining Chip and SALT." *Political Science Quarterly* 92 (Spring 1977): 65–88.

Broyles, J. Allen. *The John Birch Society: Anatomy of a Protest.* Boston: Beacon Press, 1964.

Bucklin, Steven J. *From Cold War to Gulf War: The South Dakota National Guard, 1945 to the Millennium.* Sioux Falls, S.D.: Pine Hill Press, 2004.

Chenoweth, Richard R. "Francis Case: A Political Biography." Ph.D. dissertation, University of Nebraska, 1977.

Chernus, Ira. *Eisenhower's Atoms for Peace.* College Station: Texas A&M University Press, 2002.

Cherny, Andrei. *The Candy Bombers: The Untold Story of the Berlin Airlift and America's Finest Hour.* New York: Penguin Group, 2009.

Coben, Stanley. *A. Mitchell Palmer: Politician.* New York: Columbia University Press, 1963.

Cole, Wayne S. *Senator Gerald P. Nye and American Foreign Relations.* Minneapolis: University of Minnesota Press, 1962.

Cooper, Jerry. *Citizens as Soldiers: A History of the North Dakota National Guard.* Lincoln: University of Nebraska Press, 2005.

Cummings, Richard H. *Radio Free Europe's "Crusade for Freedom": Rallying America behind Cold War Broadcasting, 1950–1960.* Jefferson, N.C.: McFarland and Company, 2010.

Dallek, Robert. *Harry S. Truman.* New York: Henry Holt and Company, 2008.

Danbom, David B. "A Part of the Nation and Apart from the Nation: North Dakota Politics since 1945." In *Politics in the Postwar American West,* ed. Richard Lowitt, 174–84. Norman: University of Oklahoma Press, 1995.

Davis, Lynn E. *The Cold War Begins: Soviet-American Conflict over Eastern Europe.* Princeton: Princeton University Press, 1974.

Day, Samuel H., ed. *Nuclear Heartland: A Guide to the 1,000 Missile Silos of the United States.* Madison: Progressive Foundation, 1988.

Doenecke, Justus D. *Not to the Swift: The Old Isolationists in the Cold War Era.* Lewisburg: Bucknell University Press, 1979.

Dyson, Lowell K. *Red Harvest: The Communist Party and American Farmers.* Lincoln: University of Nebraska Press, 1982.

Ellis, Richard J. *To the Flag: The Unlikely History of the Pledge of Allegiance.* Lawrence: University Press of Kansas, 2005.

Emmons, David M. *The Butte Irish: Class and Ethnicity in an American Mining Town, 1875–1925.* Chicago: University of Illinois Press, 1990.

———. "Irish Miners: From the Emerald Isle to Copper Butte." In *European Immigrants in the American West,* ed. Frederick Luebke, 49–64. Albuquerque: University of New Mexico Press, 1998.

Etulain, Richard W. *Beyond the Missouri: The Story of the American West.* Albuquerque: University of New Mexico Press, 2006.

Field, Bruce E. *Harvest of Dissent: The National Farmers Union and the Early Cold War.* Lawrence: University Press of Kansas, 1998.

Filene, Peter G. *American Views of Soviet Russia, 1917–1965.* Homewood, Ill.: Dorsey Press, 1968.

Fite, Gilbert C. *American Farmers: The New Minority.* Bloomington: Indiana University Press, 1981.

Fixico, Donald L. "Dislocated: The Federal Policy of Termination and Relocation, 1945–1960." In *The American Indian Experience: A Profile,* ed. Philip Weeks, 260–77. Arlington Heights, Ill.: Forum Press, 1988.

Frazier, Ian. *The Great Plains.* New York: Farrar, Straus and Giroux, 1989.

Fried, Richard M. *Men against McCarthy.* New York: Columbia University Press, 1976.

———. *The Russians Are Coming! The Russians Are Coming!* New York: Oxford University Press, 1998.

Gaddis, John Lewis. *The Cold War: A New History.* New York: Penguin Press, 2005.

———. *The United States and the Origins of the Cold War.* New York: Columbia University Press, 2000.

———. *We Now Know: Rethinking Cold War History.* New York: Oxford University Press, 1998.

Gallup, George H. *The Gallup Poll: Public Opinion, 1935–1971.* New York: Random House, 1972.

Garrison, Dee. *Bracing for Armageddon: Why Civil Defense Never Worked.* New York: Oxford University Press, 2006.

George, Alice. *Awaiting Armageddon: How Americans Faced the Cuban Missile Crisis.* Chapel Hill: University of North Carolina Press, 2003.

Gerson, Simon W. *Either the Constitution or the Mundt Bill, America Can't Have Both.* New York: New Century Publishers, 1948.

Goldstein, Robert Justin. *Political Repression in Modern America: From 1870 to 1976.* Chicago: University of Illinois Press, 2001.

Graham, Bradley. *Hit to Kill: The New Battle over Shielding America from Missile Attack.* New York: Public Affairs, 2001.

Graham, Thomas W. "The Polls: ABM and Star Wars: Attitudes toward Nuclear Defense, 1945–1985." *Public Opinion Quarterly* 50 (Spring 1986): 125–34.

Griffith, Robert. "Old Progressives and the Cold War." *Journal of American History* 66 (September 1979): 334–47.

———. *The Politics of Fear: Joseph R. McCarthy and the Senate*. Lexington: University of Kentucky Press, 1970.

Gross, Paul S. *The Hutterite Way*. Saskatoon: Freeman Publishing Co., 1985.

Harris, Mark J., et al. *The Homefront: America during World War II*. New York: G. P. Putnam's Sons, 1984.

Heale, M. J. *McCarthy's Americans: Red Scare Politics in State and Nation, 1935–1965*. Athens: University of Georgia Press, 1998.

Heefner, Gretchen. *The Missile Next Door: The Minuteman in the American Heartland*. Cambridge, Mass.: Harvard University Press, 2012.

———. "Missiles and Memory: Dismantling South Dakota's Cold War." *Western Historical Quarterly* 38 (Summer 2007): 181–203.

Heidepreim, Scott. *A Fair Chance for a Free People: A Biography of Karl E. Mundt, United States Senator*. Madison, S.D.: Leader Printing Co., 1988.

Herman, Arthur. *Joseph McCarthy: Reexamining the Life and Legacy of America's Most Hated Senator*. New York: Free Press, 2000.

Herzog, Jonathan P. *The Spiritual-Industrial Complex: America's Religious Battle against Communism in the Early Cold War*. New York: Oxford University Press, 2011.

Hofer, John. *The History of the Hutterites*. Altona: D. W. Friesen and Sons, 1988.

Hoover, J. Edgar. *Masters of Deceit: The Story of Communism in America and How to Fight It*. New York: Henry Holt and Co., 1958.

"How Russia Can Strike: An Enemy Air Force Has the Power to Hit Us in Three Ways." *Life* 30 (January 22, 1951): 77–89.

Hoyt, Edwin P. *The Palmer Raids, 1919–1920: An Attempt to Suppress Dissent*. New York: Seabury Press, 1969.

Hurt, R. Douglas. *Great Plains during World War II*. Lincoln: University of Nebraska Press, 2008.

———. *Problems of Plenty: The American Farmer in the Twentieth Century*. Chicago: Ivan R. Dee, 2002.

Janzen, Rod. *The Prairie People*. Hanover: University Press of New England, 1999.

Johnson, Haynes. *The Age of Anxiety: McCarthyism to Terrorism*. New York: Harcourt, 2005.

Kammen, Michael. *Mystic Chords of Memory: The Transformation of Tradition in American Culture*. New York: Alfred A. Knopf, 1991.

Karolevitz, Robert F. *Challenge: The South Dakota Story*. Sioux Falls: Brevet Press, 1975.

Kennedy, David M. *Over Here: The First World War and American Society*. New York: Oxford University Press, 1980.

Kennedy, John F. *The Strategy of Peace*. New York: Harper and Brothers, 1960.

Kennedy, Robert F., and Arthur Schlesinger, Jr. *Thirteen Days: A Memoir of the Cuban Missile Crisis*. New York: Norton and Norton, 1969.

Kitchens, James H. *A History of the Huntsville Division*. Huntsville, Ala.: United States Army Corps of Engineers, 1978.

Kraenzel, Carl F. *The Great Plains in Transition.* Norman: University of Oklahoma Press, 1955.

LaFeber, Walter. *America, Russia, and the Cold War, 1945–1984.* 5th ed. New York: Alfred A. Knopf, 1985.

Lauck, Jon. *American Agriculture and the Problem of Monopoly: The Political Economy of Grain Belt Farming, 1953–1980.* Lincoln: University of Nebraska Press, 2000.

———. *Prairie Republic: The Political Culture of Dakota Territory, 1879–1889.* Norman: University of Oklahoma Press, 2010.

Lawson, Michael L. *Dammed Indians: The Pick-Sloan Plan and the Missouri River Sioux, 1944–1980.* Norman: University of Oklahoma Press, 1982.

Lee, R. Alton. "McCarthyism at the University of South Dakota." *South Dakota History* 19 (Fall 1989): 424–38.

Lillehaugen, Nels. "Survey of American Policy in the Cold War, 1945–1950, as Reflected by the North Dakota Press." Ph.D. dissertation, University of Idaho, 1971.

Lonnquest, John C., and David F. Winkler. *To Defend and Deter: The Legacy of the United States Cold War Missile Program.* USACERL Special Report. Rock Island: Defense Publishing Service, 1996.

Malone, Michael P., and Richard B. Roeder. *Montana: A History of Two Centuries.* Seattle: University of Washington Press, 1980.

McCumber, John. *Time in the Ditch: American Philosophy and the McCarthy Era.* Chicago: Northwestern University Press, 2001.

McDonald, Verlaine Stoner. *The Red Corner: The Rise and Fall of Communism in Northeastern Montana.* Helena: Montana Historical Society Press, 2010.

McNeill, William H. *Mythistory and Other Essays.* Chicago: University of Chicago Press, 1986.

Miller, William D. "Montana and the Specter of McCarthyism, 1952–1954." M.S. thesis, Montana State University, 1969.

Morgan, Mark L., and Mark A. Berhow. *Rings of Supersonic Steel: Air Defenses of the United States Army, 1950–1979.* Bodega Bay, Calif.: Hole in the Head Press, 2010.

Nash, Gerald D. *The American West Transformed: The Impact of the Second World War.* Bloomington: Indiana University Press, 1985.

———. *The Federal Landscape: An Economic History of the Twentieth-Century West.* Tucson: University of Arizona Press, 1999.

Newman, Connie Mack. "A Study of the Beliefs, Methods of and the Impact or Effect of the John Birch Society in the Nation and Particularly in North Dakota." M.S. thesis, Northern State College, 1968.

Nichols, Roger L. "Something Old, Something New: Indians since World War Two." In *The American Indian Experience: A Profile,* ed. Philip Weeks, 292–312. Arlington Heights, Ill.: Forum Press, 1988.

Nolan, Rich J. "The Air Force Comes to North Dakota: A Study in the Site Selection of Grand Forks and Minot Air Force Bases." M.A. thesis, University of North Dakota, 1990.

Nuefeld, Jacob. *The Development of Ballistic Missiles in the United States Air Force, 1945–1960.* Washington, D.C.: Department of the Air Force, 1990.

Oakes, Guy. *The Imaginary War: Civil Defense and American Cold War Culture.* New York: Oxford University Press, 1994.

Oberdorfer, Don. *Senator Mansfield: The Extraordinary Life of a Great American Statesman and Diplomat.* Washington, D.C.: Smithsonian Books, 2003.

Oblinger, Joseph B. *My Priests Can Do Anything: The Bishop's Story.* Stevensville, Mont.: Stoneydale Press, 2011.

Powers, Richard Gid. *Not without Honor: The History of American Anticommunism.* New York: Free Press, 1995.

Pratt, William C. "Farmers, Communists, and the FBI in the Upper Midwest." *Agricultural History* 63 (Summer 1989): 61–80.

———. "The Montana Farmers Union and the Cold War, 1945–1954." *Pacific Northwest Quarterly* 83 (April 1992): 63–69.

Putnam, Robert D. *Bowling Alone: The Collapse and Revival of American Community.* New York: Simon and Schuster, 2000.

Rieselbach, Leroy N. "The Basis of Isolationist Behavior." *Public Opinion Quarterly* 24 (Winter 1960): 645–57.

Robbins, William G. "The 'Plundered Province' Thesis and the Recent Historiography of the American West." *Pacific Historical Review* 55 (November 1986): 577–97.

Robinson, Elwyn B. *History of North Dakota.* Lincoln: University of Nebraska Press, 1966.

Rose, Kenneth D. *One Nation Underground: The Fallout Shelter in American Culture.* New York: New York University Press, 2004.

Rose, Lisle A. *The Cold War Comes to Main Street America in 1950.* Lawrence: University of Kansas Press, 1999.

Rovere, Richard H. *Senator Joe McCarthy.* New York: Harcourt, Brace and Co., 1959.

Schaffel, Kenneth. *The Emerging Shield: The Air Force and the Evolution of Continental Air Defense, 1945–1960.* Honolulu: University Press of the Pacific, 2004.

Schell, Herbert S. *History of South Dakota.* 3rd ed. Lincoln: University of Nebraska Press, 1975.

———. *History of South Dakota.* 4th ed. Pierre: South Dakota State Historical Society Press, 2004.

Schwartz, Stephen I. "Excerpts from Atomic Audit." *Bulletin of Atomic Scientists* (September/October 1998): 36–43.

Schwiebert, Ernest G. *A History of the U.S. Air Force Ballistic Missiles.* New York: Frederick A. Praeger Publishers, 1965.

"Scientific Blueprint for Atomic Survival." *Life* 42 (March 18, 1957): 146–62.

Shannon, Curt. "Malmstrom Air Force Base Traces Its Beginning Back to 1939." *Great Falls Rivers Edge Journal* 38 (February 2007): 18–21.

Smith, Norma. *Jeannette Rankin: America's Conscience.* Helena: Montana Historical Society Press, 2002.

Spence, Clark C. *Montana: A Bicentennial History.* New York: W. W. Norton and Co., 1978.

Spritzer, Don. *Roadside History of Montana.* Missoula: Mountain Press Publishing Co., 1999.

Stock, Catherine McNicol. *Main Street in Crisis: The Great Depression and the Old Middle Class on the Northern Plains.* Chapel Hill: University of North Carolina Press, 1992.

Stolley, Richard B. "Defense Fantasy Now Comes True: In an Exclusive Interview, Secretary McNamara Explains in Full the Logic behind the ABM System." *Life* 63 (September 29, 1967): 28a–28c.

Sutherland, Jon, and Diane Canwell. *The Berlin Airlift: The Salvation of a City.* Gretna, La.: Pelican Publishing Co., 2007.

Tanaka, Toshiyuki, and Marilyn Blatt Young. *Bombing Civilians: A Twentieth-Century History.* New York: New Press, 2009.

Thompson, Francis H. *The Frustration of Politics: Truman, Congress, and the Loyalty Issue, 1945–1953.* Madison, N.J.: Fairleigh Dickinson University Press, 1979.

Thompson, Lindsay. "In the Shadow of Nuclear War: Montana's Reaction to the Cuban Missile Crisis." M.A. thesis, Carroll College, 2006.

Thompson, Roger J. "Legislation from the Past Speaks to Us Today: The Mundt-Nixon Bill." *Law and Society Review at University of California, Santa Barbara* 1 (2002): 81–87.

Tristam, Pierre. "American Impression: North Dakota, a Life in Missile." *Ledger,* January 25, 1999.

Walker, James A., Frances Martin, and Sharon S. Watkins. *Strategic Defense: Four Decades of Progress.* Washington, D.C.: U.S. Army Space and Strategic Defense Command, 1995.

Wheeler, Burton K. *Yankee from the West.* New York: Doubleday and Co., 1962.

White, Richard. *It's Your Misfortune and None of My Own: A New History of the American West.* Norman: University of Oklahoma Press, 1991.

Whitfield, Stephen J. *The Culture of the Cold War.* 2nd ed. Baltimore: Johns Hopkins University Press, 1996.

Wilson, Gill Robb. "Interview with General Chidlaw: Air Defense." *Flying: The World's Most Widely Read Aviation Magazine* 57 (August 1955): 30–32.

Zaloga, Steven J. *The Kremlin's Nuclear Sword: The Rise and Fall of Russia's Strategic Nuclear Forces, 1945–2000.* Washington, D.C.: Smithsonian Institution Press, 2002.

Web Sources

"Agriculture and Biosystems Engineering." http://www.ag.ndsu.nodak.edu/abeng/cropsplans.htm.

"Ellsworth AFB." http://www.globalsecurity.org/wmd/facility/ellsworth.htm.

"Ellsworth Air Force Base History." http://www.ellsworth.af.mil/library/history.asp (no longer available: see Palyan site below).

"Logical, But Not Practical." *Time,* May 31, 1948. http://content.time.com/time/magazine/article/0,9171,798670,00.html.

"Malmstrom AFB." http://www.globalsecurity.org/wmd/facility/malmstrom.htm.

"Minuteman Missile: National Historic Site, South Dakota." http://www.nps.gov/mimi/index.htm.

Palyan, Hrair H. "Silent Sentinels: 44th Missile Wing." http://www.ellsworth.af
    .mil/news/story.asp?id=123296728.
Proc, Jerry. "Omega." http://www.jproc.ca/hyperbolic/omega.html.
"Ronald Reagan Minuteman Missile Site." http://history.nd.gov/historicsites/minute
    manmissile/index.html.
"Safeguard: Local, Regional, and National Attitudes." http://srmsc.org/int2020
    .html.
"Safeguard System Components." http://srmsc.org/cmp0000.html.

Newspapers

Aberdeen American News (Aberdeen, S.Dak.)
Beulah Independent (Beulah, Mont.)
Billings Gazette (Billings, Mont.)
Billings Herald (Billings, Mont.)
Bismarck Capital (Bismarck, N.Dak.)
Bismarck Mandan Shopper (Bismarck, N.Dak.)
Bismarck Tribune (Bismarck, N.Dak.)
Cavalier County Republican (Langdon, N.Dak.)
Daily Argus Leader (Sioux Falls, S.Dak.)
Daily Capital Journal (Pierre, S.Dak.)
Daily Inter Lake (Kalispell, Mont.)
Daily Missoulian (Missoula, Mont.)
Daily Plainsman (Huron, S.Dak.)
Daily Republic (Mitchell, S.Dak.)
Dickinson Press (Dickinson, N.Dak.)
Drake Register (Drake, N.Dak.)
Evening Tribune (Hornell, N.Y.)
Fargo Forum (Fargo, N.Dak.)
Glasgow Courier (Glasgow, Mont.)
Golden Valley News (Beach, N.Dak.)
Grand Forks Herald (Grand Forks, N.Dak.)
Great Falls Rivers Edge Journal (Great Falls, Mont.)
Great Falls Tribune (Great Falls, Mont.)
Great Plains Examiner (Bismarck, N.Dak.)
Helena Independent Record (Helena, Mont.)
Huronite and the Daily Plainsman (Huron, S.Dak.)
Jamestown Sun (Jamestown, N.Dak.)
Independent Record (Helena, Mont.)
Ledger (Lakeland, Fla.)
Lewistown Daily News (Lewistown, Mont.)
Lima News (Lima, Ohio)
Lincoln Star (Lincoln, Nebr.)
Miles City Daily Star (Miles City, Mont.)
Miles City Star (Miles City, Mont.)

Minneapolis Tribune (Minneapolis, Minn.)
Minot Daily News (Minot, N.Dak.)
Missoulian (Missoula, Mont.)
Montana Standard (Butte, Mont.)
Montana Standard-Post (Butte, Mont.)
New York Times (New York, N.Y.)
Oneota Star (Oneota, N.Y.)
Portsmouth Herald (Portsmouth, N.H.)
Rapid City Journal (Rapid City, S.Dak.)
Rocky Mountain News (Denver, Colo.)
San Francisco Examiner (San Francisco, Calif.)
Sheboygan Press (Sheboygan, Wisc.)
Syracuse Herald-Journal (Syracuse, N.Y.)
Wall Street Journal (Washington, D.C.)
Ward County Independent (Minot, N.Dak.)
Watertown Public Opinion (Watertown, S.Dak.)
Williston Herald (Williston, N.Dak.)

Index

Page numbers in *italic* refer to illustrations.

CPSIA information can be obtained
at www.ICGtesting.com
Printed in the USA
LVHW030616060922
727611LV00017B/105